MW00811777

# THE LOST LIBRARY

# THE LOST LIBRARY
gay fiction
rediscovered

tom cardamone,
editor

Haiduk Press / New York

Copyright © 2010 by Tom Cardamone

ISBN 978-0-9714686-3-4

Library of Congress Control Number: 2009944172

Cover art "First Eyes" © Mel Odom 1982
Cover design by Kate Shanley

A version of Aaron Hamburger's essay on J. S. Marcus's *The Captain's Fire* appeared in Tin House #36.

**About Haiduk Press**
The haiduks were quasi-legendary folk heroes who to this day are regarded as romantic, Robin Hood figures; they are an integral part of the folklore of Hungary and Romania. Inspired by their example, Haiduk Press was formed to publish works that gently challenge the cultural status quo and conventional wisdom.

www.haidukpress.com
haidukpress@gmail.com

Readers who would like to encourage reprinting of titles appreciated here are invited to contact us; please mention any preference for electronic, softcover, or hardcover format.

*Printed in the United States on acid-free, part recycled paper.*

I often think of the men who planted the orchard, and I have done so many times in the last week while surveying the damage. They must have known they would never have seen the trees mature themselves, but must have hoped that their children and indeed children's children might one day pick the fruit on summer evenings, and think of them as they did so.

— *Neil Bartlett, Ready to Catch Him Should He Fall*

# CONTENTS

# Chronological Contents

# Introduction

## Tom Cardamone

I took my first steps out of the closet in bookstores and libraries. Tentatively, I touched chipped and creased paperbacks and discovered books that let me know I was not alone. Before I knew who *the* gay authors were, or at least the usually prescribed volumes, I intuited from coded titles, from the allure of certain book covers, the stories that I soon made mine. These literary wanderings were as splendid as they were haphazard. The more I read the more I craved. And I wanted a conversation, a dialogue, a list of *gay* books that *gay* writers adored and championed. Novels and stories and characters that changed readers' lives, woke them to their rights and futures and destinies and lovers. Books that cried to be passed down from one man to the next, hand to hand, with whispers of sincerity, "you *have* to read this." Books that were used, re-read, bookmarked, dog-eared, highlighted, footnoted, forgotten, spines broken, out-of-print, history. *Gay literary* history. These books whisper back, "Remember what you felt the first time you found me?"

As gay culture is absorbed into the mainstream, our history has been quickly forgotten or simplified, history that always existed in the margins, passed along from one generation to the next in bedrooms and smoky bars. Television, a few films every year, and the Internet have replaced the thrill of visiting a gay bookstore. Now these bookstores are closing. Chain bookstores have ceded us a few rows in the nether regions of their gigantic barns; for every episode of *Heroes* and rerun of *Will & Grace* today that speaks directly to a young gay man, there are a multitude of neglected books, consigned to used bookstores and boxed in attics, collecting dust.

After I started sketching out novels and sheepishly submitting short stories and attending book readings I met other gay writers. Inevitably, we would recommend texts to one another. Time and time again, I was struck by how often the novels and short story collections that I was breathlessly

urged to read were then just as speedily lamented as out-of-print and hard
to find. Worse, I surprised myself when recommending relatively recent
titles only to find that the book I deemed so important, so solidly valuable,
was already remaindered. Often I ended up buying multiple copies of these
favorites whenever I stumbled across them, storing them like talismans to
push hopefully on fresh converts. Of course I read some brilliant gay books
that continue to stay in print, have won awards, and have been adopted into
a gay canon, but I was increasingly curious as to whether they represented
the whole of gay literature; were these titles the genuine pinnacle? So many
of the books that came up in conversation embodied a diversity and history
that was either pre-Stonewall or went far beyond the available urban story.
The current canon does not make room for campy pulp paperbacks from the
fifties and sixties, so unrepresentative of our current lives yet so important
as historical documents and, in their day, as proof of our very existence.
Serious pioneer texts from these periods and even earlier have been
obscured by more forward, modern works. Transformative novels were lost
as the dark and dangerous eighties were consumed by the heady nineties.
Yet contemporary novels can have a fleeting existence within the current
multiplication of medias and the technological rapidity with which art is
delivered and consumed. A cultural lacuna has opened, one that needs
arresting. So I dug deeper. I sifted for more fiction in non-fiction books like
Michael Bronski's *Pulp Friction* and Gregory Woods' *A History of Gay
Literature* (both writers accepted invitations to contribute to this collection). I
researched small presses come and gone. I made lists of obscure or forgotten
titles and rushed to the Strand bookstore to comb the stacks on my lunch
break. What I also required, though, was for the conversation to continue. I
wanted to *hear* what books mattered, from writers I liked and knew or
wanted to know. I wanted a gay version of Anthony Burgess' *99 Great
Novels* but from a multitude of voices, different generations and ethnicities
and backgrounds -- meaning this wasn't a book I wanted to write, but one I
wanted to *read*.

This project was and is completely organic. When I decided to
embark upon this anthology, I simply looked at my bookshelf and e-mailed

the authors I had recently read and the writers I knew personally. Of those who were immediately struck by a title and author they wanted to write about (and I do mean immediate; I rarely had to wait more than a day before I received an enthusiastic response) I then asked "Can you think of anyone else who might be interested?" And they did. So straight away I let the contributors drive this project. They even suggested the title.

While waiting to collect their essays, I gathered the books they were writing about and in doing so decided that this anthology should be organized alphabetically by author covered, to best honor and illuminate these writers whose work deserves our attention, reconsideration, and possibly a place, once again, in the realm of the printed and read. I envisioned this collection as more of a round table; writers discussing, defending, remembering and explaining favorite out-of-print gay books or forgotten titles. As I read these books I was constantly surprised. I certainly did not expect to discover a book concerning a gay teen published in 1969, much less a *second* gay young adult novel from that period. The searing epistolary Vietnam War-era novel that was too hot to read in public; books about a gay black detective and a Roman Emperor's marriage to his favorite gladiator. These stories spanned centuries and took me from Rome to Boston, Capri to New Orleans, South Africa to Canada, Lebanon to Franco Spain, from the Golden Gate to Times Square. These are the books that challenged young minds, shaped careers, and saved lives.

Certainly there were authors whose work everyone here thought should be covered but regrettably was not (which led to an appendix of memorable books). As contributors were approached and possible publishers contacted, a few of the titles covered actually came back into print, a sure sign that the books we discussed deserve a permanent place on our shelves or at least wider attention. Contributor and gay literary historian Philip Clark wrote the closing essay on significant works returned to print, demonstrating that what is lost is not always unrecoverable.

This collection, meant to entice new readers and encourage publishers to bring back a few forgotten classics, is more the start of a conversation than the final word. We have to keep sharing our memories and discoveries and in doing so broaden the definition and diversity of the gay text. We must expand our cultural memory so that, in rushing from one century to the next, we carry with us the experience and knowledge that keeps the light burning for all.

Books about books are a rare species, special tomes for writers and book lovers. More than an affirmation of taste, a book about books is often a spirited celebration and sincere investigation. Quickly coveted, it remains on that particular shelf, guarded and revered,  and eventually slips out of print.  What good company we will keep then, among a library lost, only momentarily invisible, waiting patiently to be found again.

# Rabih Alameddine
# The Perv:Stories
## Picador, 1999

## Michael Graves

One great writer led me to another. My mentor had said something like, "I think you'll really dig his work. He's fantastic." I said something like, "And *how* do you spell his name again?"

Out of print? Yes. Difficult to find? Certainly. After a great deal of Internet prowling, I finally ordered *The Perv: Stories* by Rabih Alameddine. Two weeks dragged by (much to my hissy-fitting), and, at last, this collection of short stories was lying on my stoop. The box was beaten, scratched up. It looked as though it had been gang raped by other packages (possibly from Pottery Barn or LL Bean). I promptly ripped it free and delved into Alameddine's fiction. But there was a problem: my copy was a defect and a screw-up. Many pages were absent from the book. After page 55, I stumbled upon page 70 (enter additional hissy-fits). I was forced to re-order, re-read and start at the start again. All this agitation, though, was well worth it. *The Perv* has become the trusted comrade I turn to whenever I feel moody. Whenever I feel talentless. Whenever I feel dulled by the writing of others. *The Perv* waits for me on the shelf, by the bedside, near the toilet.

Rabih Alameddine's batch of eight stories is a tight, cohesive, well-stitched gathering. Still, he demonstrates diversity. In all areas. Considering both style and content, the author's pieces are sometimes loud or sometimes quiet. They are post- modernly chic or classically traditional. They are straightforward or even puzzling. Alameddine avoids any sort of limitation.

He is, by no means, a two-trick pooch. He employs countless methods to construct his tales and, craft-wise, the author's endowments gleam in every sentence.

*The Perv* reveals a homosexual voice, as well as a unique queer experience. As an artist, Alameddine refuses to be constrained by the trappings of gay literature (sex/shock/sex/shock). He showcases much much more. *The Perv*, although somewhat sexualized, remains to be a collection that is propelled by its hefty use of emotion. There is longing, loss, triumph, liberation. Amply described blowjobs and anal scenes may stigmatize gay writers, but Alameddine busts straight through these literary road blocks. The author exhibits multi-colored, multi-dimensional stories that are seasoned with Lebanese culture, political musings and crisis.

*The Perv* boasts many standout stories. Choosing a favorite would prove to be a rather laborious task. "Whore" stuns readers. This selection follows Rana, a thirtyish woman who journeys home to attend her father's funeral. Here, Alameddine deftly pulls readers into his bold setting. He writes, "Beirut spreads behind me. Interminable, a sprawling, disheveled city of mottled, self-conscious buildings ... I can see the azure of the Mediterranean, the tides, the flux, the struggle of a town in bloom against its web...The city sheds its shackles only to find that chains held its soul." Beautiful. His imagery. His hint of politics. But Alameddine juxtaposes the struggle in Beruit with the strife his protagonist carries. Rana is a painter, just as her father once was (Rana, however, is quite a success). Artistically and personally, she is enslaved by the patriarch's cultural ideals and expectations; therefore, she builds her life around a somewhat hushed rebellion. Rana tells readers, "I was such a disappointment." She becomes a single spinster who abandons her family (mother and four sisters included). Rumored to be a lesbian, she lives with her cousin Zouzou whom she allegedly sleeps with. The catty, gossiping townsfolk surreptitiously call her a whore. As Alameddine concludes this piece, all questions are answered. Most importantly, with flare, with grace, the writer offers his portrait of a

Lebanese woman who battles societal restrictions and forges ahead on her own quest to be free. Empowerment courses through each line in this dazzling story.

With "Remembering Nasser," a gay protagonist peers back at the loving relationship he once held with his cousin. This scattered, non-linear selection is crammed with tenderness and yearning. They shared a bed and a toilet at age three and stole cars in their teen years. Full-grown, the unnamed narrator and Nasser part ways; the main speaker flees to America and his cousin remains in Beirut. Still, these cousins remain fiercely connected. Alameddine writes, "Fred, my lover, was jealous of him. It completely confused me. Fred used to say my face lit up whenever I spoke of Nasser." Eventually, the protagonist grapples with the task of revealing his homosexuality to Nasser. Such moments are wonderfully profound. Alameddine writes, "When Nasser had come to the United States for a business meeting, he thought he should come stay with me . . . I tried to clean up, to remove any trace of gayness in the house. Fred was livid. . . . I told Fred there was no way Nasser would accept the situation. Once he knew, all he would be able to see when he looked at me was someone who takes it up the ass." He finally does expose himself to Nasser. Alameddine simply writes, "the wall went up." As the narrator and his cousin continue building their own lives (the main speaker ushers Fred through a terrible ordeal with AIDS and Nasser decides that he must marry and leave his bachelorhood behind), they drift further and further apart. But the protagonist still embraces his comforting memories. "Remembering Nasser" rouses readers. While avoiding sentimentality, this story knocks on one's soul with a full fist.

"A Flight to Paris" expertly utilizes dual points of views: a young gay man and an older Lebanese woman. This is somewhat perplexing, though. Coyly, Alameddine doesn't unveil his chosen form in an overt, immediate manner. He, instead, requires the audience to read carefully, backtrack a bit and discover this devise. Once in fluid motion, the author's flight mates kindly clash. They both possess strong initial impressions of one another. The man says, "For whatever reason, I found her somewhat offensive," and the woman proclaims, "He must be a homosexual. My son must know him." "A Flight to Paris" affords readers a possible glimpse into Rabih Alameddine's reality. The older woman discusses her son who has written a novel. She proclaims, "I read it. They tell him its literature. I think its trash." This may be related to Alameddine's own life experiences and the publication of his first novel, *Koolaids*. True or false, this injects a bit of cheekiness into an otherwise heavy piece. The plane soars on and Alameddine amps up the tension. The duo discusses a bevy of topics, including plastic surgery, marriage, commitment and, somewhat uncomfortably, queerness. The man asks her, "Do you think humans can choose who they love?" And the cordial debate meanders forward until the gentleman blurts out, "my lover died of AIDS." The woman begins to sob, tears streaking down her face and Alameddine's clever story, like a symphony, captures this storm of sadness. And a spot of hope too.

The title story "The Perv," is, by far, a very exceptional effort. This piece surprises readers with a brisk bitch slap. It begins, cryptically, with a salacious personal advertisement. The audience is quickly confronted by the abrasive main speaker (who we assume is named Bill). The author writes, "I know you think of me as a pervert. You judge me. By your standards, I am a pervert. But who are you to judge? If I am a pervert, it is God who made this way." While "The Perv" unfolds, Alameddine constructs his story with chunks of narrative, as well as letters between middle-aged Bill and a 13-year-old boy, Sammy. Bill writes, "My other interests include world travel and languages . . . you said you have a really slim and hairless body; that really turns me on." Young Sammy tells Bill, "I like soccer . . . I like reading . . .I like computers." The atmosphere is uncomfortable, unsettling. Readers squirm and shift. But then, Alameddine ignites a nuclear bomb of sorts and this story begins to back flip. The narrator is not the narrator. Bill is not Bill and likewise for Sammy. With his words, Alameddine performs an enchanting, road side magic show and readers are left, awestruck. The author concocts pure brilliance. But the secret to his tricks cannot be revealed for you here. You must discover it for yourself.

In America, writers are afforded the freedom to express themselves in unlimited manners. Creative liberty is a privilege. Rabih Alameddine fully acknowledges this, nabbing the opportunity to offer the world a work of importance. *The Perv* is inimitable. *The Perv* is distinctive. *The Perv* is smashing, relevant, weighty. By fiercely creating his own voice and his own vision, Rabih Alameddine astonishes readers with a very special gift: These stories. I ponder Mr. Alameddine and I often remark, "Fuck! I wish I could be *this* good."

Always a student of others, I have captured a great deal from Mr. Alameddine's words. He reinforced what I already believed about fiction and art. Be gallant. Be yourself. Create without a filter. Create without fear.

Sometimes we need fellow radicals to remind us of what we, as writers, have set out to proclaim. He has nudged me and he has almost cradled me. And I am utterly grateful for this book.

# Allen Barnett
# The Body and Its Dangers

St. Martin's, 1990

## Christopher Bram

This book of six short stories created a nice little stir when it first came out in 1990. It not only won both major gay literary prizes, the Lambda Book Award and the Ferro-Grumley, it received a special citation from PEN's Ernest Hemingway Foundation. It was widely reviewed in the mainstream press. One story, "Philostorgy, Now Obscure," even appeared in the *New Yorker*.

AIDS was a major reason for the attention. Four of the stories deal directly with the epidemic, which casts its shadow over the other two. The plague was still in its first decade and readers — gay readers especially — were looking for fiction that addressed what was devastating their lives. This book did exactly that, not in raw slices of pain but with quiet craft and perfect prose.

That was the other reason for the attention: it was so beautifully written, the language stylish yet warm, with solid rhythms and well-constructed sentences.

> You let go of people, the living and the dead, and return to your self, your own resources, like a widower, a tourist alone in a foreign country. Your own senses become important and other people's sensibilities a kind of Novo-

caine, blocking out your own perceptions, your ability to
discriminate, your taste.


But Barnett was not afraid to be funny or smartass. The AIDS quilt
is described as "a foldable, dry-cleanable cemetery." A lesbian mother tells
us about her boy-crazy daughter: "My daughter thinks that lesbianism is
next to laziness. She thinks this requires no effort."

Short stories are often treated as the poor cousins of novels, yet the
stories here are rich and full, like concentrated short novels. The digressive
episodic construction of each tale recalls Alice Munro at her best. The panels
of story don't always come in the pattern we expect, but can suddenly swing
left or right, like the movement of a knight on a chessboard. Two stories
follow the same set of characters, but the others stand free. Nevertheless,
like Munro, the repetitions and variations on certain experiences create the
fuzzy outline of an author, like the Invisible Man seen walking in the rain.

No, I'm sorry, I wanted to write pure literary criticism here, but I
am leaving out something important: I knew Allen. I thought I could
discuss his work in the impersonal language of high literature, but it doesn't
feel right. It feels false even to call him "Barnett." Allen and I were good
friends during the last year of his life. We began by talking about books, our
own and other peoples'. When he became sick with AIDS, I visited him in
the hospital. Later at his apartment I tried to help him figure out the
complicated IV drip and bags of saline solution and the syringes needed to
clean out the port in his chest. Allen could no longer write once he was ill.
All the experience in his book came from his warm imagination and the
illness of friends. When he died in 1991, he left me his computer. I wrote my
next three novels on it, including *Gods and Monsters*. My protagonist, movie
director James Whale, served in the trenches during the First World War. I
gave Allen's last name to one of Whale's dead comrades. It's strange now,
and wonderful, too, to hear Ian McKellan in the movie deliver his
extraordinary speech about dead friends and speak of "Barnett on the wire."
I did not reread Allen's stories for years, perhaps because I feared they
might not be as good as I remembered. Yet it's been a joy to go back to his

book for this essay and see Allen the author as well as Allen the friend. He was an amazing writer, even better than I thought at the time. I would love these stories even if I had not known him. They deserve to be read and reread, not only because they capture life in the age of AIDS so well, but because they have a moral weight that transcends their moment in time.

I'd like to discuss a few stories at length to suggest their quality and strength. Allen's work wasn't really about plot, but I should warn you in advance that I'm going to give away a lot.

"The *Times* As It Knows Us" is the best known of Allen's stories, reprinted in anthologies and often cited. It's about a weekend on Fire Island in a house of gay men during the epidemic, an overload of characters we can only slowly distinguish from each other, much as if we were visiting the house ourselves. The story is haunted by the times: both the spirit of the age and the newspaper. The narrator, Clark, keeps a folder of clippings from the *New York Times*, a public history of the epidemic. Clark wants to dig beneath the shallow, two-dimensional accounts of gay men with AIDS propagated by the media and find a fuller, more human reality. That is exactly what the story does. It's like a Chekhov play where nothing major happens, but everything important is revealed. The men bond and bicker, help and hinder. One comes down with a fever; Clark takes care of him with help from housemates. Some people behave well, others badly, but everyone has his reasons. It's a very rich, densely textured story that captures lived lives without glib judgments or false nobility. Needing to give the feverish man a rubdown with vodka, Clark jokes, "Not the imported, get the domestic we use for guests," without making the reader doubt his genuine fear for his friend.

"The Body and Its Seasons" and "The Body and Its Dangers" are the two linked stories, following a trio of college friends into adulthood. In the first story, a gay student, Gordon, goes to bed with a female friend, Sara, as an experiment. While they lie in bed, we get pieces of his life, chiefly his Catholic upbringing and sex with two different priests, and sex with Sara's friend Marie followed by ideas about innocence and the Fall as illustrated by a play he just performed in, *The Garden*. In the second story, Sara narrates. Seventeen years have passed. She lives with her lover Marie and their daughter Rachel, whose father was Gordon. Sara has had a breast removed for cancer yet is still stricken with the disease. All bodies are in danger, not only the bodies of gay men. Sara spends the story musing to herself, gathering together the pieces of her life: her difficult daughter, her more difficult lover, her dead friend Jake, her absent friend Gordon. (We're never actually told that Gordon is dead, but we can't help assuming so.) Her voice is quiet and mature and clear. She imagines Gordon reappearing, talking to her and touching her scar tissue. "What he cannot make whole again, he will convince me doesn't matter."

This story narrated by a woman is the most overtly sexual in the book. Allen celebrates sex throughout *The Body and its Dangers*. Where another writer might condemn the desire that kills his characters, Allen treats sex as a valuable intimacy. Yet the act itself is presented more frankly here than elsewhere. From a woman's point of view, penetration becomes wonderfully matter-of-fact in one of my favorite descriptions of a sex act: "He opened himself with his fingers, and straddled Gordon, sitting back and guiding him in at once. He smiled."

"Philostorgy, Now Obscure" follows Preston, a gay man recently diagnosed with AIDS, when he returns to Chicago to say goodbye to his friends, in particular the two women he used to live with, Roxy and Lorna., who echo the female friends in the "Body" stories. Lorna is married to Sean, their favorite teacher, and pregnant with her second child. Preston goes to the faculty steam room with Sean and they talk about philosophy, in particular St. Augustine. He contacts an old lover, Jim. They meet for lunch and go to bed together. The story ends with Preston and Roxy talking about her own ex-boyfriend while they wait for Lorna to return.

It's a strange, crowded, slightly elusive story yet very beautiful. Allen's death has given it a weight it didn't have when I first read it. This farewell to friends and lovers was never sentimental or melodramatic, but it is now terribly real. Preston thinks about his dead and remembers desire before we're told:

Preston believed that he would survive, not the illness, but death itself. It was one of those things that one believes despite one's self, a tiny bubble of thought that hangs suspended somewhere between the heart and mind, fragile and thin as a Christmas tree ornament yet managing to last decades. He believed in his consciousness, that it would do more than last, but would have impact and consequence, that wherever it went there would be discourse and agitation; decisions would be made and adhered to.

Which Allen managed to achieve in his single, wonderful book. He can still affect how we think about our lives. His bubble of consciousness survives.

# Neil Bartlett

## Ready to Catch Him Should He Fall

Serpent's Tail, 1990

## Philip Clark

Containing Fragments from and Reworkings of Neil Bartlett's *Ready to Catch Him Should He Fall* (1990).

> [I]ndeed, the whole book seemed to him to contain the story of his own life, written before he had lived it.
> — Oscar Wilde, *The Picture of Dorian Gray*

Of course, it was several years before I met my own Boy, my very own Boy, that I read *Ready to Catch Him Should He Fall*. But thank you for that book, Mr. Bartlett. In another of your books, *Who Was That Man: A Present for Mr. Oscar Wilde*, you quote That Man himself:

> It is quite true. Most people are other people. Their thoughts are someone else's opinions, their lives a mimicry, their passions a quotation. — Oscar Wilde, *De Profundis*

And is this quite true? This book you wrote, this *Ready to Catch Him Should He Fall*, this story of Boy and O, the bar where they met, the woman who helped bring them together, the marriage they shared: have I not only read and reread it, given it to others, written about it, quoted from it, but has it also, consciously or not, served as pattern and image for my most important relationship? Has life, as Wilde so famously said, imitated art?

Had I said to my Boy, *I love you, I love you, my heart is a rose!* — would it have been any less true because I was not the first to say it?

I. *In which the Narrator describes Boy for the reader:*
"I could tell you that he had white skin, black eyes, and black hair, but you can see that from the photograph. I could tell you that the eyes were so beautiful they could actually make you feel giddy when he suddenly looked up from the floor and straight at you."

I have described my Boy three times as looking like a drawing by Aubrey Beardsley, all black and white: once in a journal, once retelling a story, and now. As Wilde knew, if a line is good enough to use, it is good enough to plagiarize from oneself and use again. Besides, it is appropriate. It is right. My Boy's eyes were emerald, a cat's eyes, but in my mind and memory, they are as dark as his bright black hair. They made my stomach tighten with a pleasurable nervousness. I believe I was looking for a Boy whose eyes might make me feel that way.

He was not unlike the 19-year-old Boy who enters The Bar in that book.

II. *In which the Narrator explains The Bar's ritual of naming:*
"One thing Boy never said, the line . . . he would never have used, was *don't call me Boy*. He loved to be called Boy. He smiled whenever the name was used. He loved it that we had christened him and he knew that he was special to us."

Long after it had started, we argued playfully about who had first begun our custom. He thought he had, but I knew that couldn't be true. This ritual was in place well before the day I had him read *Ready to Catch Him Should He Fall*, and I knew I must have initiated it. We never used our Christian names. We each called the other "Boy."

And if this sounds too precious to you, if it makes you want to stop reading, then I'm sorry. Perhaps you think that this sounds like an affectation, that no two people you would want to spend time with would act this way. Well I have to say that much of the impact of this story depends upon your realizing that this felt entirely natural to us. That "Boy" also meant *I love you* and *I am near* and *we are safe with each other*.

And that when he stopped calling me "Boy," I knew it was over.

III. *In which the Narrator explains a detail of The Bar's decorations, as designed by Madame, the proprietress:*

"And whatever else the décor was . . . the one thing that was always the same and that Madame never got rid of was the ceiling. The design of the ceiling of The Bar was very wonderful. She'd had it inlaid with a hundred, several hundred small white fairy-lights, and it gave the effect of a real fantastic night sky, especially on a good night. I always loved that. The bulbs weren't just scattered, but were arranged in the correct pattern — so that if you looked up you could see (if you knew which star was which), up there amongst all the dragons, bulls, and poisonous scuttlers of the Heavens, right in the centre you could see the constellation which I always thought of as our special one, a solitary man walking with his faithful dog, the high summer constellation of Orion, the Hunter, stretched and striding above us. But I never knew what all the other stars meant, just that one constellation."

It is easy to identify The Hunter, spreadeagled on the night's black bed of sky. He is a man making his own path, always moving toward some unknowable goal. But for a dog, he is alone. This does not stop his progress. I imagine him, the protector, looking down on the heads of The Bar's patrons.

We had no Bar to turn to. We had no single space in which to be together, and so we turned outdoors, made every place our proving ground. Early on, we saw that nature welcomed us. We could not cross the college campus we first called home without encounters. An evening stroll near fraternity row led to a thick-flanked raccoon waddling across our path, eyeing us with complacent tolerance before drifting into the dusky woods. On the bridge between the cafeteria and the library, we were treated to the spectacle of five deer crashing about the undergrowth. They settled and browsed the leaves while we watched with quiet pleasure. And while neither of us knew the sky's shining map, every night we found Orion launched above our heads, watching over us, a blessing.

IV. *In which a patron of The Bar has been attacked*:

"This time there was no knife, they just got him on the floor and it was just a fist which had come down on the man's face again and again. And it happened just two streets away from The Bar. He came into the bar with blood everywhere . . . He wasn't as badly hurt as he looked, actually, but it was enough to make us all think at least twice.

People say to me that I must be keeping a list of all the attacks I hear about. They say it's morbid, they say what are you trying to prove anyway. They say why do you have to talk about that just now. They say to me, how many of them do there have to be before you think you've got enough on your list. They say when are you going to stop it, and I say, when am I going to stop it, when am I —

Not long after we began dating, one of our favorite professors screened the movie version of *Bent*, Martin Sherman's play about the claiming of gay identity, set amid the brutality of the Holocaust. Having read and been stunned at the play's power in high school, I knew what to expect of the movie. But when I walked into the darkened classroom, I was too distracted to think much about the film. I knew we would be together that evening, and in the sweet daze of one newly in love, my thoughts were always at least half with him.

But after the opening cycle of scenes, the tightening net, the knowledge that there will be no hiding, no passport, no border, no cloak of night, and after the inevitable arrests, the main character, Max, finds himself in the cattle car with his friend. When the Nazis choose his friend to mock, to abuse, when they bash their clubs against this man's ribs with the sickening thud of metal to flesh, Max stands still, knowing that to react will only invite his own destruction, paralyzed by self-protection. And I — I who do not cry at movies, who know the line between what is real and what is on the screen, who affects, like any proper boy, not to feel — I am thinking of him, thinking of his being touched for so slight a reason as petty hatred, and I cannot stop the tears no matter how I try to hold them in.

Together, we had yet to hear more than a few words tossed from cars as we made our way through the town's grid of gently curving streets. But did he notice that I held him extra-long in our welcoming embrace that night? That stepping back I examined his face, half-expecting swollen lips, a cut or bruise below those emerald eyes?

V. *When Boy reappears in The Bar with O, with whom he has spent six days:*
"In the week of their absence, we had decided that their lovemaking would be extraordinary, legendary. Since so many of us had made love to either O or to Boy, we felt that by comparing notes, we knew a great deal about how they behaved when making love, and so when we saw them reappear so obviously as lovers we were pleased to see that our predictions had been correct. We had assumed that their affair would in some way be a violent one, because O was known to be violent, and because Boy made you feel strange when he gave himself away to you, a strangeness, and a feeling that you always wanted more, that often came out as violence. And now here to prove our thesis was Boy, silent, stunned, extraordinarily tired, ravaged by intimacy, shattered by sex, dazed with sex."

Beginning that first time, shivering in my arms from nerves and the February cold, he gave himself away. Some nights he would lie on his belly, legs slightly spread, and turn his face toward me, expectant. I could lower myself on top of him, chest to back, could whisper to him any words I wanted. But even buried inside him, my teeth on the back of his neck, I still wanted more, to thrust deeper, for his flesh and my flesh to meld. This did not even have to be during sex, a touch of the hand, an embrace would find me desperate to take his body with me right down into the deep, under the earth, to drag his body beneath the sea, the heavy waves. Of course none of this made sense, I could not tell him how I felt, this desire for union, this desire to be inside his bones.

He didn't even have to say those words "Do *anything. Do anything you want to me, you can do anything you want, I give you entire permission over me*" for I knew I could take him, I could fuck him any way I could imagine, I could take all of him. But no, I never lost that feeling of strangeness, of wanting more, and no, of course, I never could get far enough inside.

VI. *From the early days of the courtship of Boy and O*
"Their daily, repeated intimacy at this time was astonishing for Boy because it had never happened to him before. And it was astonishing for O, because he did not really think that this was ever going to happen to him again. When O was in the bath, he would call out to Boy, *put that record on again will you?* or *Put some music on, whatever you like*, and then he'd leave the bathroom door open while he toweled himself dry. This was so that he could hear the music, but also so that Boy could see him naked if he wanted to, just as he was, just naturally naked from the bath, not for some pornographic scenario this time. In fact both of them found that sort of scene extraordinary, though in a way of course these were the most ordinary moments of their intimacy."

Within six months, we were living together, our own apartment, a ten-minute walk from campus along the tree-lined road. Just to be able to sit at my desk, writing, to be able to then look over and see him reading on the couch, his legs curled beneath him, to be able to pick up a book of my own and, running a hand through his spiky black hair, kiss him and sit down beside him to read, this was wonderful. It is a true wonder at any age, but particularly as young as we both were. To be able to hold his hand as we sat before the television in the evenings, to be able to buy food at the market and, shoulder to shoulder, cook our dinner together, to wake beside him in the morning and, rolling over, to stretch an arm along his stomach, my hand resting at his heart, if you cannot imagine how this would feel, if you do not understand how extraordinary these things are, then you know nothing, nothing, nothing.

VII. *In which the Narrator describes the marriage of Boy and O, their ceremony having been arranged by Madame — I'm sorry, arranged by* Mother
"It was complicated enough. Some people were not comfortable with the ceremony and half left, ending up in the kitchen while they exchanged the rings and made the actual vows, which was all done in the living room.

The vows were read very slowly, as if there could be time enough in these pauses for us all to think about what those famous and infamous words might actually mean on this particular occasion, and how you could make them mean what you wanted them to mean with regard to this person who you wished to spend time with and honour in some way, to cherish, to care for in some real way for whatever time. I do understand why they said all that out loud."

He was formally dressed in the black suit I loved to see him wear, and he stood quietly near his sister as she prepared to say the vows. Were it not for him, I would not have been there — not at his sister's wedding, of course, not in this far corner of Virginia, but also not at any wedding. Too awkward, too religious. Too painful, perhaps, to know I could not speak those vows to him.

But when I gazed at him, when I saw him look at her with such pride, *bursting with pride*, that's the phrase they use, when I heard his sister and her new husband recite these words, I began to understand. Not only to know these things to be true, this *have* and this *hold*, this *care for* and this *honor*, but to speak these things aloud, to declare them in front of the world, yes, I understand.

These words were still hard to hear, they were still complicated, but they were, for once, also mine. I gazed at him, and my lips moved with the cadence of the vows, saying them aloud and meaning every one.

VIII. *After letters Boy receives from 'Father'*
"This letter made Boy so angry that he stayed silent all day after reading it. Since Boy never replied to these letters, he had no real reason to expect that they would ever refer to O or congratulate him on his new life with O, or even mention it, how could they; the man who wrote them knew nothing of all that, nothing. But still Boy was angry, white with anger."

*And after Boy and O have taken 'Father,' now ill and infirm, into their flat:*
"Why he had to prove himself like this wasn't entirely clear. Sometimes his eagerness to do everything properly, to get it right, was so constant that it seemed fierce; his way of caring for the old man seemed as close to anger as it was to care somehow, and the silences in the flat seemed almost like the intervals in a long and violent argument. . . . All O could think of doing was to support Boy in this task or effort. . . . But he was determined never to be defeated by this man, O could see that."

Dear Boy,

I am at the window on the second floor, the top floor, and you stand in the wet grass at the very edge of the street, head down. Mostly you listen to the man who stands at his car door, the door open, the door in hand, leaving. If there is conversation, there is little of it, or maybe you respond with your head still down, barely ever meeting this man's eyes. Maybe you are, after all, still a boy sometimes.

I have met this man. When it became clear what I am, who I am to you, that was all. He would not look me in the eye again, he would not ask you about me. After each phone call, you are tense with the energy required to speak without saying.

I want to ask, "What did he do to you?" What did he do to turn you, so alive, into this shell I see standing in the grass?

You have not lived in this man's house for years. I do not understand why you continue to see him. He is everything you do not want to be: rough, brutal, silent. He works the farm you will never return to, that you will remember so strongly, that you may visit, but that you will never return to. You owe him nothing.

But I also know you cannot choose whether you owe him anything. You cannot put 19 years of knowing him away, as though they never were.

When he slams the car's door and drives away, you turn toward our building. I meet you on the stairs, halfway up and halfway down, and follow you into our apartment. There is silence that I cannot interpret: sadness? anger? Or are you simply, profoundly tired? I turn you toward me, place my arms around you. I will stay near, near for as long as you need me, ready to catch you should you fall.

IX. *From the aria O sings for Boy*
*"I can't see you weep except through tears of my own,*
*And when I can't see you, I worry about you; take good care of yourself."*
Boy, I am lonely without you.
I love you, I love you, my heart is a rose!

# George Baxt

# A Queer Kind of Death

Simon & Schuster, 1966

## Larry Duplechan

When I began writing my first novel back in 1984, it was largely in reaction to the near absence of black characters to be found in gay-themed fiction up to that time. Harvey Fierstein has said, "There are lots of needs for art. The greatest one is the mirror of our own lives and our own existence."[1] And as a young black gay man in the 1970s and 80s, I was painfully aware of a lack of fictional characters that reflected me. Weary of waiting to read a story about a man like me, I wrote *Eight Days A Week*, a story about a man almost *exactly* like me. It was, after all, *my* mirror.

In 1972, during my Sophomore year in high school (Westchester High in Los Angeles), I happened upon a public library copy of Mort Crowley's Broadway play, *The Boys in the Band* (which I had heard of but not yet read or seen). I checked the book out, read it, renewed it several times, committed much of it to memory, and quoted from it extensively in schoolyard conversation (imagine if you will a small 15-year-old black boy referring to a classmate as a "*sunt* -- that's French, with a cedilla"). In retrospect, it seems the virulent self-hatred of Crowley's group of gay friends circa 1968 escaped me all but completely. What struck me most about this, the very first piece of gay popular art ever to make its way into my young hands, was that I now had written evidence that there were other gay people (to my knowledge, I had yet to meet one in the flesh), and that they had friends, lovers, birthday parties, and lightning wit. Not only did other gay men actually exist (in New York City, anyway), but there were other *black* gay men. I wasn't the only one.

---

[1] *The Celluloid Closet* (film), 1995

True, Crowley's one black character, Bernard, was a pathetic mess (I could see that, even at 15). But as Harvey Fierstein has said regarding the portrayal of gays in Hollywood movies, "visibility at any cost. I'd rather have negative than nothing."[2] (Last Harvey Fierstein quote, I promise!)

Around 1975, a college friend lent me his copy of Gordon Merrick's 1970 man-on-man bodice-ripper, *The Lord Won't Mind*. Aside from our shared appreciation for man-meat, I could not have had less in common with Merrick's protagonists, Peter and Charlie, a pair of tall, handsome, hyper-masculine donkey-dicked Aryan *über-menchen* who not only fucked one another, but women, as well, the obvious message being that Peter and Charlie were in love with one another, but they were no girly-men. The only black character in *The Lord Won't Mind* was the maid, an old-Hollywood mammy stereotype who overcomes her religious convictions enough to allow that if Peter and Charlie truly loved one another, then "the Lord won't mind."

In 1976 –– America's Bicentennial year, my sophomore year in college, and 10 years after the publication of *A Queer Kind of Death* –– Patricia Nell Warren's *The Front Runner* was published. Like so many of my friends from UCLA's recently-founded Gay Students Union, I read, re-read and re-re-read Ms. Warren's debut novel, discussed it *ad nauseum*, carried it and quoted from it like the kids in Jews for Jesus did the New Testament. In its own way, *The Front Runner* (the story of a young gay track star and his somewhat older track coach lover) was as much a romance novel as *The Lord Won't Mind*, and as old-school as *The City and the Pillar* or *Giovanni's Room* –– its beautiful gay male protagonist is killed at the end. But for me and my colleagues, Ms. Warren's portrayal of gay male life and lovemaking seemed so true to life (she seemed to know so much about how we mid-70s gay men dressed, how we cruised one another, even how we dirty-danced) that it was rumored that Patricia Nell Warren was really a gay man writing under a *nom de plume*.

---

[2] *Ibid.*

Still, the only black character in *The Front Runner*'s world of muscular, masculine "macho gays" (a term I'm pretty sure was a Warren original -- certainly, my friends and I never used it) was Delphine de Sevigny, a middle-aged femme queen who wore diaphanous caftans and called everyone "*chérie*" in a voice borrowed from Marilyn Monroe. Now, I wasn't the world's most masculine man, but I was no Delphine, and I recall being a tiny bit miffed that Patricia Nell (as my friends and I called her, as if she were an old pal) had not seen fit to write a black "macho gay."

It may well have been in the midst of one of my diatribes about the dearth of black gay characters in gay fiction when someone (I don't remember who, but God bless whoever it was) handed me a copy of *A Queer Kind of Death*, very possibly with the announcement that the protagonist of the book was a black gay man, a police officer, didn't die at the end, and wasn't a drag queen. While I don't recall the cover art (and a bit more about cover art later), it was very likely the initial trade paperback edition. I do recall being pleasantly surprised that someone had finally written a black gay character with which I might be able to identify (that is, not crazy, not wearing a frock, and not dead), and just plain surprised at the publication date of the book: 1966.

When *A Queer Kind of Death* was first published, Lyndon Johnson was President of the United States. The Beatles released the *Revolver* album, then retreated into the studio to record *Sgt. Pepper*. Nancy Sinatra's knee-high white vinyl go-go boots were made for walking. *The Sound of Music*, released in 1965, was still the box office champ and won an armload of Oscars. *Peyton Place* and *The Dick Van Dyke Show* were among the most popular television shows, with Emmy awards to prove it; and *Star Trek* made its debut (I missed it and cared not -- I was a *Patty Duke Show* fan, and *Star Trek* was on at the same time).

Notwithstanding the much-touted "sexual revolution" of the time (by 1965, an estimated 6.5 million women were on The Pill), the mid-1960s was a difficult and dangerous time for gay people, even in New York City, where *A Queer Kind of Death* is set. The Stonewall riots were still three years in the future, and the notion of homosexuals as a downtrodden minority and/or a political force was all but unknown in America. Early homosexual apologetics groups The Mattachine Society and Daughters of Bilitis existed, but were small, underground, and little known outside their own memberships. New York's sodomy laws were very much in force (and ultimately would not be repealed until the year 2000). New York City gay bars were Mob-owned, and often run without benefit of a liquor license, as the State Liquor Authority had free reign to refuse them; and despite the bribes to local police necessary to keep them open, they were routinely raided, and their clientele jailed (and their names and home addresses listed in the newspapers, often resulting in loss of jobs, family shame, and sometimes suicide).

All things considered, I find it no less than amazing that journeyman screen and television writer George Baxt should have begun writing a murder mystery novel starring a black gay detective in 1965. No less a giant than Simon and Schuster published the first edition in 1966. There quickly followed a trade paperback edition (1966), the one I most likely read a decade later. As I remember, I read the book ravenously, despite being no big fan of the mystery genre (*A Queer Kind of Death* may well have been the first murder mystery I'd ever read), so great was my joy at finding a novel with a black gay protagonist. Over thirty years and many black gay novels (several of them my own) later, I found my recent re-read of *A Queer Kind of Death* a good deal less joyful.

In brief, *A Queer Kind of Death* concerns the death (apparently by foul play) of Ben Bentley (née Benjamin Bernheim), a handsome 20-something actor/model/hustler. In the ages-old tradition of the genre, nearly everyone in the immediate orbit of the deceased had some reason to want him dead, among them Seth Piro, failed writer and Ben's ex-roommate (and ex-lover); Seth's estranged wife, Veronica; the wealthy but elderly Jameson Hurst, with whom Ben had also previously shared digs (and presumably a bed); Adam, Hurst's current caretaker/kept boy; a native American (called Indians in 1966), ex-masseur/call boy; and Hurst's mysterious, reclusive, and oddly powerful sister, Ella. It falls to Detective

Pharoah Love ("Negro and homosexual," to quote *New York Times* reviewer Anthony Boucher[3]) to ferret out Ben Bentley's killer.

The 1986 "20th Anniversary Edition" of *A Queer Kind of Death*, a copy of which I recently bought on the cheap from Amazon, sports one of the most egregiously designed covers ever executed (and I freely admit that a couple of my own book covers qualify as eyesores): a pale purple background from which emerges a drawing of an African-American man's mouth -- wide, full lips open to reveal somewhat overlarge upper teeth; in the foreground, a human skeleton wearing a black jacket, pink open-collar shirt, a blue-and-gold-striped neck scarf, and a curly black wig, a long-stemmed red rose between the skull's teeth. Granted, the cover art has nothing really to do with the quality of a book itself, but still -- not pretty. The original 1966 paperback and 1969 British paperback versions of *A Queer Kind of Death* are considerably more attractive: the former featuring a close-up of the face of a good-looking, bespectacled black man in the background, with an abstract design of a sprawled male body superimposed. The latter, a skeleton of a hand with a pink carnation between the finger bones.

More importantly (and disappointingly), my revisiting Pharoah Love, Baxt's protagonist, 42 years after his debut, revealed a character who is little more than a funny name and the habit of calling everyone "cat." In his preface to the 20th Anniversary Edition, Mr. Baxt claims to have based Pharoah (Egyptian monarch deliberately misspelled) Love on "a very hip black man" he'd "occasionally had a drink with at Elaine's famous celebrity hangout" in New York. Apparently, either this black man called people "cat," or calling people "cat" was Mr. Baxt's idea of something a "very hip black man" might do. In any case, Mr. Baxt has Pharoah Love do this an irritating number of times in the course of 249 small, tiny-type pages: "Seth cat," "Seth baby cat," "Adam cat," "Jameson cat," "snotty cat" (Love's name for Veronica) -- face-to-face and in reference, Pharoah Love calls everybody "cat," a habit so annoying (at least to me) that he probably could have extracted confessions from suspects using that tactic alone. By the time Seth

---

[3] *The New York Times*, June 12, 1966, as quoted on the back cover of the 20th Anniversary Edition of *A Queer Kind of Death*

Piro picks up the habit, calling Love "Pharoah-cat," I had had more than enough ( according to his 1986 Preface, Baxt's original and preferred title for his first novel was *Dead Cat*; overkill anyone?).

I found myself wondering if Mr. Baxt's occasional drinking buddy might have been his only black acquaintance as of 1965. At one point in conversation with one of the white characters, Pharoah makes a reference to the Indians having sold Manhattan "to us." Granting that I was only a kid at the time, it is hard for me to imagine a black man circa 1966 who wouldn't have added something like, "Well, to *y'all*, anyway." I have no historical documents handy to back up my claim, but I don't believe there were any black folk among the men who walked away with Manhattan for a box of beads. In fact, Pharoah Love seems to be the only black person (hip or square) in the New York City presented by Mr. Baxt. Perhaps realizing he hadn't the first idea of how black New Yorkers might actually speak and behave, he chose to create one "very hip black man" character and leave it at that.

The good news about Pharoah Love, in addition to the good news that Mr. Baxt chose to write him at all, is that (unlikely as it seems for the time and place he inhabits) Love is a detective with the New York police force; he's black (he is called "dinge," "blackamoor" and such by other characters, though never to his face), and he is, by my own working definition, bisexual, and as open about his sexuality as anyone he encounters (straight, bent or undecided) is about theirs. Considering homosexual acts were still illegal in New York in 1966, and the Civil Rights Act was all of two years old, Pharoah Love is one very liberated black queer man. For a black bisexual in a straight white world, he is amazingly comfortable in his own skin. He treats the white people he deals with as his equals (professional, social, and sexual), not his betters. For the 18-year-old black gay boy I was when I first read *A Queer Kind of Death*, Pharoah Love was a welcomed addition to Merrick's Peter and Charlie, and Patricia Nell Warren's Billy and Harland, and an antidote to Mort Crowley's pathetic Bernard.

Post-Stonewall, post-gay liberation movement, post-AIDS, post-Elton, Ellen and Aiken, it is also interesting to witness the attitudes of Mr. Baxt's characters to non-heterosexual leanings and behavior. In the social milieu in which *A Queer Kind of Death* takes place, homosexuality (or, to be more accurate, bisexuality) seems almost to be the norm: while Pharoah Love is outspoken about his desire for Seth Piro (not just as a sexual partner, but as a possible steady date/housemate), he claims he could just as well "care for some chick." Detective Love is an equal opportunity flirt, turning on the charm not only for Seth, but for bar owner Ida, and a pretty blond "chick" dancing with her date at Ida's joint. Seth is sleeping with men while still legally married to Veronica. Both the hulking Adam and the movie star-handsome Ben have sex with both men and women, for fun and/or profit. Only the women seem to be exclusively heterosexual (and one of them has a Sapphic indiscretion in her past); and of the men, only Ida's bartender (Ward, née Moishe, Gabriel) seems to be unerringly straight, and only the swishy Jameson Hurst is totally homosexual. Certainly, no one in the story is talking about the possibility of same-sex marriage or homosexuals as a voting block -- sex and sexuality haven't been politicized yet -- but the pervasive attitude seems to be that sex is just sex, whoever's doing what to whom. There is a matter-of-fact sexual fluidity that seems oddly sophisticated and adult as compared with the currently pervasive strict gay/straight dichotomy and "get off the fence" attitude towards bisexuality and those who practice it. Whether this is a true refection of the "homosexual otherworld" with which Mr. Baxt claimed (in his 1986 Preface) to have been familiar, or simply wish fulfillment on the part of the author, I could only conjecture.

While Mr. Baxt exhibits an admirable way with plot (the outcome of Detective Love's investigation took me by surprise 30 years ago, and despite having read the book before, I didn't see it coming this time, either), his characterizations are not nearly as strong. With the exception of Jameson Hurst (effeminate, imperious, lascivious and somehow oddly sympathetic), the denizens of Mr. Baxt's mid-60s New York City are mostly one-note Johnnies -- their entire personalities can be reduced to a sentence: Pharoah

Love is the black guy who says "cat;" Seth Piro is weak and neurotic, moored to his Viennese psychoanalyst; Veronica is perpetually unpleasant and just as perpetually horny; literary agent Ruthelma is fat, gluttonous, and effusive (indicated by the use of *lots* of *italics* in her dialogue). Even given that murder mysteries as a genre tend to be plot-driven rather than character driven, I could not help wishing the characters were fleshed out a bit more.

As an openly gay fictional sleuth, Pharoah Love is the godfather of Joseph Hansen's Dave Brandstetter, Michael Nava's (gay Latino) Henry Rios, Katherine Forrest's Kate Delafield, and others. But Hansen (beginning in the late 1970s), Nava (in the mid-80s), and Forrest (80s-90s) wrote considerably better mystery novels than *A Queer Kind of Love*. Fortunately, so did George Baxt. He even wrote better Pharoah Love novels, in sequels *Topsy and Evil* (1968) and especially *A Queer Kind of Love* (1994). I don't believe I ever recommended *A Queer Kind of Death* to anyone the first time I read it; and I would only do so today to a mystery novel fanatic (someone who reads the genre indiscriminately), or a student of black gay literature (in spite of Mr. Baxt having been white). To the extent it works at all anymore, *A Queer Kind of Death* works as a period piece, a relic of a very different time, its allusions to short-skirted blonds dancing the frug, the Beatles wanting to hold your hand, and of course, those millions of "cats" giving the book a paisley-print "Austin Powers" campiness 40-plus years after its initial publication.

The cover of the 2000 edition of *A Queer Kind of Death* indicated that the book had at that time been optioned for a major motion picture to star Laurence Fishburne. Nearly a decade later, I see Taye Diggs in the part, or maybe Cuba Gooding Jr. or Rockmund Dunbar; with Jake Gyllenhaal as Seth, and maybe Gwynneth Paltrow as Veronica. Bette Midler could chew scenery and canapés as Ruthelma. And the part of Jameson Hurst fairly *screams* David Bowie. Of course, the screenplay would have to kill most of those "cats."

# Bruce Benderson
## User

Dutton, 1994

## Rob Stephenson

I first read Bruce Benderson's novel *User* a couple of years after its debut in 1995. Stirring, seductive prose sucked me right into this exhaustive portrayal of urban prostitution and drug addiction in early 1990's Times Square. From the first page, a soiled, silken procession of words rendered me weak-kneed, incapable of pulling out until long after its final avian image had flown.

Reading it again ten years later confirmed my original feelings. This is a remarkable novel.

Benderson's decadent, viscous language oozes through the novel much like the many liquids held inside it. We encounter a catalog of suggestive fluids: the rich fading potency of sperm underfoot, the staining and sustaining attributes of blood, the grit of old bath water and mud, the disorienting hazes of heroin and booze, the welcome buzz of hot coffee, the jolt of salt water on the tongue, the sour displeasure of diarrhea, spittle, urine, and vomit on the streets, the relentless pounding of the rain.

He offers us the sordid tale of a nineteen-year-old, self-named mulatto hustler and the people in his life. Apollo is a junkie. He dances at the Ecstasy Male Theater and lures men into giving him cash for sex in the private booths behind the stage. After a flubbed attempt to get extra money from his prey, he punches out the doorman of the theater and flees the scene. For the rest of the novel, Apollo is on the run from the police, while hustling just enough cash to cop his bags of dope.

Mrs. Huxton is the eighty-six-year-old Portuguese widow who owns the theater as well as the building that houses it. She lives stories above it. Like a ghost, she haunts the novel, materializing in the background only once to assist the police in their fumbling search for Apollo. Otherwise, she remains a trumped-up authority figure in Apollo's fantasies about his own importance and his fate. He accepts that she has control over his life. It gives him comfort and hope to believe this, similar to the way many people feel God is a tangible benefactor, remaining close in their thoughts, even though he is locked out of reach in the heavens above them.

The other main characters include Casio, the doorman who ends up in the hospital and back in jail because of Apollo's punch. Casio's son, Baby Pop, is only fourteen, a drug-free hustler. He is determined to avenge his father's sorry condition at Apollo's hand. Angelita, Casio's lover and partner in crime, performs and hustles in drag. He's working towards a sex change operation. Detective Pangero searches for Apollo, enjoying his questionable methods of extracting information from the transvestite hookers he's attracted to on his beat. Tina, a power-hungry bar owner, runs the main hustler bar. Apollo's unnamed friend with AIDS gives him shelter and pills. He is the only one with anything like a relationship with Apollo, but it never quite solidifies.

The narrative moves through the minds of many of these characters. Their stories coalesce and break off into personal historical fragments interrupting each other as they zigzag along. Inevitably, they circle back to Apollo's dire present. He is the unsettling center, often without his own center, as he drifts into ever foggier drug-induced illusions.

If, as Nabokov said, realism is a style (I suggest that it is many styles), then Benderson's longtime friend, the author Ursule Molinaro, may have given the world a great recipe for actually making it. In his lengthy essay on her writing in *The Review of Contemporary Fiction,* (2002, vol. 22, No. 1) Benderson says that she never used "paint-by-numbers details meant to give a *realistic* feeling of the setting. She chose instead the judicious placement of spare, sensuous details that enhanced the particular consciousness of her protagonist; and it is the consciousness of her characters that is mostly responsible for startling evocations of setting. . . . She just did not believe in the concept of the tourist."

*User* approaches realism of this sort. Benderson has gone to great lengths in his exploration of the motivations and lack of motivation that befuddle the carnival of denizens in his story. In his recent memoir, *The Romanian*, Benderson admits he spent a lot time with "midtown Manhattan hustlers, ex-cons, and junkies sponging up their speech and vampirizing their emotions to write about." These days, he frequently leaves the USA to escape an ever-encroaching gay mentality that he feels eagerly and publicly assimilates itself into a pathetic version of family values, part of the same exclusionary mentality that helped change Times Square into its current scrubbed-up Disneyfied incarnation.

There is one extended focus on sound in the novel: a reverberant passage that lingers in the mind. When Casio is in the ambulance on the way to the hospital, he hears a familiar ringing in his ears that initiates a chain of memories. The sound first entered Casio's mind years before in prison. While checking for contraband, the guards repeatedly hit metal pipes with rubber mallets. A change in the ringing indicated where things were hidden. As a result of the search, Casio ends up taking the rap for another prisoner. For days in solitary, he hears the ringing internally and imagines it as birds or insects buzzing around him. From then on the ringing is a recurring trigger that sets off a chain of foul memories, a collation of his worst times that threatens to draw him back into darkness.

The hard edges in this novel lie not in its structure, but in the mental boundaries of the main characters. They are all hemmed in by difficult living situations and the necessity of escaping painful aspects of every day life.

Benderson's mode of writing is enhanced by the frequent use of a device: he inserts italicized sections that are the verbalized thoughts of the character into the narrator's depictions. These thoughts are internal monologues in the voice of that character, given as if they are occurring in real time. For a few seconds, the reader feels he is inside the head of that character. The strength of these sections carries a heightened sense of reality back into the narrator's non-italicized flow.

Regardless of Benderson's success in making a novel that looks from the inside out, the reader is always an outsider looking inside the world of the novel. And in that sense, each reader is a tourist, now even more so, because the novel refers to a Times Square that no longer exists. Though it was written as a fiction, *User* has become partly a historical document of a world that has vanished or at least has been dispersed into small pockets of activity elsewhere. In this sense, it is kin to Samuel Delany's frankly stunning documentation of pre-sterilized Times Square, entitled, *Times Square Red, Times Square Blue*.

Nearly all of the characters are ruthless as the pain of living presses in on them. They need it to survive the daily onslaught of poverty or drug withdrawal, as well as betrayal from the other desperate ones around them. Yet, Benderson has compassion for each character, he rounds them out with surprising warmth and elicits our sympathy as we delve deeper into their troubled situations. They all have loyalties to others and help each other at times, but these tendencies are easily overridden by the fierce urges of day to day survival. Even the police are portrayed with complexity. Detective Pangero shows compassion for Angelita, the drag performer, by leaving him untouched and unconscious when he arrests Casio, Angelita's junkie boyfriend and crime partner. Abuela, Casio's grandmother, who navigates through a sea of religious visions and tries to save her family, is the most compassionate of all, but dies alone with no one to take care of her.

Intelligence alone never saves people from dire circumstances. Apollo readily absorbs information from everything around him and recycles it to make himself appear more attractive to a variety of men who return for his services, but only temporarily. Baby Pop has a knack for math and creates elaborate internal scenarios adapted from the popular novels he reads. But both are unable to imagine a usable framework for changing their situations.

Angelita does willfully overcome addiction to get his operation and moves out of the neighborhood. During the course of the novel, she is the only true survivor.

No matter how much Benderson seeks to reveal to us the otherness of this world, it isn't difficult to understand Apollo's need to share his pain in unusual ways with his johns and the other junkies. He blames the stomping he gives his only friend on the withdrawal from drugs. He's trapped in vicious circles that must be attended to at the sacrifice of others. In this novel, redemption comes only momentarily, if it comes at all: and then, more as a hint of whimsy than a destined eventual outcome.

Apollo's unnamed friend is an almost middle-aged educated man trying to stay alive in a pre-AIDS cocktail world. He takes strong prescription drugs to prolong his life, but it is a losing battle. Their jerky relationship continues because Apollo trusts him more than his other contacts. Apollo can only admit he needs help when he's desperate. Full acknowledgement of his helplessness would destroy him. His friend helps him because he has nothing to lose. He is already lost and he thinks for a time that some involvement in Apollo's world has more meaning than the literary life he's left behind on full shelves that line the walls of his apartment.

Benderson contrasts the abuse by the cops that Apollo receives for his drug use with his friend's unpleasant dependence on legal medication. Apollo gives in to the numbing effect dope; and his friend desperately clings to life by taking sanctioned poison.

After Apollo's valiant effort to kick and work a real job as a doorman for Tina, the pressures drive him back to dope. It's nearly impossible to stay clean when he's surrounded by the same environment that fed his habit in the first place. His comeback high gives him a surge of confidence as he puts the make on two blonde out-of-towners. They succumb easily to his macho display and take him back in their hotel room.  He takes every advantage of them by strutting, rutting, and degrading them as bitches. He stuns them for hours with super human endurance and his dope stick: the blood engorged penis that stays erect for hours at the end of a high. He completely humiliates them after the sexual frenzy by demanding sixty dollars, which they do reluctantly pay him.

This act is Apollo's pathetic revenge on the girly tourist gays who are seeping into the neighborhood, hanging out in new trendy clubs in greater numbers. Few of them are looking for a hustler. In fact, they fear him or ignore him. He has become the alien who no longer belongs, a clown to be laughed at by the passersby. Eventually, his inability to deal with this change inflates the wishful fantasies in his mind, pushing out the last remnants of rationality.

Benderson shows us that everyone is a user and is used as well. To be used is not always to be abused. At times, it benefits the used more than the user. Sometimes, both parties benefit, sometimes neither. There is the temptation to wonder who benefited more in the making of this novel, Benderson or those who were used as the basis of its characters.

No matter how we might pretend otherwise, even a cushy life can be viewed as day to day survival through the use of others and their use of us. The question is not whether this is so, but how is this so. Ironically, as entertainment-seeking tourists approaching Benderson's passionately drawn world of lowlifes, freaks, and criminals, our rapt stares may transform this novel's exquisite portrait into an elegant and filthy mirror, inside which any one of us will catch a few glimpses of his own reflection.

**Addendum:**

It was in late March of 2007, shortly after finishing this review, that I went to a celebration for the Romanian writer Ruda Popa at the Russian restaurant Samovar in Manhattan. The friend I was to meet there didn't make it. Upstairs in the salon, I took a seat at the white U-shape made of long tables pushed together. I could not avoid noticing the garish makeup of the 60-or-so-year-old woman who sat next to me. Adroit with a worn down pencil, she calculated her way through several puzzles in a small Sudoku book. Her cloying perfume mingled mercilessly in my head with the mind-altering shot glasses of vodka I downed as they were offered to me on silver trays. As soon as the guest of honor finished talking, she sighed and pushed her chair back away from the table. I recognized Bruce Benderson sitting on the other side of her. I had heard him read years before during one of the many readings hosted by C. Bard Cole in the East Village. This time I introduced myself and we spent the next several hours together talking about all manner of things including his desire not to be labeled gay and the sad fact that his new novel, *Pacific Agony* would probably not be published in English. Benderson's caustic yet cavalier wit did not disappoint.

# Christopher Coe
# **Such Times**

### Harcourt, Brace & Co., 1993

## Jameson Currier

Christopher Coe's critically acclaimed first novel, *I Look Divine*, published by Ticknor & Fields in 1987, was the witty and luminous portrait of a rich, gifted, über narcissistic gay man who believed he was exceptional from the moment of his birth. Jet-setting across the affluent and au courant landscapes of Rome, Madrid, Mexico, and Manhattan, *I Look Divine* recounted the tragedy of Nicholas, the divinely sophisticated "affected creature" of the title, and his swift downfall when he realizes that aging has erased both his youth and beauty. As narrated by his older brother in a cleverly succinct manner, Nicholas's life was marvelous and stylish right up to its end.

That same sort of elegant and eloquent stylishness reappears in Coe's second novel, *Such Times*, published by Harcourt in 1993 and reprinted by Penguin in 1994, but the journey on which the author propels his characters this time is not merely through the process of growing older but of navigating the bleak and haunting realities of the first decade of the AIDS epidemic. This time Coe slowly strips his archly observant gay narrator, Timothy Springer, of his wealth, health, and good looks, and, in the process, infuses this novel with a humanity that was often absent from *I Look Divine*; *Such Times* becomes, then, a sort of riches-to-rags tale, a Job-like tumble from the demands an unexpected life-altering circumstance can produce — in this case, an AIDS diagnosis. As in *I Look Divine*, Coe tells this tragic tale of a vain and self-involved man's breakdown from a grand, clever, witty and distinctly gay point of view.

The narrative structure of *Such Times* finds Timothy and Dominic, friends for twenty-plus years, catching up with one another over *risotto frutti di mare* in a trendy Los Angeles restaurant after viewing Dominic's taped appearance on a television quiz show. Dominick and Timothy share many traits with the brothers of *I Look Divine*. Dominick, like Nicholas, "has always made up laws for life." He knows a true daiquiri cocktail requires a few drops of maraschino liqueur, adores his set of Baccarat tumblers, and can recall verbatim Elizabeth Taylor's Academy Award acceptance speech for *Butterfield 8*. Timothy, overly articulate and "desperate to be glamorous," shops for a baby spoon for himself at Tiffany's and desires to be "irresistible to every man who looked like anything." Together they drink Gavi dei Gavi la Scolca and find it "acceptable." Everyone in *Such Times*, in fact, seems to be well-bred and well-educated and well-traveled, even our protagonist's more lugubrious conquests and acquaintances. Throughout the novel there are illusions to reading John O'Hara, Socrates, and Henry Miller, tasting soufflé Rothschild and smoking Montecruz 210 cigars, shopping on the via del Babuino, living on the Ile Saint-Louis, and drinking Muscat Beaumes de Venise or Château d'Yquem.

But it is 1992 and Dominic and Timothy have both been through personal battles with AIDS; Timothy knows of Dominic's struggles, but Dominic is unaware of Timothy's illness and of the recent death of Jasper, Timothy's older and wealthier lover of 18 years, from AIDS. That night is full of reminiscing for Timothy, flashbacks of his friendship with Dominic, his own life in Manhattan, his travels to San Francisco, Rome, Puerto Vallarta, and Sitges, his brief affair in Paris with a musician, but most of these memories are regarded in the context of his long-time love for Jasper. And contained within these recollections are Timothy's astute elucidation of the polar differences between gay life during the decades of the 1970s and '80s.

At the emotional center of *Such Times*, however, is the issue of sexual monogamy of gay men. Jasper, 41 and 22 years Timothy's senior, was in another relationship the night in 1974 that he first met Timothy, 19, at the Continental Baths in Manhattan, though it is made clear that Jasper and his official lover, Oliver Ingraham, an older and wealthier man than Jasper, have not had sex in years. During the entire 18 years of Timothy and Jasper's affair, Jasper never gives up his relationship with Oliver. Timothy, a would-be actor with a trust fund turned portrait photographer, and something of a prudish "coy maiden," learns fairly early on in his desire to be solely with Jasper that he is not able to satisfy all of Jasper's sexual appetites. "Can't I be enough for one night," Timothy says when he discovers Jasper's unsatisfied libido when they spot each other by accident one night at the waterfront piers of Manhattan's west side after celebrating Timothy's 21st birthday together at Lutèce only hours before — Timothy has shown up at the piers drunk and to be a voyeur of the parade of gay men, but Jasper, a "straight-forwardly handsome, virile" man, is looking for as much sex as he can find — and with partners other than Timothy.

As the years progress and change, however, so does Timothy and Jasper's relationship, becoming sexless itself, though the love they have crafted and developed for each other has not diminished. The era of AIDS brings to Timothy's mind, among many things, the nature of sexuality and the ability of gay men, in particular, to find and maintain emotional attachments, or, in his sentiments, love, *monogamous* love. "People make a mistake," he muses, "love wrongly when they love without demands. Jasper always told me that he loved me in his fashion, that he was true to me, in his fashion. It may be to his credit that he made no promise on which he didn't deliver."

And throughout the years of their relationship Timothy has been mostly monogamous with Jasper; his infidelity, though, is rather calculated. Fearing that he may have become infected with the virus because of Jasper, Timothy decides on a liaison with another man so that if he does become ill, he will not have to hold Jasper accountable. "It is only of my case I can say that everything that has come to me has come because I loved without demands."

Love without demands, Timothy believes, has killed more than a million men in a decade. Coe is careful about not making this issue a moral statement, though the lush, romantic sweep he imbues *Such Times* with proves that Timothy is a man who only wants to love just one man. Jasper believes that "monogamy is antithetical to the homosexual life." He refuses to attach an emotional need to sex; he is a man who appreciates it for its particular pleasures. But Coe is also careful about showing how Jasper, in his own fashion, cares for Timothy, from the table and bookcases he builds for Timothy at the onset of their affair, to the special sugar, easily dissolvable in cold liquid, he buys once Timothy becomes ill.

What buoys *Such Times* above its haughty locales, pretentious characters, and its simple and melodramatic plot, is Coe's playful but concise use of language, which is the same technique which lifted Coe's first short novel, *I Look Divine,* into the literary stratosphere. Timothy narrates the *Such Times*, like Nicholas's brother in *I Look Divine*, in a clever, deadpan tone. Evasiveness and repetition are Coe's primary techniques, but the sentences are crisp, spare, and full of shrewd, elegant observation. In *I Look Divine*, clothes become "frocks," photographs are "shots," *joie de vivre* is retitled as *suave de vivre*. In *Such Times*, dessert is always "pudding," sex is "toss and catch," improvisation becomes first improvision and later improvositable, a well made daiquiri is "perf," an affair is a *frisson*, a particularly handsome man is continually referred to as "The Hot One." Timothy forbids Jasper calling him "Tim" because he hates "being called a monosyllable." In fact, Timothy, as a young man, attempts to woo Jasper with words. "I had a richer vocabulary than I have now," he remembers. "It was a time of life when I did not run out of words. I'm always running out of words now, and things have become harder to describe. I can't pin them down as I used to. There wasn't an adjective I wouldn't use, misuse, abuse. I also spoke with my hands. Years later, Jasper told me he had been startled that night by the way I spoke. He told me he hadn't before heard anyone speak quite as I did, and he told me that he had thought for a while that I might be the smartest person he'd met in his life. This made me wonder more than a bit about his life, but it was, of course, nice to hear. He took it back, naturally, once he got to know me."

As in *I Look Divine*, Coe uses a lyrical, elliptical construction in *Such Times*; subjects are examined as if through a prism, revealing a succession of delicate and fine-tuned details. "There is something just to proximity, to having known a man's body by touch, to loving the forces behind it, the voice that comes out of him, the words he selects, and then, too, something to having been away awhile — a week, a day, an hour, time in which you were removed, briefly free of him, even — and to coming back into a room and finding him still there, unchanged, the same as he was when you left him. There is something to this, to finding that you cannot possibly fill in what the man was in your absence, cannot imagine him as having been anything at all, even just alive, lying motionless without you, and something about this is bound to overcome you."

*Such Times* pulsates with the confusions and heartbreaks of attempting to understand the different types of gay men and their relationships — from the well-built to the unattractive to the uninhibited and disposable to those hopeful and unrequited — and chart them in an era when every blemish was a suspect of something else and the medical mystery of AIDS was spiraling into hysteria. Anyone who has found himself as the third party in a triangular relationship — and that is not altogether uncommon in the modern gay milieu — will certainly empathize with the pleasures and pains Timothy finds in his love for Jasper. And anyone who witnessed the changes of gay life during the first decades of the AIDS epidemic — the individual and collective pain and dislocation and strength and heroism — will find *Such Times* a must read; and any reader with a taste for gay history and sociology and the way things were will also find the novel worthwhile today. Coe covers a multitude of subjects before and during the onslaught of the epidemic, from riffing about fisting to musing about taking the HIV test. He perceptively charts many of the physical and psychological changes the plague brought to the gay community. "The appearance of the people with the virus, how they look physically, is more widely documented than what they feel under their skin, inside themselves," Timothy observes.

In fact, Coe spends as much energy pondering science and medicine and health as he does on sex and gay men and relationships. There are scenes of lumbar tests, tales of hospitals overcharging patients, and explanations of the thymus gland. In lesser hands, this sort of diversion could potentially bog down a contemporary novel, but throughout Coe is able to maintain Timothy's cleverness, particularly on a section about retroviruses. In attempting to explain nucleotides to Jasper, for instance, Timothy conjures up a metaphor of precious stones. "My virus may begin with an emerald, and then go: diamond, diamond, sapphire, ruby, emerald, emerald, ruby. Your virus may begin with a sapphire, and if read from end to end, which they can do now in a laboratory, it might go something like this: sapphire, diamond, diamond, sapphire, ruby, emerald, diamond, ruby, ruby."

Even ill and recuperating, Timothy refuses to shed his sophis-tication or his appetite for a good life, enjoying the meals Jasper cooks for him: "a rare rack of baby lamb, not yet a month old, a wonderfully thick veal chop sautéed with chanterelles, a two-pound lobster, which he took out of the shell for me and served with fresh tarragon mayonnaise, tiny soft-shell crabs crisp with garlic and capers."

But it is Timothy's attempt at uncovering and understanding the mysteries of science and medicine that provide him with a reason to live. Jasper, however, allows himself to succumb to the virus without even a fight. When Timothy finds a drug that might counter Jasper's AZT anemia, Jasper refuses to take it because it has not been approved by the FDA. In literary merit, this is the true test of character — showing how a person reacts to conflict or change. And in showing the contrast by which Timothy and Jasper react to their diagnoses, Coe demonstrates how AIDS forced a whole generation of men into directions they might never have taken, and the positive and negative forces of each individual spirit.

> Every morning now, when I come to life again, it amazes
> me to be in the world, that in the day ahead I will be able to

witness some event, to hear on the telephone what friends are doing, where they dined the night before, to hear their menu and what they said to each other about someone else. . . . I may not extrude enthusiasm or effervesce with cheer, but buildings do go up, money changes hands, nations prosper and fall; possibly someone's friends grow cherries in their gardens, handsome men eat peaches; sounds come into being that are heard for the first time; new music is made with them; cuisines are reinvented; new machines come along, new techniques for old things; diseases are conquered, history happens, and movie stars still have babies.

Timothy refuses to see either himself or Jasper as victims, unwilling to yield to the randomness of fate or to the misery of lost romance. What he does is find a redemptive power from his memory, and, as he unfolds his story, his voice elevates *Such Times* into a transcendent classic that deserves to be discovered and re-discovered.

I first read Coe's *I Look Divine* in 1988 after a recommendation from a writing workshop. A few years later, in 1993, I was asked to review *Such Times* for *The Washington Blade*, a weekly gay newspaper. It was my second paid assignment as a literary critic. (James McCourt's novel, *Time Remaining*, was the first.) I knew nothing of the personal facts or the life history of Christopher Coe, nor did I attempt to discover them, although I knew through editors and publicists at the time that Coe was ill and struggling with AIDS. Coe was also sketchy about revealing facts about himself. In a 1993 interview that ran alongside my review in the *Blade*, when editor Trey Graham asked Coe about the autobiographical inspiration of *Such Times*, the author responded, "Quite a bit of it is autobiographical, but I don't get into that — you'll forgive me. I resent those questions because people are trying to peg you in one category or another. If I say it's all made up, it's all fiction, then they'll say, 'Well, what does it matter then?' And if I said it's all autobiographical, it's all from the truth, then they'll ask, 'Then where's the art?' So you can't win."

Eventually, Coe and I shared an editor at Viking Penguin, Edward Iwanicki, a man who championed many gay male writers writing about AIDS, including David B. Feinberg and Richard Hall. Christopher Coe died shortly before the paperback publication of *Such Times*, on September 6, 1994, at his home in Manhattan. He was 41 years old.

In re-reading *Such Times* 14 years later for this anthology of lost gay fiction, I found Timothy's line, from which the novel derives its title, particularly poignant. "I really do find it hard to believe that there used to be such times," Timothy says in 1992, referring to the uninhibited past of glory holes and bathhouses and sex with other men inside the empty trucks on the streets of the meatpacking district in the West Village. Ironically, the same can be now said of 1992 and those first horrific years of the epidemic, when every HIV-positive diagnosis was a potential death knell. Who knew then that such times would change again? Who knew this could happen? Who knew such *extraordinary* times would turn into history?

# Daniel Curzon
# Something You Do in the Dark

Putnam, 1971

## Jesse Monteagudo

The years after the Stonewall Riots (1969-73) were the lesbian and gay community's "heroic age," a period of great achievements in gay politics, society, religion, culture and thought. But when it came to creative literature by or about gay men, the "heroic age" left much to be desired.  This was a period when fact was more exciting than fiction. As the later Roger Austen wrote in *Playing the Game: The Homosexual Novel In America* (1977), "One of the most obvious results of the politicization of gayness has been the publication of scores of nonfiction books which have quite dramatically overshadowed the output of traditional gay fiction. . . . As closet doors have been flung open, men who had had neither the time nor the talent to write novels have not hesitated to dash off personal reminiscences, and altogether the movement has produced very little fiction but an avalanche of con-essions, interviews, essays, diaries, and polemics." What novel could compete with the true-life adventures of Arthur Bell, Lige Clarke and Jack Nichols, Wallace Hamilton, Merle Miller, John Murphy, the Rev. Troy Perry or "John Reid" (Andrew Tobias)? Outside of pornographic fiction — and "non-gay," gay novels by the likes of James Purdy and Gore Vidal — gay fiction in the years between 1969 and 1973 could only produce Joseph Hansen's first two Dave Brandstetter mysteries (*Fadeout* and *Death Claims*), Gordon Merrick's first two Charlie and Peter romances (*The Lord Won't*

*Mind* and *One for the Gods*), Merle Miller's autobiographical novel *What Happened*, Frank Hilaire's prison yarn *Thanatos* and Leo Skir's quaint *Boychick* — and Daniel Curzon's first novel, *Something You Do in the Dark*.

I am a non-fiction kind of guy, so I did not read *Something You Do in the Dark* when I went through my own coming out process in 1972-73. Rather, I came out fine by reading some of the aforementioned true-life memoirs, as well as "gay 101" books like Peter Fisher's Gay Book Award-winning *The Gay Mystique*. I first read about Dan Curzon and his book in early 1977, thanks to an Oscar Wilde Memorial Bookshop catalog. I immediately ordered a copy of the Lancer paperback, read it with mounting excitement, and became a fan for life of Dan Curzon. Cole Ruffner, Curzon's gay anti-hero, was a man whom I could relate to, though thankfully I did not suffer any of the trials or tribulations that Cole Ruffner went through within the pages of this book. When I began to write a book review column ("The Book Nook") for Miami's newly-published, gay community newspaper *The Weekly News* (Nov. 1977), one of the first articles that I wrote was a review of *Dark* and of Curzon's second novel, *The Misadventures of Tim McPick* (1975). The following year I had the opportunity to meet Curzon when he spoke at a Florida Gay and Lesbian Conference in Tallahassee. I still have with me my autographed copy of *Something You Do in the Dark*, dedicated by the author "To Jesse, a nice guy, nice to meet you. With people like you, good gay literature can't lose. Dan Curzon may 29/78" Since then I have kept in touch with Dan Curzon, most recently by e-mail, and have been fortunate to read and enjoyed all of his subsequent novels, short stories, memoirs and satires, though sadly none of his equally-acclaimed plays.

*Something You Do in the Dark* has been described (in Amazon.com) as "the first gay protest novel" and as a "revenge novel with a social protest theme." Georges-Michel Sarotte, in his literary study *Like a Brother, Like a Lover: Male Homosexuality in the American Novel and Theater from Herman Melville to James Baldwin* (1978), called *Dark* "a well-written, lucid, intelligent *and* militant novel" and Cole himself "the faithful image of the American — the Western — homosexual of the 1970s." When I first read *Dark* 29 years ago, I viewed Cole Ruffner as a post-Stonewall, "angry young gay" who was informed by the new gay militancy. However, as Curzon himself said in a recent published conversation with his life partner John W. Gettys,

> When I wrote *Something You Do in the Dark*, I had never heard of the Stonewall Rebellion in NYC or gay liberation. People wrongly think one event caused all the subsequent events. I just knew that I was a good person and the world was saying I was so despicable that we couldn't even discuss what 'you people' do sexually. It took me until the age of twenty-six to overcome this social disapproval and become a sexual human being.

Like Curzon himself, who came of age in the 1960s but managed to hit his stride in the 1970s, Cole Ruffner is both pre-Stonewall and post-Stonewall. Sarotte described him as being "a creature in transition; still a prisoner of social taboos and fears, he resolutely looks toward the future, a future where bisexuality (more hetero or homo according to the individual) will be the rule" — an apt description, if you leave out the part about the future of bisexuality. A pre-Stonewall Cole Ruffner would have dealt with his problems by killing himself, or by going to a shrink. A post-Stonewall Ruffner would have taken his problems to a gay activist or support group. Ruffner resists oppression, but does so as an individual and not as an organized member of a persecuted minority. Only occasionally does he interact with other members of the tribe. Early in the book Cole tries to help a gay man who, like himself, was a victim of police entrapment. Later in the book Cole tries to help his fellows after the bathhouse that he and they were in was raided. But nowhere in the novel does he join or seek the assistance of a gay or gay-friendly organization. Cole has no political platform or beliefs, save for the wish to be left alone.

*Something You Do in the Dark* begins with a fantasy sequence, set in a world where homosexuality is accepted and heterosexuality is persecuted. From that starting point, Curzon sets out to describe and condemns what he perceived to be the negative consequences of being openly gay in a

homophobic society, as they were experienced by one particularly
unfortunate individual. Though all of Cole's misfortunes really happened to
somebody somewhere, they did not all happen to the same person, as
unfriendly critics were quick to point out. Had AIDS been around at the
time Curzon wrote this novel, no doubt Cole would have had it (which
Curzon confronts in 1984's *The World Can Break Your Heart*). To a large
degree, *Something You Do in the Dark* is one big tale of woe. Cole Ruffner is
entrapped in a men's room, and is sentenced to six months in jail, to which
the judge then adds two years for contempt of court (even then Cole's
temper was a wonder to behold). Later he is gang-raped in prison, an act for
which his sentence (along with those of his rapists) is extended for six more
months. For all his troubles, Cole loses his government job, his family
practically disowns him, and his lover Teddy deserts him. All this turmoil
makes Cole Ruffner a very angry man; and he directs his anger at those who
tried to destroy him, at those who love him, and at himself. The main target
of Cole's anger is Officer Keel, a particularly homophobic vice cop who
entrapped him in the rest room and who has made it his life's goal to
persecute gay men everywhere. Killing Keel, it seems, becomes Cole
Ruffner's primary goal in life.

      Though Cole's misfortunes are real, to a large extent he is his own
worst enemy. His post-prison visit with Teddy — who now has a new lover
— is a disaster. His reunion with Angie, his old girl friend, is equally
disastrous, and not just because Cole's attempt to rekindle their old sexual
relationship is doomed to failure. Angie sympathizes with Cole, even invites
him to a party, but to no avail. Another friend, Bud, is a closeted
homosexual who (like many other men, then and now) is engaged. When
Cole presses Bud to accept his true feelings, Bud runs away. Later, Cole is
reconciled with his invalid father, and moves in to help the older man. This
effort, too, ends disastrously when the older Ruffner catches his son having
sex with another man, Jerry, in his own home. Cole seeks solace in a
bathhouse but that, too, gets raided, and by his old enemy Officer Keel. Cole
then tries to kill Keel, but this too fails; and Cole ends his tale wailing, "My
God, why don't I die!" An inferior author would have made Cole Ruffner a

more lovable and thus more sympathetic character. Curzon instead makes Cole Ruffner thoroughly unlikeable, which is why some readers found it hard to relate. Critic James Levin may be forgiven for thinking, in his study *The Gay Novel in America*, "that capricious fate more than homophobia seems responsible for [Cole's] plight."

Through the novel, Cole (or Curzon) makes some interesting points about himself and other gay men. In spite of all his militancy, Cole and his oppressors agree that gay men are basically promiscuous, and incapable of maintaining a stable relationship. For example, while in the midst of his disastrous reunion with ex-lover Teddy, Cole viciously asks if "we [Cole and Teddy] represent the usual homosexual 'marriage'? A brief couple of years of pseudo-fidelity and lots of cheating and lying about it, and then the break-up, quarrels and sniveling and backbiting?" Later, while actively cruising Jerry, Cole is delighted that he doesn't have "to pretend that our two bodies are the only ones that you and I will ever need." At the baths, Cole places the gay community in a "pecking order" where "Homely has to suck Unattractive and Unattractive has to suck Ordinary and Ordinary has to suck Handsome, and even Handsome does to Handsomer." Later, after having had a three-way with a rather Unattractive pair, Cole comes to the conclusion that he is just an object to them, as he is with every other man that he has sex with at the tubs (and vice versa). Even so, Cole muses, it is "better [to be an] object than in love. Here there was no pain, for any of them. There was uncomplicated lust. They were using one another's bodies, but thoughtfully; it was simplistic to call it selfishness." Like the hero of John Rechy's *The Sexual Outlaw*, Cole Ruffner seeks anonymous sex at the baths or in public parks, both as a sexual release and as an act of defiance against a society that prosecutes homosexual acts as criminal. Cole's attitude is very different to those of closet case Bud or Cole's parole officer Mr. Schultz, who insist that straight marriage is the solution to all of their problems.

Almost three decades after I first read it, *Something You Do in the Dark* is still a powerful and provocative reading experience. Having matured a bit since then, I don't perceive straight society with the same anger or frustration that Cole and I felt in the 1970s. Perhaps, if he had survived his misfortunes, Cole would have mellowed a bit, too. Though *Something You Do in the Dark* is dated to some extent, in many ways it is as relevant as it was when Dan Curzon first wrote it. Gay men still get arrested in public parks and at the baths, though now the officers of the law have added "AIDS prevention" to all of their other excuses. Prison conditions in America today are, if anything, worse than ever, and "sexual offenders" are branded for life by our crime-obsessed society. And closet cases like Bud continue to use religion and a fraudulent marriage as crutches. On the other hand, a book like *Something You Do in the Dark* is taught in gay studies courses (by Curzon himself and others). Today's Cole Ruffners seek and enjoy a supportive GLBT community that helps them in their hours of need. And many gay men — Curzon included — now enjoy stable, long-lasting relationships, even if state and federal governments refuse to recognize "gay marriage."

After making allowances for its time, and in spite of its less-than lovable protagonist, I enjoyed *Something You Do in the Dark* as much now as I did when I first read it. Like Curzon's other great novels — 1978's *Among the Carnivores* and 1984's *The World Can Break Your Heart* — *Something You Do in the Dark* is a hard-hitting novel that tells it as it is, not as we want it to be. This novel's (and its author's) refusal to compromise is perhaps why it has been out of print for much of the past 35 years. Most recently republished by Curzon himself through his own IGNA Press, *Something You Do in the Dark* deserves to be back in print, and to be read by a new generation of avid gay readers.

# Melvin Dixon
# **Vanishing Rooms**

Dutton, 1991

## Ian Rafael Titus

I bought my paperback copy of Melvin Dixon's *Vanishing Rooms* on September 8, 1994. I remember this because I used to deface books by writing my name and the book's date of purchase on the inside front cover (I no longer commit such crimes against books, except for the occasional highlighting of reference texts).

An ad in the Voice Literary Supplement first drew me to the book. In one of the blurbs, Melvin Dixon's novel was favorably compared to James Baldwin's writing. I had read Baldwin's *Giovanni's Room* and *Another Country*; never before had I experienced such unflinching prose dealing with same-sex relationships and interracial desire. To a young black male who had dated and slept with white men, those books, especially *Another Country*, were a revelation. Baldwin created complex, breathing characters whose explorations of race and sexuality mirrored some of my own concerns about gay interracial attraction. *Vanishing Rooms* promised to pick up where those works left off.

Set in 1970s New York City, the novel (first published in 1991) is narrated in alternating chapters by three characters: Jesse Durand, a black dancer whose white boyfriend Metro is beaten, raped and murdered by teenage thugs; Ruella McPhee, a black dancer who falls for Jesse as she provides a haven for him to work through his grief; and Lonny Russo, a troubled 15-year-old who takes part in Metro's assault.

The book's original dust jacket illustration, by Alain Gauthier, features the moonlit silhouette of a black man cradling a white man whose mouth bleeds a heart-shape onto one black forearm, while in the background stand three ominous male figures before an urban landscape; a crescent moon tinged red hovers in the sky. It's an illustration that daringly shows the novel's central elements and one of the reasons why I was drawn to *Vanishing Rooms*. In comparison, the cover of the Cleis Press 2001 edition is a photograph of a handsome bare-chested black man in profile. A sensual, attractive cover, yet there is no hint of the gay interracial issues at the heart of the novel.

I have read this book three or four times, and returned to favorite passages more times than I can recall; each reading has brought new insights or raised questions not considered before. A book often changes in recollection and when revisited there can be a conflict between our memories of the book and the book's reality. When I first read *Vanishing Rooms* I was eager for stories depicting gay interracial relationships, a subject that I rarely saw portrayed convincingly (if at all) in the art, books or films that I would come across. Through imaginative works like those of Baldwin and Dixon, I sought like-minded spirits who were exploring this subject as well as the various challenges faced by individuals in such relationships. How did others feel about their attraction to someone of a different race? What are the various implications of desiring people of a certain color? And in the case of *Vanishing Rooms*, can two men, one black and the other white, love each other in a world that condemns not only their sexuality but also their difference in race?

Melvin Dixon was born May 29, 1950 in Stamford, Connecticut to parents originally from the Carolinas. A Professor of English at Queens College from 1980 to 1992, Dixon was a poet, translator, and novelist whose books include the poetry collection *Change of Territory* (1983), *Ride Out the Wilderness: Geography and Identity in Afro-American Literature* (1987), and *The Collected Poems of Leopold Sedar Senghor* (1990), a translation of poetry by the one-time president of Senegal. His first novel, 1989's *Trouble the Water*, combines Dixon's urban upbringing with his family's southern roots for a tale featuring his talent for creating the gritty, layered realities and surreal lyricism that would be explored further in *Vanishing Rooms*.

While the protagonist of the first novel is a married teacher at a celebrated New England college, Jesse Durand in *Vanishing Rooms* is a young dancer sharing a Greenwich Village apartment with his white lover. The subject of gay biracial relationships was controversial not only during the novel's 1970s setting but also at the time of *Vanishing Room*'s publication in 1991, and still to the present day. I admit my own hesitation at approaching the subject; disapproval and misunderstanding remain in the minds of many individuals gay and straight. Maybe part of why I read Melvin Dixon's book was because at the time I needed some form of validation for my desires, to see an interracial couple explored with the same depth of imagination and complexity as lovers in other works of literature.

Yet from page one, the reader knows that Jesse and Metro's romance is anything but idyllic. Metro, a night shift reporter for the *Daily News*, has summoned Jesse to a warehouse on a rotting pier where men meet for sex. They emerge covered in dust and splinters, and Jesse is appalled by the experience but will not admit it. Late for a dance class, Jesse leaves Metro to get in a cab, not realizing it will be the last time he sees him alive.

> I'd be gone only a few hours. Metro would be home when I got back. Yet I missed him. My stomach fluttered. Maybe it was that empty, searching look in his eyes, or his suddenly pale skin against my oily brown hands. I missed him and searched the rear window. Metro was standing in the middle of West 12th Street, oblivious to the traffic veering around him. He scared me. I wanted the cab to turn around and pick him up, but it was too late.

As the story unfolds through the voices of Jesse, his fellow dancer and brief love interest Ruella, and the disturbed youth Lonny, we learn more about Metro, his relationship with Jesse and what led to his brutal murder. What first attracted a black dancer from Hartford, Connecticut to a white farm boy from Lafayette, Louisiana? At a campus demonstration to memorialize Malcolm X's death, Jesse describes his first sight of Metro:

> Thick, wavy brown hair, angular forehead and chin, horn-rimmed glasses, stubby fingers clutching a reporter's steno pad. Eyes like reaching hands. When he looked straight at me, I felt pulled into his whole face. His stare made me feel weightless, light, angled toward him on wings suddenly fluttering from inside me and begging for air. I wanted then to get under his skin, travel at break-neck speed through his veins and right to his heart.

Suddenly the demonstration seems unimportant to Jesse compared to the emotions given wing by the force of his attraction. It's a mutual hunger that brings them together, yet what is the basis of this need? Dixon did not aim for definitive answers to this question; the subject is too complex for cut-and-dried explanations. When I first reread *Vanishing Rooms*, I was struck by how much I'd idealized or forgotten regarding Jesse and Metro's relationship. The ugly moments between them, including a disturbing sexual flashback, startled more than the first time. Was their bond doomed to be severed even before Metro's murder? When Metro joins Jesse in New York after a trip back home, something has changed but we never find out what, though one suspects it has something to do with Metro's parents, Jesse's race, and an erotic childhood memory recalled by Metro involving a black maid's son.

While pursuing their respective dreams, Jesse and Metro have different schedules and see different aspects of the city. Jesse's world involves dance studios, part-time work for a choreographer, the ceaseless awareness of prejudice. Metro's job as a night shift journalist constantly exposes him to the poverty, crime and corruption in the city, and when it takes its toll on him he begins abusing drugs and pursuing anonymous sex in the streets, trying unsuccessfully to make Jesse understand the guilt, rage and disappointment that he feels.

Dixon does not make his characters one-dimensional or stereo-typical. Therefore Metro is not some unsympathetic racist using Jesse for his pleasure and Jesse is not entirely blameless in the downward spiral the relationship takes. In the novel's first line, we learn, "Metro wasn't his real name, but I called him that." His real name is Jon-Michael Barthe but to Jesse he is Metro for "the fast, slippery train we were on," for having traveled underground, to places where Jesse wanted to go. Metro, increasingly frustrated with life in New York City, questions Jesse's refusal to call him by his true name. Does he believe that by calling him Metro his lover is denying his identity, not truly seeing him for who he is? In his worsening emotional state, does Metro come to associate Jesse's blackness with the criminals that he fears, with everything he comes to hate about the city?

*Vanishing Rooms* makes it clear that other factors work against the success of Jesse and Metro's relationship, not only the issue of race. The uglier side of urban life, with its teeming masses, homelessness, crowded subways, rampant crime and racism also play a significant part in affecting the novel's characters.

Having lived in New York City since I was12, one of the thrills in reading Dixon's book was recognizing the streets and locales his characters inhabit, being able to relate to the city's vibe and to its potential for countless wonders and terrors. I've known the restlessness that drives Jesse to ride the subways at night, the deadly allure of the train tracks when one is desperate. I've also known the hunger that ultimately leads Jesse to the Paradise Baths, the setting for some of the novel's more hypnotic passages.

The Paradise is the amusement park of sex clubs, a seven-story building with rooms catering to all kinds of fetishes, from scout camp showers and barred cells to army barracks and a completely mirrored room where images of coupling men are repeated as if "extended into infinity." Jesse goes because Metro had been there once and he feels that somehow he'll be close to him this way. He's also there to test something in himself. Metro, as anxious as he'd been regarding the city's dangers and miseries, fell under the spell of anonymous sex, embracing its thrills and perils; yet bewildered by Jesse's refusal or inability to understand him, he escaped further into that world. By stepping into the Paradise Baths, Jesse is not only seeking to understand his dead lover but also to see how far he can go himself.

Like a twisted version of Dante's *Inferno*, Jesse's guide through the seven levels of the bathhouse is a tall and overweight black man, "old as sin," who calls himself Clementine. As they make their way up and visit the various rooms, Jesse flashes back to his times with Metro in college, where they first met, and to the months in New York following Metro's return from Louisiana. The narrative takes on a feverish urgency as Jesse explores both the Paradise and his memories. Men emerge like ghosts out of steam rooms, sniff open lockers while masturbating to boyhood memories, fill the many rooms with the smell and heat of their bodies, the sound of their moans and sobs. And Clementine changes throughout the scenes; appearing as a friendly, sharp-tongued wise man at first, he takes on a somewhat sinister aura when he seems to know things about the nature of Jesse and Metro's relationship, insisting that Jesse had been Metro's "nigger" and chiding him for being a "snow queen" (a derogatory term for a black man attracted to white men). It's when Jesse finds the room of his ideal fantasies that his grief over Metro's death and Clementine's increasingly aggressive words and actions send him over the edge.

In *Vanishing Rooms*, Melvin Dixon chronicled the failure of an interracial couple to triumph over the specters of racism and homophobia. One finishes the novel unsure of what Jesse's (or the author's) stance is on the subject. Does his dating Rodney, a black dancer, at the end of the book signify a rejection of biracial desire? When he flees the Paradise Jesse declares, "I wasn't Metro's nigger, or Clementine's. I was my own beautiful black son of a bitch." Despite it all, Jesse uses his passion for dance and the wonderful and terrible times with Metro to transcend the pain of his experiences.

> It wasn't always like this, I told myself. A quick fuck in an
> abandoned warehouse. It wasn't always like this. Once, we
> strolled across campus holding hands. Once, underneath the
> streetlamp behind the library at the marble stairs leading onto
> the quad, he kissed me. Once, anyone studying all night in the

reserve room or just getting high late that night could have
seen us. Once, someone did. Once, we marched together in the
commencement procession.

Metro's murder interrupts a relationship initially built on a promise of
love and comradeship. Victims of America's racist history, Jesse and Metro are
brought together by a hunger to know the other, a deep need to connect
regardless of sex, race and upbringing. *Vanishing Rooms* creates a dialogue still
needed in our so-called progressive times, where people still oppress or kill
others because of their skin color or for whom they choose to love. Years after
my first reading, I continue to admire Melvin Dixon's courage in tackling such
troubling subject matter with haunting grace and moving immediacy.

Dixon died of AIDS-related complications in 1992 at age 42 (one year
after the publication of *Vanishing Rooms*, the same year Dixon's partner Richard
Allen Horovitz passed away; the novel is dedicated to him). As with James
Baldwin's death, Dixon's absence leaves an empty space for other brave writers
to fill and undertake the still divisive topics brought to light by Dixon and his
literary ancestors. That *Vanishing Rooms* was brought back into print seems to
indicate not only that its significance to gay and African American literature has
been recognized but also that "Jesses" and "Metros" of the present and future
will still have this novel as part of their literary heritage, perhaps helping them
move beyond the traps of racism and homophobia to a place where they can
see each other in unfiltered light.

In his college senior year, Jesse performs a spooky solo to "Strange
Fruit" at the spring dance concert. The next day someone asks him for the
meaning of the dance.

Then he asked if I wasn't really saying something about
people ostracized from society, outcast, martyred, some fruit
unpicked and rotting in its sugar. I didn't know what to say. I
promised to think it over. And I promised myself that I'd keep
on dancing no matter how hesitant the applause, how rooted
the tree, how strange the fruit.

# John Donovan
## I'll Get There. It Better Be Worth the Trip

Harper & Row, 1969

## Martin Wilson

Published in 1969 — the year of the Stonewall Riots — John Donovan's *I'll Get There. It Better Be Worth the Trip.* was the first Young Adult novel to deal with homosexuality. Ushered into print by the legendary children's book editor Ursula Nordstrom (she has been called the Maxwell Perkins of children's literature), the novel is an honest, sensitive, funny, sharply written, and very moving coming-of-age novel narrated by a 13-year-old boy who is, most likely, gay.

I was well past my own adolescence when I first read about Donovan's book. I had recently finished graduate school, in fact, and was about to attempt my own first novel. One Sunday, while I was reading *The New York Times Book Review*, I came across a review of a book called *Dear Genius: The Letters of Ursula Nordstrom*. In the course of the piece, the reviewer mentioned Donovan's book as one of Nordstrom's ground-breaking achievements. Indeed, Nordstrom, in a letter to Donovan that is included in the book, writes, "the whole experience of publishing your book has been a most rewarding one for me." It is clear she was aware of the risks in publishing such a book, but she persevered: "We're going to meet a lot of resistance to this book and we will be eager to fight that resistance as intelligently and gracefully as possible." I was astonished: There had actually *been* a book for teenagers with a gay character way back in 1969? Why hadn't I heard of this book, with its catchy but oddly long title?

I had spent my own young adult years (in the 1980s) reading writers like Beverly Cleary, Madeleine L'Engle, E. B. White, Louise Fitzhugh, and Lois Duncan, not to mention those Choose Your Own Adventure books and Richie Rich comics. Of course, back then I hadn't known I was gay, though I realized that I was attracted to other boys and their bodies. But I couldn't connect those feelings with "being gay," which was so foreign, scary, and invisible, especially in my home state of Alabama. If I'd discovered Donovan's book at the time, would I have figured out what these urges meant? Would I have seen that there are other "normal" boys out there with such feelings? That's hard to say. More likely I would have freaked out a little, the same way I did when I started reading *The Picture of Dorian Gray*. All those paragraphs about male beauty just made me nervous, for now-obvious reasons.

As a writer just starting out, I was curious about this all-but-forgotten Young Adult novel. I had actually considered writing a novel for a YA audience — it made sense, I thought, because many of my characters were tormented, angst-ridden teenagers. But at the time I wasn't sure if, as a gay writer, there was much of a place for me, or for my characters, in the genre. But here was this author, John Donovan, who had found such a place, before I was even born.

I *had* to track down a copy of *I'll Get There. It Better Be Worth the Trip*. I checked first on Amazon.com to see if it was in print, but it wasn't. Then I searched for it among the shelves at the local used bookstore, where I'd found countless out-of-print treasures in the past. But *I'll Get There. It Better Be Worth the Trip* was nowhere to be found — neither in the "adult" section nor on the children's shelves. It wasn't even at the local library. I finally tracked it down through an online used book dealer. I ordered my copy, a hardcover, for about eight dollars.

It arrived a few days later. The copy I had purchased was what you call a library-bound edition — a glossy hardcover without a jacket, made for wear and tear. The dust jacket copy was glued inside the front of the book,

as was a little pouch for the library card that was stamped with
DISCARDED in black ink. Someone had taken a blue marker and tried to
cover another stamp that said this book was PROVIDED BY THE
ALABAMA PUBLIC LIBRARY SERVICE. So, I thought, this book came
from Alabama, just like I did.

The cover art was modeled clearly (and cleverly) after a yellow
piece of lined writing paper, the kind you might use in elementary school.
The novel's title was printed incompletely in a loopy font (starting with I'LL
GET THERE. IT BETT. . .), from top row to bottom row, all the way down
the page, where it culminated, finally, in the complete title (including the
period) in pink letters, followed by "a novel by John Donovan" in aqua-blue
lettering.

*I'll Get There. It Better Be Worth the Trip* is narrated by thirteen-year-
old Davy Ross, who from the very first page has an appealing sardonic
voice, one that suggests both toughness and vulnerability. Davy has lived
with his grandmother — not with his divorced parents — since he was five.
But as the novel opens, his grandmother has just died, and now Davy must
move to New York City to live with his mother. "There aren't many adults I
have anything to *say* to," Davy tells us, "and now there is one less, with
Grandmother dead."

Reluctantly, his high-strung and fussy mother allows him to bring
along his beloved dog, Fred, a lick-happy dachshund. But she resents his
presence — the way he barks when Davy leaves, the way he pees on the
floor when he gets excited, the way he playfully gnaws on her bathrobe. She
refers to him as "a little bastard" and, addressing Davy, adds that "there's
something wrong with you animal-lovers." She also finds living with her
son difficult, and copes by going heavy on the evening cocktails, something
she unsuccessfully hides from Davy — he's no fool. Davy's father,
meanwhile, lives in the city with his new wife, and though both of them
seem very supportive and kind, Davy sees them only on occasional
weekends. Really, in Davy's new life, Fred is his only friend.

His mother enrolls him in a private Episcopal school, even though
Davy notices a lot of public schools nearby. On his first day, as he's

introduced to his classmates, Davy says, "I smile as though I'm friendly, and about everyone smiles back except the kid in the seat in front of me, who doesn't even turn around to see what I look like." That kid is Douglas Altschuler, the sullen class jock. Things start out frosty between the two, but soon they inch their way toward friendship — and maybe something more. "There's one thing about this guy; he's not modest," Davy says of Altschuler after they become friendly. "The second thing is that he says exactly what's on his mind. I never met anyone like Altschuler before." To Davy, Altschuler is a breath of fresh air, anything but a phony. He's also good looking, a fact Davy remarks on a few times in the novel.

Throughout, as Donovan develops their friendship, you can sense a tension between the boys — the moments of vulnerability sprinkled with bravado, the kindness followed by petty arguments, misunderstandings, pouting, then reconciliation. This well-crafted tension — subtle but insistent — finally reaches a head. One day after school, Altschuler accompanies Davy home. Davy's mother is still at work. They take Fred for his walk, then return to the apartment, where they chase Fred around the furniture until they both collapse on the floor, laughing. What follows is their first encounter:

> I feel unusual. Lying there. Close to Altschuler. I don't want to get up. I want to stay lying there. I feel a slight shiver and shake from it. Not cold though. Unusual. So I open my eyes. Altschuler is still lying there too. He looks at me peculiarly. I look at him the same way. . . . I guess I kiss Altschuler and he kisses me. It isn't like that dumb kiss I gave Mary Lou Gerrity in Massachusetts before I left. It just happens. And when it stops we sit up and turn away from each other.

The two boys pull apart, feeling awkward and confused. In the end, they simply laugh their actions off. Still, Davy ends the chapter by directly responding to what has just happened: "I mean a couple of guys like Altschuler and me don't have to worry about being queer or anything like that. Hell, no."

Typically, Altschuler avoids Davy at school the next day, but the two can't avoid each other forever, and soon they are back on track. Before too long, Altschuler ends up sleeping over one night. Donovan skips over what happens that night, but in Davy's reflections the day after, it is clear that "goofy business" has occurred again between the two — kissing, for sure, and perhaps more. Davy's ambivalence and confusion about what has happened are spot on: "There's nothing wrong with Altschuler and me, is there? . . . It's not dirty, or anything like that. It's all right, isn't it?"

Things carry on between them, until Davy's mother catches the boys asleep and embracing each other on the floor. Later, she grills Davy about what is going on between the two: "Nothing . . . unnatural . . . happened this afternoon with you and Douglas, did it?" Soon, Davy's father is called over, and he is a surprisingly level-headed voice to counter the hysterics of Davy's mother. But Davy is in denial and swears to his father, "I'm not queer or anything, if that's what you think."

While Davy is having his heart to heart with his father, his mother takes Fred out for a walk. The tragedy that ensues — Fred gets loose and is struck and killed by a car — has been used by contemporary critics to dismiss Donovan's novel as an example of a kind of self-hating gay novel, where tragedy is meted out as punishment for gay activity. But this dismissal is wrong-headed and simplistic. Sure, Davy blames himself for Fred's death; more specifically, he blames what happened between him and Altschuler: "Nothing would have happened to Fred if I hadn't been messing around with Altschuler. My fault. Mine!" But Davy is reacting the way many young gay kids might have acted at the time — indeed, the way some kids might *still* react. He is guilty, afraid, and confused. I remember being homophobic when I was a teenager, which I can see now was a reaction to the feelings I secretly had for other boys. Like Davy, I was afraid of it, didn't want it — it couldn't possibly be true about *me*. Indeed, I wasn't ready to accept the fact that I was gay until I was twenty. Davy, at thirteen, is still in search of himself. While it is clear to the contemporary reader that Davy is likely gay, the narrator can't yet truly see that about himself. The territory is still too strange, fraught with uncertainty.

As the novel draws to a close, Altschuler and Davy are walking together, talking about all that has happened between them. Altschuler says, "What happened to Fred had nothing to do with us." "Maybe it did," Davy replies. Altschuler, showing that he, at least, is more comfortable with his budding sexuality, says, "Go ahead and feel guilty about it if you want to. I don't."

In the end, Davy is still confused by his feelings. But the two friends agree to respect each other. Whether that respect will lead to deeper feelings isn't clear. But it is clear that Davy, though conflicted, has crossed a threshold into maturity. He's prepared to face whatever the future holds. Sure, some readers might prefer to see Davy and Altschuler rolling around passionately, affirming their love. But such an ending would ring false — this is a novel about growing up, not coming out.

Since *I'll Get There. It Better Be Worth the Trip.* was published, many YA novels about gay youths have entered the marketplace — books by David Levithan, Nancy Garden, Alex Sanchez, and Jacqueline Woodson, to name just a few. In fact, the gay YA novel is now pretty commonplace. Sure, the quality of the titles varies, but even the fluffiest of these books are worthwhile, because now, finally, gay and lesbian young people can find mirror images of themselves in literature. I've read a number of these books, but so far none have affected me the way that *I'll Get There. It Better Be Worth the Trip.* did. It's a subtle and honest story told by an appealing and confused young man. Again, remember that this novel was published in 1969, just as gays were becoming more visible in this country, standing up for their rights, refusing to be invisible. Donovan's book, in that light, is remarkable and daring. But now, with gays more visible in "mainstream culture" than ever before, it is even more remarkable that this eloquent novel still rings true as a portrait of a young gay man, inching toward adulthood, searching for his place in the world. I like to think that Davy got there — and that it was worth the trip.

# Robert Ferro
# **The Blue Star**

Dutton, 1985

## Stephen Greco

I've just reread *The Blue Star*, Robert Ferro's third novel —or his second-to-last, to use a method of ordering that felt inescapable in the year when the novel came out, 1985. It was a time when all the young gay authors I knew were thinking that their next books might well be their last. Robert certainly thought that; he told so me many times, when working on *Second Son*, a thoughtful and surprisingly entertaining AIDS novel that appeared in 1988, the year Robert died of the disease just six weeks after his partner of many years, the novelist Michael Grumley, died of it, too. For Robert, I think, *Second Son* had to be about AIDS. He was constantly sick by then, and the prospect of his death was too momentous to leave unexplored. *The Blue Star*, on the other hand, seems about life and the forces that drive it, unhaunted by "a death out of order," which is how Robert referred to AIDS fatalities.

According to the slightly yellowed flap of my copy's dust jacket, *The Blue Star* begins with "two heroes, reflective Peter and Byronic Chase, indulging their youthful appetites in Florence." By day, the boys feast on *la dolce vita* in conspicuously well-tailored clothing — this is the early 1960s — and by night, after hours, they cruise along the Arno and find love and violence. Then they are invited to tea by a worldly, lecherous old aristocrat, Count Niccolo Virgiliano.

The next afternoon, after an extensive toilette, we presented ourselves at Palazzo Virgiliano, which abutted the Pitti and was favored with a private entrance to the Boboli Gardens. A butler in a striped coat took us up in a small mahogany elevator, delivering us into a three-storyed paneled library in which the floor, tables, and all the chairs were covered in bright green baize cloth.

"Numbers three and five," muttered Chase [who has previously explained that some statements are needed so often in life that numbers make them easier to use: three meaning "Do you love it?" and five, "Where will it all lead us?"] A door opened and the count came in.

Virgiliano was over sixty, very tall, thin, and grey, and he had crossed over that line between the truly aristocratic and the truly effeminate. In the fifteenth century his family had had its historical moment with the Humanists and lived in the reflected glory of this moment ever since. Grandmère Chase and Count Niccolo's mother were contemporaries and had met in the forties. Chase said Niccolo had known every gay tourist to visit Florence since the Brownings. English translations were his hobby, American boys his passion. . . . Tea was brought in, on a tray with thirty objects for three people, and Niccolo asked if I would be mother. I had no idea what he meant and gave him a perfectly stupid look.

"Pour, Peter," Chase said, and Niccolo smiled.

From that tea, over the next 20 years, everything follows: Peter's loss and rediscovery of his first love, Lorenzo, who grows from a stunning teenager into a beautiful man; Chase's marriage to Olympia, Niccolo's princess niece, for the express purpose of joining bloodlines and fortunes; and the voyage of several of these characters up the Nile on a yacht named La Stella Azzurra — The Blue Star — in a climactic chapter that happens to elucidate a similar though shadowier voyage that Robert described years before in his first novel, *The Others*.

As the passage above suggests, time was second only to family as an important theme in Robert's work. (He inscribed my copy of *The Blue Star* "through the years …") Not far into the story a temporal shift occurs that I remember finding jarring at the time, partly because the author's voice, already authoritative, ascends into infallibility: "To tell the story it is necessary to jump back a hundred years, to New York City in 1857, to an ancestor of Chase Walker — his great-great-great-grandfather Orvil Starkweather, and to begin with a brief history of Central Park, and something of the Masons."

It is at this point that *The Blue Star* blooms into a tale of a family conspiracy spanning centuries — generations!— as Orvil leads the building of a secret Masonic temple beneath Central Park. Secrets, conspiracies, and cabals are at the core in *The Blue Star*, as they were for Robert at the core of human existence. In fact, the depiction of hidden powers and arcane knowledge — to be revealed only to those worthy of seeing how such stuff spins into history (i.e., readers and other initiates) — is what makes *The Blue Star* so distinctly a gay novel, gayness for Robert being a kind of revealed knowledge. Yet like *The Others* and Robert's second novel, *The Family of Max Desir*, *The Blue Star* is more than a gay novel. It appeared just at the moment when one could feel so-called gay literature stepping beyond genre, into the mainstream — an arrival merited by authors as masterful as Robert and his Violet Quill colleagues, who didn't merely write about gay life, but drew on the gay imagination to write about "life as a whole." Transcend convention.

*The Blue Star*, in particular, shows the gay imagination catalyzing the observation and description of things both common and mysterious, like sex and love, which affords the reader a fresh appreciation of the breathless thrill of existence. "Euphoria" is how Robert's friend, the poet and translator Richard Howard, described this quality, in his blurb for the book:

Robert Ferro possesses that rarest gift in a fabulist, euphoric imagination. He may revel of course in quite the

> darkest of double-plots, in crone-princesses and epicene
> wizards, in a cloud-cuckoo gaiety where no one is ever sick
> or hurt, where work is heresay, and all are witty (gallows-
> humor without the penalty is Ferro's forte), but his real
> achievement is to detail the contents of happiness.

"The contents of happiness." Isn't that a felicitous phrase? It applies not only to Robert's approach to literature but to his understanding of life and the exacting way he pursued life's nicest possibilities. The blurb was printed on the rear cover of the novel's original hardback edition, which depicts an azure sea at dusk, as seen from a terrace, through an elegant stone archway. On the front over, through another archway, is more sea and a stylish white yacht, along with title and author. If I am not mistaken, Robert worked closely with the artist on that jacket illustration. He might also have sweet-talked Richard Howard for the blurb and worked closely with Dutton, the book's publisher, to polish the jacket copy. Some might have thought Robert a control freak, but he was really a perfectionist, attentive to the smallest detail, like the placement of an amethyst-glass vase on a windowsill in the beach house in Sea Girt, New Jersey, that Robert and Michael often shared with friends on weekends. That house — another story, I'm afraid — had been his mother's, and its maintenance as an idyllic escape for himself and loved ones was one of Robert's greatest pleasures and perhaps one of his greatest achievements. The walls of the downstairs powder room were specially muraled with stone arches and a tranquil blue sea, just like the book cover.

That house helped make *The Blue Star* possible, in a big way. He often went there to work, and completed large portions of all his later novels there. Moreover, Robert had a talent for living well, which deeply informed the voluptuous living in his novels — the kind of good living that is sacramental, not consumerist. Robert and Michael traveled with their own bed sheets, for instance, just in case, because *one has certain standards*. Lots of people have written about the legendary tea salons the boys hosted at their West 95th Street apartment — again, another story, except to mention that the teas seem, in retrospect, to have taken place in a kind of temple: the long living room of the boys' graciously-proportioned, pre-War apartment, made even more palatial by a pair of towering *faux marbre* columns that Robert had installed at great expense.

Those salons were always packed with cultural luminaries, gay and otherwise, and it was at one of them that Robert first told me of the new book he was writing.

"It's going to be beautiful, Muzzy, if I can just pull it off," he said in a whisper. "But let's not speak of it here, among *these* people."

He might have been fetching a plate of crab puffs from the kitchen at that moment, and might well have been confiding the same thing to everyone else, but Robert did take care to make me feel special. He called me Muzzy, after the Carol Channing character in *Thoroughly Modern Milly*, a nickname I felt was an immense honor. Then he accorded me a more important honor, early one morning, down at the shore. I came downstairs and found Robert outside, on the terrace, with the manuscript of a story I'd given him. He had read the thing that morning, instead of working on *The Blue Star*. It was the first real fiction I'd ever written, a story entitled "Good With Words," and I was delighted that he'd agreed to look it over, even if apprehensive.

"*You*," he said, pointing his finger decisively, when he spotted me at the bottom of the stairs. Everyone else in the house was still asleep. "Come over here." I was too terrified to pass through the kitchen and pour myself a cup of coffee, from the steaming batch Robert had already prepared for his guests.

For an hour we sat on the terrace and talked of writing, as the waves crashed away beyond the thicket of rugosa and a scrawny strip of beach. Writing was sacred, Robert reminded me. Writers were priests, and a calling was not to be ignored. He explained that he'd found my story good, and that this meant I should stop monkeying around in magazines — I was senior editor of *Interview* at the time — and start taking myself more seriously as a writer.

My little story was printed in *Advocate Men* and eventually made its way into *The Penguin Book of Gay Short Stories*. And I wrote other stories. But it would be years before I completed my first novel, *Dreadnought*, and even then it was Robert's spirit that helped me get through the ordeal of writing it — much as Chase in *The Blue Star* takes his time becoming the vessel he was meant to be, and does so after a tap on the shoulder by fate, in the form of Niccolo, whose chief talent is taking one's self seriously.

Yet not too seriously. *The Blue Star* also expresses what might be called a respect for fun as a supernal quality — fun when it's combined with pleasure and joy instead of substituting for them, as often happens in American life. This side of Robert was often on display during weekends at the beach house, when gossip had to be shared and games played. It was customary, for example, for Robert and Michael to welcome me and my boyfriend, Barry, for a weekend with a little note they'd secreted away beforehand in a certain rabbit-shaped box in the room of the house that I preferred, the Suite Orientale, so-called because it boasted a pair of extravagantly exotic, red-black-and-gold lamps in the form of Chinese courtiers. Upon departing at the end of a weekend, Barry and I would leave a note for our hosts. One weekend, I had planned ahead. The note we left was the first clue in an elaborate treasure hunt that led to further clues — ten of them, I think, in the form of parts of a map, which I had hidden throughout the house all weekend, right under Robert's nose. The last of the parts led directly to the treasure: a miniature casket brimming with fake gemstones I had collected from shops in New York's button-and-bauble district, off Seventh Avenue. I had placed the casket in the powder room — the one with the Blue Star murals.

The reason I speak so much of the beach house is that both it and Robert's writing reflect a deeper quality that was essential to him as a man and an artist. Robert always said that the key to life was rearranging the furniture. Consider that statement's practically Victorian resonance — imperial in its ambition to remake Nature in accordance with our needs, our beliefs, even our esthetics. Indeed, in his personal life Robert did as much decorating, landscaping, and commissioning of suits as his characters do, and this all reflects an urgent faith Robert had in an individual's pure agency.

   In the years since Robert's death, I've re-read his novels frequently, just to stay in tune with his wavelength. I also direct the annual literary prize that bears his and Michael's name, the Ferro-Grumley, which I co-founded a year after they died. I guess you could say that the prize itself is a kind of conspiracy, devised in Robert's name to draw attention to the kinds of truthful, luminous writing he aimed for in his books and sought in those of others, books that continue to sit upon our shelves, as seductively incandescent as a blue star.

John Gilgun

# Music I Never Dreamed Of

Amethyst Press, 1989

## Wayne Courtois

**Thirteen Short Essays**

1. *What I Meant to Do, I Think*

I meant to write a conventional critical essay on John Gilgun's novel *Music I Never Dreamed Of.* But who was I kidding? I'm not a literary critic. Perhaps instead I can write a series of impressionistic pieces that will magically coalesce in the mind of the reader into some of kind of magnificent whole . . .

Or something like that.

2. *Days of Our Inner Lives*

In the title essay of her collection *The Din in the Head,* Cynthia Ozick — who really is a literary critic, as well as a fiction writer — refers to the novel, a perennially dying art form, as "the last trustworthy vessel of the inner life." As I mulled over this apt description it occurred to me that the conflicted protagonist of a gay novel may have more than one inner life. There's the one that we all recognize, the inner life that runs on autopilot, dictating the character's thoughts, observations, and emotions throughout the day; then there's the *inner* inner life, which is telling him that he is living a lie — that the world is upside down and will stay that way till he corrects it. The author of a coming-of-age gay novel faces the difficult task of giving two inner lives their due, as they battle it out with each other.

### 3. *Homo = Werewolf*

If you are Stevie Riley, then it's like it is 1954, you live in South Boston, you're nineteen years old, and you know you're homosexual. But there *are* no homosexuals. They don't exist, except in dirty jokes. The word *homosexual* is never heard on TV, or used in newspapers or magazines except in the most furtive, negative contexts. The few films and relatively few books that have dealt honestly with the subject are so out of reach that they may as well be on Mars. Here is the only kind of information that Stevie Riley can get his hands on, as he explains to a female friend:

> During a full moon we go crazy. We have 'periods' the way
> women do, except it's in our minds. We get incredibly
> horny. We can't control our impulses. We become sex
> crazed. The jails fill up. They round us up and throw us in
> jail. It's the only way the police can control us. I read it in
> *Washington Confidential* while I was killing time in a
> drugstore on Saturday.

Stevie has just returned home to live with his family, after spending a year and a half in seminary like a good Irish Catholic boy. He was dismissed from there for not having a vocation — a verdict he agrees with, though there's more to it than that. Stevie is a product of his place and time: he knows he's queer but he can't accept it. Who can blame him? Maybe, if he manages to get laid with a woman, the queerness will go away. That seems to be the conventional wisdom, and he has no friend or mentor who can tell him otherwise.

### 4. *Next He'll Be Pissing in the Holy Water*

Recently I saw an old Brazilian horror flick called *At Midnight I'll Take Your Soul*. The monster / protagonist is a snarky mortician who has qualities of both a vampire and a ghoul. His first horrific act in the film is to eat meat on Good Friday. Yes, ladies and gentlemen, there he is, gnawing on a leg of lamb in his window while a holy procession passes on the street below. I was reminded that Brazil is the largest Catholic country in the world; no doubt many viewers of this film were sincerely horrified by the maniac's sacrilegious act.

I was reminded, too, of Stevie's mom — how she verbally abuses and slaps her sons around at the merest hint that they might be committing sacrilege. She says that Stevie's older brother Brian is endangering his "immortal soul" by reading *Studs Lonigan*, for Christ's sake. And while she doesn't seem to be disappointed that Stevie left the seminary, she seems haunted by the question of *why* he had to leave. In one terrifying scene she explodes at him, calling him an "introvert." It's probably the worst word she knows, and its echo of *pervert* isn't lost on Stevie, who's cut to the quick. He actually sinks to his knees, right there in the living room, breaking a religious statue in the process. More yelling. The neighbors are pounding on the walls.

It's a typical night in the Riley household. Even the neighbors pounding on the walls are doing so "out of habit." They know it won't do any good.

5. *At Least He's Not Reading 120 Days of Sodom*

Like his older brother, Stevie also reads *Studs Lonigan*. When he mentions it during confession, the priest tells him to stop reading. Stevie asks why, and the priest explodes:

> Why? Did you ask why! Are you questioning my authority? Are you kneeling here in this confessional and questioning my authority? Did I hear you ask why! You can't read the book because the Church has decided that the book is dangerous for you to read. You put your soul in jeopardy when you read it. That should be enough for you.

When Stevie says it's not enough, he gets kicked out of the confessional — a painful yet necessary step in his liberation.

Note the punctuation of the priest's dialogue. "Did you ask why!" is not a question. Neither is "Did I hear you ask why!" For the priest — the ultimate authority figure in this hell on earth — exclamation points are as good as question marks, because he already knows all the answers.

That you can endanger your immortal soul by reading a book is still a widely held notion in the world. It makes me glad I'm a non-believer, considering some of the books I've read, not to mention the things I've written. Oh, my soul would be toast on Judgment Day — and not cinnamon toast, either.

6. *The Urban Death Machine and Joie de Vivre*

I laughed with delight at Stevie's first mention of *Studs Lonigan,* because that was precisely the novel I was thinking of while reading *Music.* "It's about us," is Stevie's assessment of James T. Farrell's work; and he's not wrong. By writing *Music I Never Dreamed Of,* John Gilgun placed himself squarely in the tradition of Farrell, Nelson Algren, Henry Roth, and other great chroniclers of the urban death machine. And nobody does it better. Consider this description of Stevie and his friend Luanne entering the subway:

> It was the kind of March afternoon when, as you move toward the MTA subway, your eye is caught by something bright, the first bright thing you've seen in months, and as you look up you notice some old woman selling jonquils from a pushcart. But that sensation, that flash of yellow, only lasts for a second, because people are pushing you from behind.

Down in the pit, the horror closes in:

> The subway smelled like the bottom of a diaper pail. It was like every wino in Boston had pissed in there at one time or another. And someone had drawn big hairy cocks sticking out of the pants of all the male figures on the billboards and big tits on the female ones. We pushed through the beat-up old turnstiles. This separated us for a minute, but then we came together again on the platform. The pissy smell was

> replaced by the smell from the third rail — a chemical smell
> like mothballs, fractured electricity.

But the final sentences of this passage are the most telling:

> I got those smells every day, so usually I didn't notice them.
> But today my senses were alive to them. I don't know why.
> It felt good though, feeling alive that way.

Stevie Riley doesn't get crushed by the urban death machine. He feels alive, every day of his life. That's the joy of this novel.

7. *Meanwhile, Many Years from Now . . .*

Gilgun gives us two tantalizing glimpses of Stevie in the future. Near the beginning of Chapter 6 he makes the startling assertion that it's May 9, 1989, and he's re-reading the novel *1984*, another book that he had read during his fateful 19th year. And later, at the beginning of Chapter 8, he makes the startling statement that "I'm sitting here at my Apple computer, an instrument I could not have dreamed of in 1954, writing my book. It is 5:10 a.m., May 12, 1989."

We've seen this before, the aside that tells us that the character gets to grow up and write an autobiography about his salad days — the book we are holding in our hands. It blurs the line between author and character, suggesting that the former is really writing about his own life. I would hold that no one who inhabits Stevie's life and times as thoroughly as this author does could possibly be writing anything other than autobiography.

In the case of John Gilgun, his life took some turns that allowed him to escape from South Boston, all the way to a college in St. Joseph, Missouri, where he taught literature for many years. He is now retired and divides his time between St. Joseph and Des Moines, where his partner lives.

8. *Books Are Short, Art is Long*

*Music* weighs in at 145 pages and 10 chapters. It comes at you all in one piece, with few breaks in time and only a few half-scene flashbacks. It's as if it were written in one sitting, or meant to be consumed in one sitting, like a short story. In fact, this novel's history is a long and torturous one. John

wrote the first draft in 1959, and it wasn't published till 1989, after 30 years
of effort. At one point the manuscript swelled to 800 pages; that was when
an editor at Macmillan got hold of it, chopped it down to 300 pages, and
effectively killed it. It is a testament to John's perseverance and, yes, good
fortune that the book finally saw print.

The headlong nature of the narrative — the sense that, yes, it *must*
have been written in one sitting — has a special place in my heart, because
my own first (unpublished) novel was similar in this respect. I didn't even
divide mine into chapters, because I wanted no "breaks" between the story
and the reader; I wanted the novel to be experienced as a long dream from
which the reader couldn't awaken.

9. *Compassionate Conservatism* circa *1954*

Guess what? Stevie's mother has a brother. Uncle Tim is the kind of
Republican fascist who, in our current decade, has brought our country to
the brink of moral and financial bankruptcy while making it the most hated
nation in the world. A big shot at a company that manufactures fire ex-
tinguishers, Tim has everything that a man who is "making it" is supposed
to have: "a ranch-type house with a breezeway and a two-car garage and a
patio in the suburbs, a cocker spaniel, a new Pontiac Chieftain, an attractive
wife and that daughter in dancing school." And he has a God-given mission
to make sure that Stevie and his brother Brian will "make it," too.

He promises Brian a job at the fire extinguisher company that will
lead to a management position within a year. To his credit, Brian recognizes
that this offer is nothing that he wants. But he has a wife to provide for, and
that includes buying a house; he's feeling a squeeze.

Tim has plans for Stevie, too. Unlike his brother, who has a heart
condition, Stevie is bound to be drafted any day now. Tim arranges an
interview for Stevie with an Army captain who can pull strings to get Stevie
into OTC, so he won't have to "waste his time" as a private. Like his brother
Brian, Stevie is repulsed by his uncle, yet feels he has to go along with this
plan. He can't quite make a complete break with the belief that his elders
know what's best for him.

10. *The Ubiquity of Ignorance*

The pleasure of reading this novel is exquisitely tempered by pain, as the naïve Stevie encounters one crisis after another while striving to do the right thing. Stevie keeps the appointment that Tim sets up for him with the Army captain, and for a while he feels good about doing the right thing. But his natural inquisitiveness, his yearning for growth, gets the better of him: when he meets his friend Luanne again, she mentions a counselor that she and her little boy are seeing. Stevie sees an opportunity: if he talks to this counselor, maybe he can find out *why* he's queer.

Luanne wangles Stevie onto the counselor's overbooked calendar, and Stevie, filled with anticipation and hope, walks into a familiar trap: when the counselor learns of Stevie's homosexuality, he responds with obvious contempt. He also gives Stevie one piece of information that he didn't have: at his pre-induction Army physical he will be asked if he has homosexual tendencies; and if he admits that he does, he'll be rejected. Stevie is horrified. He can't lie on the induction form, yet he'll have to, or he'll be letting everyone down. It's another crisis, and it provides the tension for the last few chapters of the novel.

The sinister counselor is the worst kind of straight hypocrite: "I despise what you are, and at the same time, I don't believe you." We may be safely removed in time from Stevie's 1954, but this type of ignorance is very much operational today. It powers, among other things, the ex-gay movement. The so-called ex-gays have even been lobbying for a voice in the public schools: imagine the damage *that* will do.

Not long after I moved to Kansas City, I became involved with a peculiar institution called the School of Metaphysics. The free classes that were held on weeknights covered topics such as meditation, kundalini yoga, and dream analysis. It was during one of the dream-analysis sessions that a female student mentioned a dream about having sex with another woman. "That's not possible," the instructor snapped. Curious, I stayed after class to ask the instructor why she had said that. "It's not possible for two people of the same gender to have sex with each other," she said. "Oh, honey," I told her, "it's not only *possible,* it's been *done.*" She continued to argue, saying that homosexuality violated the "male-female principle of the universe."

That was when I walked away from the School of Metaphysics. Who were these straight people to think that their sexual orientation could even co-opt the stars?

11. *So What Do They Do with Each Other?*

The counselor Stevie visits does him another disservice: when he asks Stevie what he does with men in his sexual fantasies, Stevie can only reply: "I hold them. We hold each other. We touch each other. Look, this isn't easy for me! We . . . We just love each other." The counselor's response is casually cruel: "You have the fantasies of a boy of twelve. They may be normal in a boy of twelve, but it's time you outgrew them."

It's true that Stevie doesn't know *exactly* what men who love each other do in bed. He does know about sucking cock, if only because that activity is such a cherished and loathed staple of schoolboy lore. Maybe his fantasies aren't far removed from a twelve-year-old's, after all. But it's 1954, and there's no shrink-wrapped *Joy of Gay Sex* waiting for him on some bookstore's top shelf.

Family and friends are no help. Stevie's friend Luanne and brother Brian both love him, but they have difficulty understanding or accepting him. Even Luanne, who knows Stevie better than anyone, won't give up on the cherished heterosexual belief that all Stevie has to do is find the right girl. Sympathetic characters like Luanne and Brian remind us that there is nothing more heartbreaking than the ignorance of decent people. And so it is, in 1954 Boston, decades before sex of every stripe becomes part of our public discourse, that the fate of a young man like Stevie depends quite literally on the kindness of a stranger.

12. *To Be Nineteen and Losing It*

If I were to fault *Music I Never Dreamed Of* for anything, it might be its title. It gives the impression that this is a lyrical kind of work, which it isn't. There are no flights of fancy; no dense, allusive, "literary" passages. Instead we find gritty realism, tempered by Stevie's lust for life and naïve observations.

Stevie is drawn toward art and literature, but there is little mention of music in this novel. This seems strange since, by the mid-1950's, American popular music had exploded with the sounds of African-American influences, and infectious beats were heard everywhere. Stevie's only encounter with recorded music appears near the end of the novel, when he spends his first night with a man.

The character of Hal, Stevie's first, whom he meets at Luanne's, is well drawn and all too believable as the kind of first lover that a naïve kid might bump into. Older — he's just graduating from college — and somewhat cynical, self-involved, and defensive, Hal has no interest in seducing Stevie or even being particularly nice to him. His first impression of the younger man is, "I thought you were a dyke" — hardly the stuff of romance.

Yet Stevie is drawn to Hal, who is handsome and has a "compact little body." We can further understand the attraction when we remember that Stevie is nineteen and dying to lose his virginity. The two men leave the party at Luanne's together, against Hal's better judgment; he declares, in his typically blunt way, "I'm not going to bring you out." After the two of them get kicked out of a coffee shop for ordering only coffee, they make their circuitous way to Hal's house. It is here that Stevie encounters Debussy's *Preludes*, which seem to speak to him.

Hal is unhappy and snarky, but in a short while he learns to be nice to Stevie. And he does, of course, sleep with him. Their lovemaking is both tentative and satisfying. Hal even drives Stevie to his pre-induction physical the next day. It's here that Stevie faces his greatest test: can he lie about his sexuality? No one who has read this far could have any doubt about what he will do, but it's still elating to see him do it. The *bildungsroman* ends as it should, with Stevie preparing to take his first giant steps away from home.

13. *Liberation: It's Not Just for Fictional Characters*

John dedicated *Music I Never Dreamed Of* to his friend Jerry Rosco, an accomplished fiction writer, literary biographer (*Glenway Wescott Personally: A Biography*) and journalist. Jerry was instrumental in getting *Music* published, because he happened to have a copy of the manuscript at the right time and place — terrifying confirmation that publication depends on luck as much as anything else.

Jerry is a friend of mine also, dating back to the time I lived in New York; it was his idea that John and I should meet, which we did, early in 1987. I had recently moved to Kansas City, and John was teaching at Western Missouri State University in St. Joseph, about an hour's drive away.

Outside of the relatively gay-friendly metropolitan areas like Kansas City and St. Louis, the state of Missouri is like so many others: just one redneck town after another. When I met John during that winter of 1987 I found him to be convivial and articulate — and bitter about the closeted life he was living in St. Joseph. Fortunately, he was about to take a sabbatical and go live in San Francisco for a while. He had visited there many times, and it felt like home to him.

When John returned to his teaching job in St. Joseph, his novel came out. So did he, in a public address. To their great credit his students were behind him, petitioning the college to add John's novel to the curriculum. As a result, John was able to teach *Music I Never Dreamed Of* to his literature classes. When I think of those students, most of them encountering an authentic gay voice for the first time in this heartfelt, exuberant novel, it gives me a great feeling. Suddenly I'm right back there in South Boston in 1954, with Stevie Riley, and we're both feeling frightened and confused, yet alive — gloriously alive, in ways we never dreamed of.

Agustín Gomez-Arcos

# The Carnivorous Lamb

Godine, 1984 (1<sup>st</sup> edition in English translation)

## Richard Reitsma

As frequently happens when bookish gay men are exploring their sexuality, I assumed the library was my best bet for discovery. Not for cruising, mind you, I was too terrified of actual human contact. No, my hope was for vicarious pleasures, enjoying the exploratory homosexual awakenings of others made vivid in books. The stacks became my refuge. Granted, I grew up in small town West Michigan, which meant the stacks were rather limited, and the gay material even more limited, but they did have some things in the HQ section (the section in libraries for cataloguing books on gay and lesbian issues, frequently difficult to find, at least in the past). Nowadays, of course, libraries are more and more online, from the card catalogue to articles and even books. There is something wonderful, however, in just going into the stacks, wandering around, pulling out a book, putting it back, only to discover that the book next to it, or on the shelf above is REALLY the book you want.

As a professor of literature today, I still find that thrill of bookish discovery to be invigorating, and am saddened at how little my students avail themselves of simply wandering among books, addicted as they are to shallow internet noodling. Young — I was a college freshman, mind you — overly literate, untouched by human hands; my censored sexuality directed me to the stacks, a particularly darkened, forgotten, and dusty corner of the library where I tremulously reached for different volumes. As Poncia says about the Alba sisters in Lorca's *The House of Bernarda Alba*, "no one can deny their true inclinations." I, of course, could not resist either. Somehow, in one of those serendipitous moments of chance, an inconspicuous book found its way into my hand. The title was intriguing — *The Carnivorous Lamb* — and immediately appealed to my hyper-Christian sensibilities associated with the word "lamb," not to mention the lamb imagery replete in Lorca's aforementioned play. First impressions are always lasting ones, and my first encounter with Gomez-Arcos was shrouded mythic possibilities which my mind has continued to romanticize ever since.

As is my custom, either out of an insatiable curiosity, or dyslexia, or both, I always start a book at the end, opening to the last pages and reading, to decide if I like it. It drives everyone I know crazy, but after all these years of reading, I've never, ever read anything without first reading the end. The end, which describes a same-sex wedding scene, and associates it with anti-Franco terrorism and filial rebellion against repressive parents, was certainly sufficiently compelling for me to take the book, sit on the floor in the middle of the stacks, and begin reading (from the beginning). In fact, the power of the narrative was so seductive that I was able to overcome all my internalized homophobic anxieties and actually check out the book. I was bewitched by its transgressions, enchanted by its beautiful prose, and utterly tempted by its violent rejection of family and country, with which I could so closely identify as a repressed and oppressed youth uncertain of what it was about me that made people withdraw warmth and affection. Of course, it helped that the title was utterly innocuous so as not to call attention to the fact that I was checking out a gay book, but still, it took courage to claim allegiance to its contents, to go on record that, however momentarily, the book was with *me*, was of *me* . . . the book *was me*.

The drama of the novel occurs in the province of Almeria, Spain, the same province where Gomez-Arcos was born in 1939, at the start of the Spanish Civil War. At the age of twenty-seven, in rebellion against Franco's fascist regime, he went into exile in 1966, and wrote all of his major works in the language of his exile. The Spanish Civil War and its fascist aftermath impact all his work, and particularly pervade this text.

The novel describes the living death of Spain under Franco's fascist rule and the ways in which a failed Republican family subverts the fascist state and the Church Politic. The drama explores the relationship among a family of self-labeled anarchists. The mother is of the aristocratic class, who marries below her station as an act of defiance to the social restrictions placed on her as an elite woman. Her husband is a Republican, who survives the Civil War a broken man, kept alive by his wife's money, but he is walking dead, repressed daily by Franco's incessant chanting of "peace and victory" on the radio. She gives birth to two boys who are groomed to fulfill their parents' abortive revolutionary activities. As they grow, the two boys commit terrorist activities by perverting Catholic rituals within their incestuous, homosexual love affair. One of the most beautifully written moments in the novel is also one of the most sacrilegious: having passed through the rituals of his baptism and first communion, allowing him to enter Spanish society, the youngest experiences his first penetrative sexual experience as the culmination of his entry into manhood. The elder brother takes his sibling to an Edenic cave full of butterflies for this deflowering:

> The taste of the body of Christ had hardly left my mouth when my brother's tongue hungrily pushed into it, wiping away the last traces . . . He pulled down his pants and took me with a thrust of his hips. The butterfly-filled air shook with my cry, and a shower of golden motes rained down on us . . . 'I love you!' My brother liked those words so much, he repeated them over and over, each time pushing a little deeper into me, appropriating the wild discovery of my body, his shout mingling with mine in my mouth . . . The water from the spring murmured in my ears, and my eyes were lost in a kaleidoscope of butterflies, the whole dominated by my brother's god-face . . . I loved the merciless pain my brother caused me, bringing me to the edge of delirium. I realized this delirium was a world he

had spent years preparing for, and that he was drawn to it
as irresistibly as I was.

The novel is replete with lyric descriptions of scenes devastatingly taboo
which function to contest, banish, and overwhelm the oppressive fascism
which engenders such graphic revolts.

Such scenes aroused me. I devoured the book. I fell in love with the
novel. I wanted to live that life. Well, not exactly, but I wanted sex like that,
love like that. I wanted to be IN the book. Alas, in Western Michigan in the
80s there was no way I could find a copy of an out-of-print book from a
foreign writer (this was, of course, before the internet and Amazon.com). So,
I photocopied it, and kept it like a rescued treasure, and returned it to the
library to let it sink back into the dark recesses of the stacks for some other
intrepid, frightened, confused student to stumble upon.

Years later, as a graduate student, I was allowed to start teaching
literature, and, once I had proven my capacities in teaching benign topics, I
was finally given the chance to design my own special topics course. The
course I designed was The Body Erotic/The Body Politic: Deviant Sexuality
as Political Discourse. I have continued to teach versions of that course
throughout my academic career, at a variety of different institutions and
departments. I don't always get a chance to teach Gomez-Arcos, but when I
do, his is always the first novel we read. This isn't merely a tribute to my
youth, it is, rather, an homage to a wonderful book that articulates
beautifully the intersections of the body erotic and the body politic, since the
core relationship takes place with the backdrop of the Spanish Civil War
and the Franco dictatorship, and the love affair exists in direct conflict to the
fascist regime. However, I am always nervous teaching the novel and feel a
need to explain it before it is read: to excuse its behavior, to justify it,
because the novel is frankly erotic, and details an intergenerational,
homosexual, incestuous love affair between and older brother and his
young sibling. Now I realize, of course, that this is ridiculous, and
judgmental, and probably homophobic, ashamed as I am to even consider
that notion. It should be noted, however, that the cover of the French edition
is decidedly reserved, representing a stern woman and two children

standing in the large shadow of a cross. This is in stark contrast to the various English language editions which are significantly more romantic and erotic. And yet, incestuous, homosexual love is not the point of the novel at all. The novel is an indictment of the Spanish Civil War, of Franco and his regime, of the powerless republicans who remain in the country, of a nation mired in a repressive, backward-looking fascism that dooms its people to the despair of a living tomb. All these themes of exile, of sexual behavior used as a political weapon, of children rebelling against a crazy mother and a passive father all coalesced in my own personal experience as something with which I could identify. The story of the brotherly love in Gomez-Arcos is both so political, and so beautifully told, that the issue of incest is almost forgotten. In fact, the beauty of the language, the poetic prose, is so overwhelming, that one often forgets one is reading something that celebrates every taboo of society, from incestuous homosexuality to parental abuse of children, to thorough desecration of all things sacred. Time and time again my students tell me how they were seduced by the prose and forgot that they were supposed to be unsettled, so enmeshed were they with the narrative exuberance.

And every year I teach this novel and am nervous, I am reminded by my students' reactions that there is no need for that fear. At the end of the semester when I've taught this novel, I ask them which book they liked the most, which book they would suggest I eliminate. Almost to a person, regardless of gender, sexuality, race, or other factors of difference, their favorite novel is *The Carnivorous Lamb*. They talk about how the body erotic and the body politic so perfectly interact in the novel; how the body becomes the territory upon which political violence is enacted, a metonym of the geographical national body. They are fascinated by the novel's terrorist critique of fascist Spain. Mostly, however, they respond to the same things I did, all those years ago: the beautifully written love story; the engaging descriptions of eroticism; the beauty of their first penetrative sexual encounter in an Edenic cave, surrounded by a colony of white butterflies, the sacrilegious exuberance of love. Mind you, the majority of my students over the years are straight, with a preponderance of females.

Gomez-Arcos' writing, despite the obvious rage against Franco and his regime, is seductive, charming his audience, luring readers in to a reality that converts them, in the best tradition of the novel, into terrorists themselves: they see the world differently after this novel. When I ask them about the impedimentary taboos of incest, of intergenerational sex, let alone the frankly erotic depictions of gay sex, they barely bat an eye. And these are not, at least initially, the most sophisticated of readers. Common comments are "I forgot they were brothers," or "It didn't bother me because it was so beautiful," or "I didn't think about it that way, I just saw it as a metaphor." Now granted, my worried introduction to the novel always includes caveats such as "The sexuality in the novel is one of the metaphors used to contest fascism, just as the color symbolism of red and yellow, which permeate the novel, is a metaphor to deconstruct the Franco regime and Spanish fascism." Those caveats are true, but they would not suffice for students to overlook the obvious taboos unless the narrative itself were so beguiling, bewitching us into accepting the closed world of the brotherly love as something transcendentally beautiful, offering that possibility of hope that compels us to wander among the library stacks, bravely reaching for forgotten texts and finding a bit of ourselves, and, perhaps, love.

Michael Grumley
# Life Drawing
Grove, 1991

## Sam J. Miller

The narrator of Michael Grumley's *Life Drawing* is an artist — an aspiring painter, we presume, although he never does any painting. Instead he draws, scribbling out pencil sketches of statues in parks or his lover in sleep. Life drawings. The novel itself is a modest work of art. Grumley is not offering a thousand-page portrait of social inequities, or a ruthlessly intimate examination of a run-of-the-mill bourgeois adulteress. His book is content, like a drawing, to depict a little bit of life. No Van Gogh sketch ever fetched tens of millions of dollars the way his big deep dramatic landscapes have. No pencil study of a posing model ever impacted popular culture in the same way as, say, *Die Zauberflote* or *To Kill a Mockingbird*. And *Life Drawing* is not *Death in Venice,* or *Giovanni's Room,* or *Our Lady of the Flowers,* or any of the other big tragic rambunctious defining works of the queer literary canon. And yet in spite of its modesty, or because of it, the book stands out as one of our most moving novels.

Published in 1991, three years after its author's death, *Life Drawing* follows its young narrator through one pivotal year. Mickey's maturation skewers the standard tropes of the coming-out story, reveling in his own power and reckoning with the responsibilities that are part and parcel of being a man. At no point does he grapple with the contempt and violence of his peers, or endure agonies of self-loathing or self-doubt. His first sexual encounter with a boy is at once matter-of-fact and astonishing — the joy of sex with none of the baggage. He is not wracked with shame or fear beforehand and afterwards feels himself "a dynamo of prowess, filled with a rare strength, able to outshine the other guards and halfbacks . . . Something like a moral invincibility cloaked me. The power of an undiscovered life — a truly adult way of being — came over me, and I out-muscled the rest of the team to set the evening's record in push-ups, sit-ups, and leg raises."

After that, Mickey's small-town high school life goes on for another five months, until one afternoon, after wrestling practice, when out of nowhere he "got drunk and headed for New Orleans." Not because he's fleeing cruelty or a broken heart or even any specific malaise, but because his hunger for life has outstripped what his small town life can feed. On the way, on a river boat, he meets a young black man named James, with whom he begins a love affair.

*Huckleberry Finn* first established a truly American literature not only through its engaging grasp of the Southern vernacular, but because it was the first book to really grapple with the racial violence on which this country was founded. Unlike *Uncle Tom's Cabin* and the pamphleteer novels that came before and after it, *Huckleberry Finn* grasped what many Americans still haven't understood: that racism's legacy is so big and broad and fundamental to American society that it cannot be encapsulated inside an "issue," and any attempt to do so will distort our understanding of who we are. Racism shapes the way people live their lives, and the way that people interact, and our attempts to form real relationships. This is one of the many secret storylines in Huckleberry Finn, and in *Life Drawing*.

Mickey does not objectify or exoticize James, and their love is neither predatory nor exploitative. But Mickey, raised in a world of social and material privilege where one rarely has to grapple with the consequences of one's actions, has been shielded from life in a way that James has not been. Mickey doesn't know how rare and wonderful their love affair is, and when he destroys it by sleeping with another man, he barely realizes he has done anything wrong.

Unable to remain in New Orleans after James leaves him, furious with himself and his own affectations, Mickey goes west. He turns his back on "the artist in the park, the lover in the bedroom, the whore in the street. Perhaps not completely on the whore on the street — let that person in me have his way, let him be led along, led by the flesh. A kind of greed commenced to grow in me, a greed of experience." Like the young men of the 19th Century, who Horace Greeley urged west to set up shop on land freshly stolen from the native Americans — like Huck Finn fleeing from his aunt's attempts to "sivilize" him. He hitchhikes through the oil towns and red deserts, watching "thoughts like tumbleweeds and tumbleweeds like thoughts flashing quick and raggedy across the road."

In California, he dedicates himself to "playing around with decadence." "Swimming in a big blue pool at night," savoring "sand from the beach, and the smell and feel of VO5 hair cream, new tastes, new smells, a new me." He becomes a kept boy; he learns about "reefer and hallucinogenic morning glory seeds;" he meets real cowboys and female impersonators; he models for Cal Tech students (the artist become the art object); he poses for beefcakey naked photographs.

But in the end, Mickey goes home. It's not that he's unable to build a life for himself in this glossy sunlit world of crocodile wrestlers and pornographers — it's just that this is not the life he's looking for. The family he finds there is not the family he needs. Mickey needed to grow up and see the world and test the extent of his appetites, but he cannot live without the family he was born into. In this respect, *Life Drawing* stands alongside James Baldwin's masterful *Just Above My Head* as one of the few great queer novels to truly show how gloriously, irremediably, and terrifyingly we are intertwined with our families; how essential their love is to our happiness. From the first sentence of *Life Drawing* — "the first thing I remember is dancing with my brother" — a note of gentle love and acceptance is sustained throughout. "We held each other by the hand and bounced along, while the war sputtered away in the distance; the only echo we heard was in the male camaraderie of the Big Band choruses, persuading America that war or no war, we were all one big happy family, healthy, optimistic, and strong."

In the book's last scene, Mickey attends an event at his father's country club. Wandering the golf course after dark, he comes upon two men setting up the fireworks that will serve as the evening's entertainment. James and his father. Subtly and poignantly, the scene underscores the gulf of class and race that lies between them. Mickey's eager to find the perfect thing to say to make everything better between them, but of course there's no such thing. There's no rapturous reunion, or acrimonious confrontation. Just two men, and the unremarkable sadness of growing up.

Does it make me a bad homo — or an ignorant one, which is maybe the same thing — if I say I never really liked the political reading of *The Wizard of Oz* that views Dorothy's adventure as a metaphor for gay identity? I was on board with it for 99 percent of the film, when Dorothy leaves drab prim Kansas for the flamboyant fabulous Land of Oz, while Glinda sings "Come out, come out, wherever you are," when the Cowardly Lion self-identifies as a "sissy," and a "dandy lion." But then there's the end, that bullshit about "there's no place like home," Dorothy desperate to leave her queer friends and rush back to sappy sepia-tinted Kansas. To me it always seemed like your standard tacked-on Hollywood ending where patriarchy, in the form of the censorial Production Code, smacks you down for enjoying transgression; where Bette Davis' triumphant bitchiness gives her cholera or condemns her to a lifetime of spinsterly loneliness; or where Jimmy Cagney, whose bloody savage antics we've been applauding for an hour and a half, gets gunned down by god-fearing G-men. After reading *Life Drawing*, though, I happened to catch *The Wizard of Oz* again, and suddenly the ending of both works made sense. Developing a queer sensibility does not necessarily mean that we can never go back to the world we came from. Sometimes it does, and that's fine. The Tin Woodsman has no place in small-town America, and I've always identified as a Tin Woodsman. Mickey is a changed man, but the change does not mean that he must turn his back on his family and their way of life, which has always been supportive and loving of him.

Why is this book out of print? Part of me wants to get angry and judgmental and say that gay audiences are just as shallow and sex-and-violence-obsessed as the straights are, and that a book like *Life Drawing* is too smart and too subtle and too radical, in its refusal to push the buttons we expect it to push, to gain a wide following. On the other hand, this book's disappearance points to a broader tragedy, where a young and thriving queer literature, like so much else, was demolished by AIDS.

AIDS did not just kill the brilliant writers and artists whose names we know. AIDS also killed the literary agents and the editors and the publicists and the *audiences* that nurtured and supported those artists, and in the process an overwhelming amount of art and talent has been lost. In a very real sense, Michael Grumley is part of a lost generation, and *Life Drawing* is only one more casualty in a tragic war whose death toll continues to mount.

But a book is more durable than a man, just ask any scholar of Soviet history. In this age of eBay and Amazon, an out-of-print book does not vanish into the sea of oblivion so easily. The estates of Michael Grumley and his lover, Robert Ferro (another unforgivably-out-of-print gay writer represented in this anthology), endowed the annual Ferro-Grumley Awards for queer writers, which, since 1989, has honored the best of queer lit, including such luminaries as Edmund White, Christopher Bram, Sarah Schulman, and Felice Picano. *Life Drawing* survives to move readers in ways at once more ineffable and more devastating than the mainstream emotional juggernauts. It's a sketch, a simple thing, really, but no less moving for being simple. *Life Drawing* has the same slow emotional impact of fireworks bursting over a suburban golf course or the sight of a boat on a river at dusk, dark against the bright sky.

# Lynn Hall

## Sticks and Stones

Follett, 1972

## Sean Meriwether

"Hey, Fairyweather. Yo, faggot! How's the weather, Mary?" The taunts, which made up in venom what they lacked in originality, started in seventh grade. It was a harsh reversal from grammar school where I'd always had a "boyfriend," that one kid that I would be infatuated with. We would talk during lunch and recess, and in the best of all possible worlds, sit next to each other on the long bus ride to and from school. My serial monogamy started in kindergarten with a shy boy named Karl, then progressed to the stoic intellectual, Robert, to rough-houser Chuck, then sincere and awkward Tom. There were a dozen other boys sprinkled in between, along with a few tomboyish girls. My parade of boyhood crushes were mutually entertained and no one, least of all me, found anything wrong with my unwavering attraction to other boys.

Everything changed in middle school. I'd shot up six gangly inches in one year and went from a charismatic boy to a waifish pimpled teen. It was more than the physical differences that divided me from the other boys — the softcore infatuations I'd harbored for them were no longer tolerated, and the girls cliqued together to discuss boys and makeup. I was left behind with a handful of outcasts who treated me like an exotic refugee, but never as one of their own.

The boys frequently called each other queerbait, faggot and homo in playful rivalry, but when they turned those words on me, they were used to attack. I looked the words up hoping I could figure out what was wrong with me and stop *being* that. Instead I discovered that I was exactly what they were calling me — a boy who liked other boys. My silence only confirmed their suspicions; the accusations grew in strength and number.

I had never considered what I felt to be wrong, nor even un-conventional. I believed my daydreams about kissing boys or seeing them naked were perfectly normal and the same jack-off fodder employed by my peers. When they confronted me with a different reality — that my desires were abnormal, even immoral — I turned to a stonewalling God and asked, *Why me?* I immediately heaped blame on my parents' divorce and my distant father; had he been a stronger masculine influence on my childhood I never would have turned out *that way*.

I read what little I could find on the subject, which amounted to one chapter of *All You Wanted to Know About Sex, but Were Afraid to Ask*. Homosexuals *cruised* dark bars, *tearooms*, and parks to have anonymous sex with strangers. These undesirables could only live out their perversions in the twilight world, while maintaining a "normal" life during the day. Worse, there were reports on the news, including an episode of *Donahue*, about an unknown disease killing gay men. I refused this future and tried to change myself before it was too late.

I tried to be "normal." I cut my hair short, competed in gym, honed an extensive knowledge of all things carnal. I learned everything I could about sex, *regular* sex, so I could lure in an audience. I even tried to dress like my tormentors to blend in, but my mother did not have the budget to wardrobe my fledgling persona. I started cutting lawns and doing odd jobs so I could afford to buy my own clothes.

My efforts were negligible. The verbal attacks escalated and stopped just short of physical violence — AIDS-inspired fear saved me from that; I might have bled and infected them. Most teachers did not notice my dilemma and one particularly ignorant one used my unpopularity as a comedic device to get the students on his side, taking every opportunity to belittle me in front of the class. I switched tactics in my freshman year of high school and tried to disappear. I slipped quietly from class to class, sat in the back, grew my hair long to hide my face, and started testing poorly to avoid the attention of good grades. My radical change in behavior was noted and my status as queer kid on campus was modified to freaky-druggie-faggot. My desire to become invisible drew more attention and authenticated my role as outcast.

I always had a passion for books, but they became my true companions during my social isolation. They allowed me to enter the insulated safety of another writer's imagination. My hometown in rural New Jersey may have been bucolic, but it was no haven for readers. The nearest bookstore was at the mall more than an hour away and the town's two-room library had a meager selection. Undeterred by the lack of literary choices, my mother and I became professional book vultures, able to rip through garage sales and thrift stores with skills honed by necessity. We'd pay up to a quarter for a paperback, a dollar for a hardback, but our goal was a dime a book. Since the toss-offs would have landed in the trash after a garage sale, we normally walked off with a bagful of booty for less than the asking price.

The summer before my sophomore year, my mother drove us a hundred miles away to a remainder sale in a small college town. She wanted to load us up with advanced texts to get a jump on the school year. I was eager to go, albeit for less academic reasons; I'd discovered Steven King and had devoured everything I could get my hands on. I'd championed King's revenge on high school bullies in *Carrie*, and enjoyed his macabre twists on the everyday. I was confident that I'd be able to increase my collection of horror and science fiction at a *real* bookstore.

I was severely disappointed in the sale, which was held in a small warehouse off campus. There were stacks of hefty college-aged textbooks and large cardboard boxes jumbled with odds and ends, but I did not find a single book of horror, sci-fi or fantasy, not even a thumbed-through paperback. I poked through the boxes marked "fiction," bypassing Joyce, Woolf and Orwell, writers that I would have no use for until I was old enough to appreciate their unique ideas and use of language. Instead, I rescued one young adult novel from the lot.

The cover had an illustration by Milton Glaser (who created the "I 'Heart' NY" logo) depicting a misanthropic boy standing alone in the foreground, hands in pockets. Two figures stood behind him at a pronounced distance, magnifying his isolation. The sticks and stones of the book's title, missiles that had fallen short of their target, littered the ground around him. There was a worry in the boy's anxious face that mirrored my own; I felt an instant affinity.

Intrigued, I flipped open the book to read the inside flap and was arrested by the repetition of the word "homosexual." A chill rushed through me with a mixture of fear and excitement; I knew this was a book about me. I looked up to make sure no one was around, especially my mother, before finishing the description of Lynn Hall's *Sticks and Stones*. The story centered on seventeen-year old Tom Naylor, the victim of a gay rumor which threatened to "shatter his life" and forced him to question his relationship with his best friend, Ward. Tom's problems were the same as mine and I wanted him to show me the way out; I had no one else to turn to.

I looked at the cover intently, staring into the hooded eyes of the boy, and calculated the risk of buying it. Owning a book about a homosexual was the same thing as admitting that I *was* a homosexual. However, something in the boy's story promised help; I decided to chance it. I fished two dollars out of my pocket, thankful that I didn't have to make my mother pay for it, and rushed up to the cashier. I slid the book to her, face down, along with the money. I couldn't meet her eyes, fearing that she knew why I was buying it and would expose me. She said nothing, and I raced outside to wait for my mother, concealing the book from her.

It was very easy to empathize with the main character from Lynn Hall's novel. Tom Naylor is a classically trained pianist and artistic type who is dropped into rural Iowa after his parents' divorce. His mother's hometown of Buck Creek has a population one point over the double digits and only a handful of kids his own age, none of whom he has anything in common with. Although he misses his life and friends back in Chicago, he sees how much happier his mother is living on her own. The buoyant youth downshifts into small town life knowing it is worth his personal, and very temporary, sacrifice; he will be off to college in a year's time.

When he first moved to town, Tom had made friends with Floyd, an overweight, insecure, priggish boy, one who was only too happy to have a male companion his own age. The book opens with Tom beginning to avoid Floyd's demands for his attention in favor of practicing the piano. The slighted youth turns against him in a fit of jealousy.

At the same time, Ward Alexander returns to Buck Creek after being discharged from the army. In him Tom finds a spirited friend to whom he can relate. Ward is a quiet and worldly writer who takes over an abandoned schoolhouse on his family's farm. The pair spends hours converting the building into Ward's writing studio and their relationship flourishes through manual labor, shared meals and quiet coexistence. The young man is adopted into Tom's family and becomes the older brother he never had.

Problems begin when the rebuffed Floyd learns Ward was discharged because of a homosexual incident. He judges Tom's artistic leanings, his lack of a girlfriend, and his very intimate relationship with a known homosexual and figures that Tom must be queer too. Floyd salvages his ego by rationalizing Tom's rejection was based on his not being queer, not because he was unlikable.

Floyd eagerly spreads the rumor to other people in town, who then use it for their own entertainment, passing it on "in confidence" to prove their nosy prowess. The gossip mill churns. Tom, an engaging boy who reads like a precursor to *The Front Runner*'s Billy Sive, is abruptly ostracized from his community without knowing why. People avoid him, giggle behind his back, treat him differently. The hardest part for Tom is that he doesn't understand why his social standing has changed overnight. He grows paranoid, can't sleep, and his grades fall off dramatically.

Tom tries to ignore the unspoken accusations to focus on his music. His goal is to win the music category in the state finals, get a scholarship to a good school, and get the hell out of Buck Creek. He cinches the prelimnaries but is informed by the principal that he can not attend the state finals. An angered Tom demands to know why. The principal informs him that a parent refused to allow her son to stay overnight with a known homosexual. The school would not tolerate that type of scandal, no matter how talented Tom is. The boy leaves school flustered. If everyone, including the principal and music teacher, believed him to be queer, perhaps it was true. He questions his being a momma's boy, his passion for music over girls, and his own sexuality, which had never been in doubt before.

Deeply troubled, Tom rushes to his best friend, Ward. After hearing Tom's predicament, Ward confesses his "homosexual tendencies" and apologizes for being the root of the rumors. Although some future woman might make him commit to marriage and family life, he accepts that he may only achieve an intimate relationship with another man. He ensures Tom that their friendship was prized, but that the boy was never the subject of his romantic interests. Tom is crushed to find his one sanctuary to be the cause of all his trouble. He leaves with an increased sense of isolation.

Tom spends the next few weeks alone and in a state of pronounced depression. He convinces himself that his chances of escaping to a good school are trashed along with his future, questions his feelings for Ward, and feels deserted by his mother, who has started dating. The world closes in on him and he gives up the fight. The rumor mongers win.

The novel ends quickly with a deus ex machina. An overconfident Floyd demands that Tom drive him home after missing the bus. Tom drives recklessly in his haste to get rid of the boy and speeds on icy roads thinking that nothing really mattered. He wrecks his car. Floyd dies on impact, but Tom takes no joy in his demise when he wakes from a coma a few days after the accident. With a new appreciation for life and time to reflect, Tom understands that he had allowed the misinformed opinions of people who didn't know or care about him to destroy his life and the one relationship he valued. Tom and Ward are reunited in friendship, but one that is strained by the circumstances.

The book was originally published in 1972 and marketed to teens, which seems incredibly controversial as it was barely three years after the

Stonewall Riots and the dawn of Gay Liberation. However, neither of the characters commits to being gay — Tom is the straight-arrow all-American golden boy and Ward's homosexual "tendencies" are reduced to a single thwarted experience that he pays for by being discharged from the army. Although Ward imagines a life shared with another man, he consigns himself to celibate bachelorhood, and writing, until he can be saved by a good woman.

Lynn Hall's original ending was "open for interpretation" but implied that the two young men did enter into a homosexual relationship. The publisher, Follet Publishing Company, did not feel comfortable marketing a book that ended with a positive portrayal of a gay relationship, which might have been "damaging to young minds." In keeping with gay literature of the period, they suggested resolving the issue by killing Tom or Ward in a "nice, handy car accident." With three days to rewrite the ending, Ms. Hall split the difference and kept both men alive, but allowed the accident to change the outcome of their relationship. [4]

Despite the editorial intervention, the end result remains daring for the intimate domestic bond the two men share. They spend time rebuilding the schoolhouse as their own world, support one another in their artistic pursuits, and stay up all night talking about their dreams and plans for the future like a newly forged couple. Ward is not portrayed with any of the stereotypical attributes of a closeted queer, but is an honest, vanilla, and decidedly masculine mentor to his younger friend. He is, and remains at the end of the novel, a positive role model.

*Sticks and Stones* hit me in two stages through high school. The first was outright denial. If Tom Naylor was really straight but only doubted his sexuality because he was accused of being gay, then perhaps the same was true of me. When I returned to school in the fall I rushed into a thankfully short relationship with a mousy girl, and then into a second relationship with a visionary punk girl, Cheré, who saw me as raw clay. She molded me into Duran Duran's Nick Rhoades to her Julie Friedman, introduced me to

---

[4] Cuseo, Allan A. Homosexual Characters in YA Novels: A Literary Analysis, 1969-1982

alternative music, pot, and a culture more accepting of differences. We started swapping clothes and makeup, and as Boy George and Annie Lennox introduced gender-bending to MTV audiences, we starred in our own controversial roles as rural New Jersey's cross-dressing ambiguously sexual couple.

Cheré and I formed the nucleus of a loose knot of outsiders: punks, Goths, and other artistically bent individuals. Together we rejected the mainstream as it rejected us. We felt superior *because* of our differences and inspired one another to be more outlandish, more outrageous, and more combative against our so-called peers. They could no longer force us out if we refused to belong.

The taunting, however, escalated through high school and culminated in my being nicknamed Rocky in honor of Rock Hudson's AIDS-related death. Despite my unflappable facade, the words and the belittling attitude of the other students, and the general negligence of the teachers and faculty, began to wear me down. I did not defend myself against the attacks knowing that there was nothing I could do or say to change their opinions, but neither did I stand up and say, "Yeah, I am a faggot. What's it to you?" That would have taken courage I had not yet developed.

The culmination of years of being singled out finally took their toll. I broke things off with Cheré — it was just one more lie to maintain — and withdrew into myself. I erroneously thought I had no one to turn to who could understand what I was going through. I didn't think I could change, and that I was doomed to a life of hatred and avoidance, where intimacy could only be found in bathroom stalls. I saw little hope for my future, and like one-third of gay teens, I tried to take my life. It was a drastic and embarrassing call for help; I downed an entire box of NoDoz thinking the caffeine overload would stop my heart; instead it only made me puke for thirty-six life-changing hours.

*Sticks and Stones* was my only gay text, so I returned to it for some answers. I reread it with a fresh perspective. Tom's life was nearly destroyed by lies, but in his case they *were* lies; in mine, the only person lying was me. It was Ward who lived in peace with his homosexuality, creating his own world where he could maintain a platonic but intimate relationship with his younger friend. Ward Alexander became a gay mentor, one with whom I shared something in common, writing.

I first outed myself on the page and wrote short stories and bad poetry about being gay; I didn't show these to anyone. Writing about my feelings helped me clarify my emotions and gain some perspective. It was also easier to have a fictional me confess his desire for straight male friends than to say it out loud and risk losing that friendship. I used my pen to recreate myself on paper before I attempted it in real life.

I came out to my ex-girlfriend, who admitted her own bisexuality. We developed a new friendship after our short affair — one where we could talk about boys *and* girls that we were interested in. Emboldened by her acceptance, I came out as bisexual to a few of my male friends simultaneously. I wasn't sure what to expect, but they accepted my confession without a hint of surprise. Although our relationships were never the same we did remain friends until I left for college two years after graduation. I would discover years later that two of them had also struggled with their own sexuality, but did not admit it to themselves until well into college. They backed away from me for fear that my outspoken desires might spill over into their lives and tip the balance.

Admitting I was gay to myself and a handful of friends gave me a little courage to face the rejection of the student body, but it did not end the feeling of isolation. I was an alternative queer kid in rural New Jersey who didn't try to fit in; I was not to be tolerated. The gay baiting continued, even after I stopped reacting to it. I found ways to absent myself from school and attended less than a half of my senior year; my loss in hindsight. Using Lynn Hall's creation, Tom Naylor, as inspiration, I kept my eyes on the promise of escape after high school. Freedom came in the shape of a car, and allowed me to drive my friends into Manhattan, only sixty miles away but another universe where possibilities thrived. We discovered the club scene where society's misfits and sexual deviants created their own world out of music, self-expression and recreational drugs. It was only a stepping stone into my future, but offered me the freedom to define myself, to kiss another boy, and to understand that only *I* had to accept myself, it was optional for everyone else.

If I had not come across Lynn Hall's book when I was struggling to define my own sexuality, I might not have survived to write this essay of my own experiences. In it I had Ward Alexander and the knowledge that there was someone else like me in the world; I wasn't the only one. Would my experience have been different if the original ending had united Tom and Ward? Not necessarily, but it would have shown me that men could commit to one another in romantic relationships built on love, trust and mutual respect. If I could return and tell my teenage self what I know now, I'd assure him that the isolation and social ostracizing that he'd experienced helped him become the person, and the artist, that he is today. I'd tell him to have enough confidence to look his tormentors in the eye and say, "I'm gay, so what?" and disempower their accusations. I have told this much of my story to my youngest brother, who is coming to terms with his own sexuality. It is both a challenge and an honor to assist him where I can while allowing him the space to learn on his own.

I am astounded at how much has changed since the early 80s when I'd first read *Sticks and Stones*. Literature plays such a minor role in our community now, when it used to be the primary means of uniting and informing our community. I grew up in the brief span between pulp fiction and the representation of gays and lesbians in the media at large, and certainly before the Internet allowed us to connect in ways we'd never dreamed of. Despite those advances, kids continue to struggle with their own questions and suffer the cruelty of their peers. Gay kids are still three times more likely to attempt suicide, develop substance abuse, and run away from home. It is up to us as a community to present positive role models in young adult literature so they know they are not alone, and that there are many ways for them to grow into gay adults.

# Richard Hall
## Couplings

Grey Fox, 1981

## Jonathan Harper

I discovered a friend of mine in a book. It was just one story out of a full collection, but until those 15 pages, I never felt that I had known Simon intimately before.

It feels rather childish to say that and I desperately want to be taken seriously. Simon is a long time friend of my husband, Gordon. They are both 10 years older than me and I've learned not to include myself in every conversation between them. Simon is used to my rambling and has mastered the art of selective listening, always with a polite smile. My husband finds my eccentricities endearing. He constantly entertains my exhausting tangents on politics, my analyzing our social circles, my ideas for novels I'll probably never write . Gordon is patient. So, when I previously pushed the book in front of him saying, "Who does this remind you of? Isn't this just like Simon? It's Simon, right?" he read a few pages, nodding his head and complacently agreed before refocusing to more important things on the TV.

Of all places, we were sitting in a diner, Simon monopolizing the conversation with his latest dramas. I had brought my copy of *Couplings* by Richard Hall with the intention of passing it along. Ever since we were introduced, Simon has been getting his heart broken on a regular basis. The latest fiasco: a young man had been living with him for a few months. What Simon had called a platonic friendship was obviously a thin veneer for infatuation. This young house guest had been living rent free and the two of

them had invested in a small online business together. Then, instan-
taneously, the young man lost interest in the business venture, the
Washington area and Simon himself. All poor Simon could say was, "It's the
companionship I miss the most."

And then, there is the book. *Couplings* by Richard Hall. The edition I
have was printed in 1982 (I was two years old), is in decent condition with a
slightly tattered cover. It was purchased on a vacation in Palm Springs; this
was the year after the Lambda Literary Foundation closed its DC offices and
I was laid off. In fact, I wouldn't have recognized the name and title if it
weren't for that job. In 2003, I had helped organize the last Richard Hall
Memorial Short Story Contest. Richard Hall was the first openly gay critic
elected to the National Book Critics Circle and the author of three collections
of short stories and two novels, one published a year before he died of AIDs
in 1991 at the age of 65. At work I was suddenly one of the facilitators of the
Lammy Awards, my name was printed on the masthead of the *Lambda Book
Report*. Each new fact learned, new acquaintance made, was flaunted among
my college friends. This was also a much-needed wake-up call: I was not the
only aspiring gay writer around. For the first time, I had to acknowledge
decades of literature and history that came before me and had to learn as
much of it as possible before I could ever hope to contribute on my own.

My involvement was over before I turned twenty-five. I purchased
*Couplings* for sentimental reasons: I missed my old job. For the longest time,
that organization had defined me. Among my partner's social circle of
government workers, lawyers and security managers, I was the young
idealistic nonprofit worker, the kid who "read queer books for a living." At
first, when I read *Couplings*, it was a reminder of being affiliated with
something distinct. It also marked those transitional years out of college
when I was learning how to be an adult. And a major source of conflict
between people is this idea of being "grown up." These words always come
into conflict: younger versus older, innocence versus experience, and so
forth. My process started long before I was giving ignorant opinions to
experts and now several years later, plenty of people my senior claim that

none of us ever really completed it. Richard Hall's stories seem very aware of this.

One story in particular, "The Servant Problem," reminds me of Simon. With all of their expectations and disillusionment, Simon and the narrator seemed interchangeable. The story follows Meade, a middle-aged "everyman," during one of his routine therapy sessions. The plot is straightforward: Meade and his therapist exchange a battle of wits throughout the session, a humorous exchange at times that shows how two people can simultaneously lose an argument. Meade punches pillows with his therapist, vents about his malevolent friends, fantasizes about everything he's not supposed to want. There is no central love interest; he has a maid and a house boy and somehow, that is an adequate substitute for romance. Meade's therapist asks him, "Is it possible that all the people in this cottage that you fantasize are really your servants? That you can only trust people who are totally dependent on you?"

So, we sit at the diner and Simon continues on about his recent boy. He makes it sound like he rescued a stray dog or cat and nursed it back to health before it ran off to find its original owner. Simon is a chubby man in his forties. He overeats to the point of obesity and complains about his constant state of loneliness. When our group of friends meets, he gets lost in the shuffle of multiple conversations. There is gossip he is not involved with and references to people he despises and desires. He usually arrives with small entourages of twenty-year-olds who let him pay for drinks and then proceed to talk only with each other. One long vicious cycle. And yet, I wonder how long Simon could function without these characters beside him. This is one of the conversations Simon and I don't have, about his obsession with youth.

What I wanted to say to him was "Look, I read this book. And it was good, for many reasons, but the reason why I want you to read it is because I learned something about you from it. I feel like all the worrying I do about you and all the times we've sat with you discussing your problems have been for nothing, because we've just not been able to put it all into context for you. Bur if you could just get a clear understanding, like I did, then at least we can figure out how to makes things better." But I couldn't say that. Not without the fear of sounding completely ridiculous. As much as I try to prove myself, he still equates me to the young men he surrounds himself with. From his perspective, I'll always be too young and naïve to understand him. And the source of my empathy was a fiction book by a deceased author who's out-of-print and that he's not even going to read. If empathy can't be forced, then neither can epiphany.

Instead, I listen to my husband and Simon kill time by talking about their jobs and I struggle to keep myself interested in business affairs of which I know absolutely nothing. My ears perk whenever a pop culture reference is made, which makes me wonder how juvenile I must still seem during serious conversation. When it's my turn to introduce a subject, I mention Hall's book and Simon slightly nods his head, as if preparing a poker face. I tell him about another story in the collection, "The Koan," in which a young man has a crisis of conscience about living off a sugar daddy in a big house on Fire Island. "My question is how do you possibly end a story like this?" I ask. "Some overgrown teenager gets to live consequence-free in some guy's house. If he leaves, what does he do with no money and no work experience? If he stays, what happens when he's worn out his welcome or somebody newer and cuter arrives?" I stopped. Simon was looking at me funny.

"Sounds interesting," Simon said with that high pitch meant to close off a conversation. I pulled *Couplings* out of my backpack anyway and put it on his side of the table. "There's a naked guy on the cover. Is this one of your porn books?"

"No," I assured him.

Throughout my childhood, books had been my escapism. I read young adult novels about orphans and Tolkeinesque fantasies. I took the job at the literary foundation thinking it was an opportunity to become a writer. Due to my employment, I was not eligible to submit to the Richard Hall Story Contest. My breakthrough novel did not materialize. But I continued to find books that inspired me. I was no longer reading to escape, but to learn. Hall's stories were lessons on how to be a gay adult.

It's not that Simon's incapable of understanding any of this. I offered to loan him the book. He shrugged and said that he wouldn't have the time to read anyway (Simon isn't a reader, many of my friends aren't). It was a defeat — I felt defeated. That is, I felt I offered something that resembled his complicated life so intimately that he might have recognized himself. Idealistically, about 15 pages might have explained his attempts to possess unobtainable boys and why he keeps losing them. But in actuality, I was offering more of my sympathies, my attempt to have an intimate connection, to share something personal. And Simon rejected me.

We got our check and said our goodbyes. It can be exhilarating having dinner with your lover's friends; no matter how integrated, you're still one of the outsiders. You analyze them differently than you usually would; and they do the same to you. I wonder if I've maintained my good reputation with Simon, if he still finds me amusing and pleasant, a good catch for his friend and a decent addition to his larger circle of acquaintances. Did he realize that I withheld an opinion, that this book was supposd to be less about me and my thoughts and more about what he should be thinking? Much like Meade, it's doubtful Simon will ever change, or even recognize the potential for change. He'll continue to bring his fantasies home and report his highs and lows like the best gossip. I'll continue finding symbolism and explanations in stories, and be hesitant to share my interpretations with others. After leaving the restaurant, I went home and placed *Couplings* on my bookcase. Richard Hall holds court with Alasdair Gray and Andrew Holleran on a shelf of select favorites. It is still a book I go back to, for nostalgia's sake. I guess I'm just growing up.

# J.S. Marcus
# The Captain's Fire

Knopf, 1996

## Aaron Hamburger

In his remarkable first novel J. S. Marcus takes us on a highly personalized tour of the fascinating mess that is Berlin.

"Berlin," Marcus writes, "a capital of dead ideas; a card catalogue for a library that no longer exists; intricate, somehow superfluous; symbolic capital of the twentieth century, or else just capital of twentieth-century symbols."

Imagine a European city with the sprawl of Los Angeles and the cultural life of New York. Something like London without the anchoring centerpieces of Oxford Street, Picadilly Circus, and Trafalgar Square, or Paris without the Champs Elysees and Arc de Triomphe.

Yet unlike that other European urban mess without a center, Rome, Berlin works. Every corner of the city is connected to each other by means of a Jackson Pollock-like network of underground and overground trains, street trams, buses, and taxis. New buildings are sprouting up all over the city like tulips after winter, including a new glass cathedral of a train station that promises to make Berlin a central transit hub of the new Europe. Tourists are flooding in from all over the globe (yet the city is constantly verging on bankruptcy).

The messiness extends to the ethnic life of Berlin, the most un-German of all German cities, which also happens to be the country's newly restored capital. Native-born Germans compete for space with Turks (some who trace roots in Germany going back two generations), Russians, Africans, Italians,

Americans, and Jews (who may be German, Polish, or citizens of the former Soviet Union). The heavy odors of beer and wurst compete with the spicy aroma of doner kebab stands on every corner. Women with spray-painted Mohawks jostle onto the U-bahn trains beside women in headscarves.

But perhaps the most important way in which Berlin is a mess is how that city's complicated past has imprinted itself on the architectural landscape. You can walk down a single street and see one of the few Baroque buildings spared by Allied bombings, now beautifully restored and freshly painted, while its neighbor lies in shambles with World War II bulletholes still pocking the remains of the façade. Masterpieces of East Berlin Communist architecture are now adorned with ads for Coca Cola and McDonald's. These compete for space with rows and rows of bland cement apartment buildings built in the 50s and 60s that look like giant air conditioners and are painted in garish shades of bright blue or orange. The latest vogue in architecture seems to be for sparkling new buildings comprised of little more than sheets of glass fitted into shining steel frames. Or sometimes, as in the case of the Reichstag, or the Café Josty in the new Potsdamer Platz, elements of old and new are fused into a new postmodern hybrid of both.

And occasionally, if you're lucky, you'll come to a point where the buildings mysteriously end, and there's a strange gap of vacant lots, which indicate you've come across that snaking belt of emptiness where the Berlin Wall used to stand.

In the middle of all this mess and trying to make sense of it is J. S. Marcus, a queer American Jew who lived in Berlin during the mid-90s, and in his first novel explored that most forbidden love of all: the love of a Jew for Berlin. It's a love I quickly learned to share during the past few years as I trekked back and forth to Germany's old and now new capital to do research for a novel. Soon I found out I wasn't the only American Jew in town. Artists, rabbis, singers, translators, English teachers, and of course, writers; here we all were, exploring the city where the Nazis once plotted our destruction, making a home for ourselves in the shadow of history.

I first discovered Marcus when I read an essay he wrote for an anthology called *Wonderlands: Good Gay Travel Writing*, which I happened to bring with me on one of those trips. I saw in his biographical note that he was living in Berlin, and contacted him by email. He wrote me back to say that unfortunately he was going to be in the United States while I was in Berlin and vice versa. Oh well, I thought, maybe next time.

But there was no next time. I finished my research. I came home to New York to stay. I lost his email address. And then one day I was in the library and happened to come across his novel. For the hell of it, I checked it out, and began to read.

The first thing a reader might notice about *The Captain's Fire* is its lack of paragraph breaks. Instead there are solid blocks of text and long sinewy snaking sentences that bleed into each other. Commas, parentheses, and words in italics do the work that is normally done by periods and paragraph breaks, in the manner of such noted German-language novelists as the late W. G. Sebald and Thomas Bernhard. The result is a densely-packed palimpsest, with fascinating nuggets of trivia, history, and characterization all fused into an interlacing pattern. The object is not to put these facts back into chronological order, but rather to experience them all at once, as a brilliant kaleidoscope that recreates the dizzying experience of an outsider delving into the city of Berlin.

Take a look at the book's opening, in which Joel La Vine, the book's narrator, has been asked by his German landlords to leave his apartment. "I just assume that they had been working for the secret police while the wall was up," Marcus lets us know casually, then adds, with even more sinister overtones, "Their note, written in the old-fashioned German handwriting that Frau Kruger must have learned in the late 1930s, told me to be out of the apartment in two months, before the first of March." The references to the old-fashioned German handwriting style (favored by the Nazis) as well as the time period of the late 1930s suggest the unavoidable creepiness of a German evicting a Jew (even an American Jew) in Berlin. Nothing can be innocent in Germany after Hitler. And yet, this encounter is entirely innocent, a simple business transaction.

This is exactly what life is like as a Jew in Berlin today: you're constantly waiting for the proverbial other shoe to drop, but it never drops because after all that's happened in Germany in the 20th Century, there are no shoes left to drop.

Here is another typically Marcusian snaking sentence, whose structure echoes the mysterious layering of contemporary Berlin existence, always steeped in often noisome fragrances from the past. Again, we hear about the Krugers:

> Both of their professions were suspect, as these things go; he was a plumber at a hard-currency hotel on Unter den Linden, and she was a librarian, though now they're both unemployed, living, presumably, off their two unemployment compensations and off the extra money I pay them, which is three times the rent they have to pay to the mysterious corporation with the Hamburg postmark that got to buy up all the buildings in this part of Berlin as part of privatization and now, in turn, is supposed to be selling them off to new owners, who tend to remain fairly anonymous in most cases, or just absent, letting the Hamburg corporation go on managing the buildings (I have never found out who actually "owns" the Krugers' building, have always paid them my rent in cash, as requested).

Any given sentence in *The Captain's Fire* can veer from its seemingly intended purpose (here, to state the jobs of the Krugers) in order to delve into questions of history, public and private. This isn't a lack of control on Marcus's part. It's the only way a sentient person can process this complicated terrain. A walk to your local grocery store can lead you unexpectedly past a statue of Lenin in full heroic mode plopped down for decoration in the parking lot of the local branch of the German version of Home Depot. On your way to a romantic restaurant for a date, you may trip over a memorial brass cobblestone set into the ground and etched with the name of a Jewish family deported from a building nearby.

Marcus's sprawling style reflects not only the confusion of its setting — a divided Berlin trying to make itself whole — but also the confusion of its narrator, Joel La Vine, a bisexual (or lately "no-sexual") American Jew attempting to make sense of himself and his infatuation with his adopted home.

"Trying not to think about Nazis all the time," he writes, "like (or not like) trying not to have an erection. (Trying not to think about Nazis in Germany: like trying not think about sex in a porno theater. Why go in at all?)"

Indeed, every interaction in Berlin is so loaded for La Vine, that the book has no space for a traditional plot. The complications begin with the most innocent of questions, the one a foreigner always gets asked, "Where are you from?"

> I don't tell people that I am Jewish or Italian or, to some people, vaguely Viennese, or bisexual, for that matter — as I haven't told them about not being able to get it up, about being no-sexual. I tell them I am from Milwaukee, which is true enough. When I do tell people that I am Jewish, they are each, in their own way, flabbergasted; they lose their facial expressions, look, really, as if their faces have collapsed, then they promptly, and quite alarmingly, ask me if I eat pork: to Germans, it would seem, not eating pork is something truly unbelievable but documented, like cannibalism.

Other notes on Germans, from the head of Joel La Vine:

> Germans seem to prefer dogs that look like other kinds of animals.

> Germans distinguish between kinds of blond hair.

> Germans, lately, often disgust me, although I am sometimes attracted to Germans who remind me of Germans whom I was attracted to when I first got here, who, in turn, didn't remind me in any way of anybody I slept with before, and, in that case, probably don't look very German and almost certainly look vaguely Jewish.

It's important to note that Marcus's narrative is a reflection of a particular consciousness and not a documentary. Isherwood's rather dubious claim of "I am a camera" does not apply here. A short-sighted reviewer for *The*

*New York Times* complained that observations like the ones above merely rehash generalizations about Germans rather than present a fuller picture of the true German character. But that complaint misses the whole point of the book, which is not to look at Germans but to look at one American Jew looking at Germans, trying to understand himself as he navigates his highly-charged surroundings, and constantly failing:

> I avoided walking over Albert Speer's bridge — I didn't know what it would mean — but then walked over it anyway on Sunday afternoon because I was late for my train, only remembering, while I was walking, that I was in a hurry; later I thought about not remembering while I was walking . . . like walking through a place where the Berlin Wall had once stood and not thinking about it, which is what people now do all the time. . . . I am walking slower, remembering faster. Or forgetting faster, walking faster. . . . A child among adults, a Jew among gentiles (a German-speaker among Jews). A homosexual among heterosexuals. A heterosexual among homosexuals. An American in Europe. Cemeteries. A visitor in a cemetery.

Marcus's voice is so crisp, thought-provoking, funny, and above all deeply poignant, that it lodges itself inside your head and stays there. Indeed, when I finished his book, I felt as if I'd just woken from a vivid dream. I wanted to hear more, so I tried to buy a copy of the novel to own and discovered that it was out of print. I searched for other books by Marcus. There was an earlier story collection, *The Art of Cartography*, but nothing after *The Captain's Fire*. I looked for Marcus's email address, but couldn't find it again, so I contacted the editor of the anthology *Wonderlands* to ask for it. It turned out the editor had lost Marcus's contact information too.

# James McCourt
# **Time Remaining**

Knopf, 1993

## Timothy Young

There are some books you read out of obligation, in the same way you go on a blind date with a friend of a friend. In both cases, though, it's natural to harbor a bit of hope that love may well peek through the blinds.

November 1995 — My boyfriend and I are staying at a friend's apartment in New York, everything is the same as I remember, except there is a book on the pillow: *Time Remaining* by James McCourt. It is inscribed to me. Why? I helped fix his computer — over the phone. There was a time when it seemed that every writer I knew was accidentally erasing his almost finished novel and I was called, in a panic, to suggest a way to resurrect faded words from stubborn hard drives. I had never met James, but he responded with gratitude — and, having been the previous overnighter on 16th Street, he left me a present of his last novel.

What could I do with it? A box of chocolates, you can eat or regift, but a book is a commitment. I put it on my bookshelf until one day, waiting for my online service to complete a download, I was hypnotized by the dialog window - a slowly creeping status bar and the words: "time remaining." It was a sign. I put the novel in my bag as I headed for my Friday trip on the Long Island Railroad from Penn Station to East Hampton, a regular commute when my boyfriend lived there full time. As I started to read, I discovered the second sign. The novel takes place on the very train route I was following. The main characters chat and tell stories as they pass through Jamaica, Speonk, Quogue and the progressively distant Hamptons. I read. I co-existed. I fell in love.

What is the book about? Categorically, it is a collection of two tales — an introductory story followed by a novella, but they are the same narrative line, so let's call it a novel. Nominally, it concerns the reminiscences of an aging performer, Odette O'Doyle, who has returned from an extended European trip, the purpose of which was to scatter the ashes of her departed fellow travelers in the great, historically meaningful rivers of the continent. The Eleven Against Heaven, an opera-loving, female-gender-appropriating (in pronoun references, clothes, mannerisms) group has been reduced by AIDS to two survivors, the aforementioned Odette and her traveling companion and interlocutor, Delancey. But before Odette can begin recounting her adventures, Delancey gets the first word, in the brief introduction to the book and to the world they inhabit, in which he/she recounts her most recent success, a one-woman show, "I Go Back to the Mais Oui," a performance/memory piece that evokes, and thus sets, the scene for the long second act.

When the two principal characters board the milk train to the East End, the action begins in earnest. Lives are delineated. Anecdotes tumble like unsecured luggage. References — classical, pop-cultural, many obscure, but enough of them parseable for the average reader — cascade from the lips of the inimitable Odette.

The language of the book is its primary beauty. McCourt uses words to make jokes and puns with an incisive and intellectual edge. He writes with real sound and fury. The narrative doesn't flow as much as it swerves and dodges and glances. Clichés are turned at right angles: "Sic transit Gloria Swanson" is heard at the end of a long anecdote. The ur-source for much of the thematic construction of the book is grand opera. The stories of each of the dear departed follow the overwrought dramatic arcs of booming stage works. One queen is poured into the Rhine; two garrulous friends/enemies are committed to the Buda and the Pest under bright moonlight by a pair of hunky hotel clerks recruited for the task; another precious character is cast into a fjord in Norway.

These concrete actions are the pinions that anchor the rambling story that encompasses Odette's life, the lives of her friends, and . . . well, it is a mini-encyclopedia of gay New York life in the second half of the 20th century. It's all there — sex, drugs, cross-dressing, politics, psychoanalysis, poetry, movies — everything that makes life worthwhile — or keeps you alive. McCourt went on to write a true encyclopedia of the sort — the incomparable magnum opus, "Queer Street" — a work that must be read almost randomly, so dense is it with facts and observations.

But what is *Time Remaining,* as a special beast among these special gay books? It's a book about faggotry — the celebration of the best qualities of gay life — self-amusement, defiance, an aggressively earned comfort with the world.

I remember a scene, decades ago, in the bathroom of a gay club in Oklahoma. Dressed in acid-washed jeans, sporting a feathered-haircut, thinking I was desirable, I entered the bathroom to use it for its intended purpose — only to find a gaggle of drag queens occupying one of the corners. As I strained to be nonchalant and go about my business, one of them made a pronouncement in my direction, "Don't be afraid of us honey, we're just drag queens." I couldn't piss to save my life. And so they, elegantly, effortlessly, gained dominion over me and the space. I assumed a bathroom was a bathroom, but in the gay world, it was a private boudoir for cool glamazons. Drag queens claimed and repurposed that little space and with a few slight words, they caused my inner organs to shut down. I began to understand.

What power did they (do they) have? Do drag queens hold sway over a middle territory, a sort of psycho-gender limbo? They understand the tears of a woman and they know the desires of men. I respect drag queens and I have learned to listen to them. Odette distills the wisdom of the ages in the pages of McCourt's book. And what wisdom it is: the history of Greek statuary; the accomplishments and entanglements of the New York School and the Abstract Expressionists, the oeuvres of Claudette Colbert and Jackie Curtis, the works of Gabriel Marcel, Leon Edel, and Alec Wilder, lives of divas and prima ballerinas (real and imagined), the geographic courses of great rivers — all subjects related to drama, eros and art, of course.

Odette claims for herself, "the lifelong necessary faggot-survival technique: knowing as much as ever you could about what *everybody* was up to — in the house, on the block" and, ultimately, in the world, it seems. What better way to gird your delicate, lady-like loins than to become a walking reference work of both popular and intellectual culture? So whether or not you get picked up and taken to a dingy dive bar or to the top of the Ritz, you can make good conversation. Fine manners, indeed. The desire for knowledge should come naturally to gay men. With so many narratives in our lives — truths, lies, soap operas, deceptions, personae — formed by Biblical stories, conflicting philosophies, and T-cell counts — who can blame us for making a few things up in our search for the truth?

Didn't Frank O'Hara desire (for all of us) "Grace, to be born and live as variously as possible?" Odette O'Doyle is living that promise. She has seen life from both sides, like Tiresias, as a man and a woman. She has been a performer and a voyeur, a maker and a recorder. She has taken in the capital letter NEWS as well as the ephemeral details of life over six decades and reassembles it in a *collage particulier* that the reader is privileged to receive.

Pity the dull majority of the world who will not receive it, the throngs waiting in airports for the next flight to . . . somewhere. If they're reading, it's some limp-covered tome by the likes of Stephen Grisham or James King or Nelson Baldacci or David Patterson or some other blended Anglo-Saxon thriller-er. How un-various can a novel be? They could be reading about a cross-dressing performance artist on a death march across the Olde World! (In either case, the theme is death — straights obsess about murder; fags about loss.)

Odette claims, early on in her narrative, that she needs only three things for a performance: "sufficient gravity, sufficient reflection, and the full consent of the will." If this statement were to feature prominently on the cover of the book, many a reader would be turned off, for it makes the story sound oh-so-serious. Admittedly, there is a strong thread of thanatology coursing through the book. Odette *is* recounting her experiences gathered while disposing of the remains of her closest friends. She has experienced enough deaths to have sufficient gravity, indeed. To quote one of her paraphrases, making reference to losses during the height of the AIDS crisis in the late 1980s/early 1990s: "There's people dyin' now that never died before!"

Speaking of death. There is a curious narrative device that turns up now and again in the book, mainly at the beginning — interrupting the story at odd junctures in the same way the train conductor's voice breaks Odette's story with the barked-out names of the stops. It's the re-telling (and re-re-telling) of the circumstances of Jackson Pollack's death (summer night, convertible, excessive speed, oak tree, sudden loss). Why does it appear? To let us know that non-faggots die, too? To mark a moment in 1956 when New York culture shifted, unalterably? To mark the place where death waits — that is, the end of the long train line on which Odette is traveling?

But back to the personal aspect of this critical narrative. Once the novel had made its way onto my all-time "best of" list — and after I had begun to buy copies as gifts for friends (finding them on discount remainder tables for a pittance — equally thrilled at the thrift, but annoyed that the book had been, for all practical purposes, cast aside), I felt I needed to be in contact with the author. I wrote him a series of letters — under the pretense of thanking him for the book, but, as I reread those letters today, I understand that I was posturing wildly, filling my paragraphs with convoluted and studied sentences I hoped would convince him that I, too, was a man of elegant verbiage. Was I sincere? Yes, but just a bit of a blowhard. I ended up sending James McCourt a draft of a novel I had written. I don't remember his response — probably polite indifference, which was a common reaction to that stillborn over-extended short story.

I eventually made a date with him in Washington, DC — a year and a half after receiving the novel. We met in a weathered old steak house off of one of those Avenues that radiate from the capitol out to the suburbs. I was still in my vegetarian phase, so I sifted through some semblance of a salad while Jimmy made his way through an impressive piece of beef. He humored me, chatting about his work, about the world of publishing, about gay life in general and in specific. I listened, as an acolyte should, and awaited whatever epiphany he could provide. He didn't give it up easily. I knew I had to work through his dense conversation as I had to work through his dense writing. He chewed his fat and I stuffed my face with lettuce leaves. I did realize something — that he was as full of life as I wanted to be. That's why we read books, right? To experience a part of life that we wouldn't otherwise have a chance to?

Read *Time Remaining* — and McCourt's other books — like installments of the thinking gay man's *Encyclopédie*. Absorb the crowded intensity of this novel: old movie plots, snippets of fine poetry (Schuyler! Auden! Ashbery!), situationist arguments, modern art, sassy banter on a midnight train, bad puns and brilliant ones. He helps explain the world, through a thousand little examples and citations. Maybe the texts won't, in the end, point to the big answer, but, to let Odette have the last word, "All a body wants, really, is a little *emphasis* now and again."

# Mark Merlis
## **American Studies**

Houghton-Mifflin, 1994

## Rick Whitaker

In 1988, while a music student at the University of Cincinnati, I decided to move to New York and become a writer. I got on a bus with a friend and in early September we arrived at Port Authority with less than $1,000 each, no prospects for work or shelter, no friends, just one contact (my friend's, not mine), no portfolio. We stayed a night or two with the generous man my friend knew who lived in a small midtown studio, and we proceeded to make our way in the big city. Despite the difficulties and poverty, we managed. I worked my way slowly into the circle of writers around Gordon Lish, editor of *The Quarterly*, my favorite literary magazine, and eventually I studied with him and worked for him at the magazine and at Knopf publishers. My first friend in New York was Yannick Murphy, one of Lish's students, whose 1987 book *Stories in Another Language*, was my favorite book. At the age of 21 or so, I began to see the kind of life I wanted. I did some writing and I read everything that appealed to me, and I developed a sensibility that seems to have been tied pretty inextricably to my being gay.

Mark Merlis's *American Studies* is the novel that demonstrated more than any other, when I found it at the age of 26, that the kind of gay sensibility with which I found myself in sympathy could, at its most sophisticated, synthesize wit (a pair of bottoms are described as "two tunnels with no train"), intellect (the literary critic F.O. Matthiessen is the model for a character, and the writing rings with intelligence throughout), eroticism (the interplay between the narrator and his young hospital roommate is quintessentially sexy), and emotional depth in a story that's riveting, memorable and fun. Merlis's novel, published in 1994 (his first and best so far), is for me the literary achievement par excellence.

The narrator of *American Studies*, a low-level bureaucrat named Reeve, has been hospitalized after being badly beaten up by a man he'd brought home for an anonymous sexual encounter, the kind of nocturnal business for which he has a long-term yen: a rough scene with a blindfold and a tight belt around his wrists. (Reeve, at 62, has become accustomed to reluctantly paying for his usually acquiescent, if rough, young men.) He shares his hospital room with a beautiful blue-collar man in his twenties whose loose-fitting gown gives Reeve a few chances to glimpse bits of his flesh, his magnificent back, his perfect ass. This forced intimacy between the older man and the younger, and the plethora of associations it inspires, is one of the main tropes of the novel.

The other is Reeve's long-ago close friendship with Tom Slater, a famous, much older professor at the unnamed university where Reeve pursued but never finished his PhD. Slater was a semi-closeted, mostly chaste übermentor to many a handsome, wholesome young student (Reeve remembers them as Slater's "Wheaties eaters"), one of whom, Jimmy, became Slater's amanuensis and companion in the year or so before Slater was exposed as a Communist and homosexual and shot himself. Slater, who was involved in a shadowy way with the Communist Party during the McCarthy years, lost his position after Jimmy complied with an official request from the university to reveal the nature of their relationship, which included some (distinctly mild) sex. Tom Slater is the character based to some extent on the real-life figure of F. O. Matthiessen, who was for many years a professor at Harvard, where he helped found the field of American Studies; he, similarly outed as both far-left-wing and gay, jumped from a window to his death in 1950.

(I recently asked Mark Merlis to confirm that he used Matthiessen as a close model for Slater. He replied with the happy news that *American Studies* will be back in print in early 2009. He declined to answer my question directly, referring me to the preface in the new edition — when it is published and available at bookstores).

Reeve, in his sick bed, is occupied by thoughts of Slater because Howard, Reeve's gay friend, has brought Slater's book, *The Invincible City*, along with *Daniel Deronda*, for Reeve to read while recovering. Slater's book, a brilliant swerve by Merlis from Matthiessen's *The American Renaissance*, is a long, erudite study of nineteenth-century American letters. Reeve has never been able to get through it, and he never does, but the book is nonetheless a potent symbol of achievement and power. Mathiessen's *American Renaissance: Art and Expression in the Age of Emerson and Whitman* has achieved classic status for its power as a critical study of a great era for American writing. His book is assertive and accurate. He could be warmer and more amusing, but he is bona fide *emeritus*.

The opening paragraph of *American Studies* could be narrated from almost any time period imaginable. The prose marches elegantly along in an almost classical mode. It could be Achilles speaking, or Alexander the Great, or Whitman, or an aging dandy from an Andrew Holleran novel.

> The boy in the next bed lies sprawled atop the sheets, his gown riding up on his heroic thighs, an inch or so short of indecency. I would stare, but he is on my blind side and it hurts a little to turn my head. They have tapped me like a sugar maple: a vial taped to my forehead, over the bandaged eye, is collecting some fluid I apparently don't require. Sap, sapience. When my head is empty it will cease to ache.

*American Studies* itself is just "an inch or so short of indecency." Reeve's lust, and the lust of all the other characters in the book, is powerfully destructive and disreputable. Everyone is rebuked and forsaken, and worn out by the mad pursuit of un-intimate sex. Merlis is among the blackest of comedians in his description, woven into the narrative, of loneliness and depression. Reeve tries to keep up his amusing tone for us, but we know he has suffered and is suffering now. Both physically in pain and rather acutely depressed, Reeve is a lonely, unsuccessful gay man with nothing much to look forward to. It's amazing he's even bothered to write this story at all; the polished narrative seems to be the sole object and product of his ambition.

At first Reeve can't see the boy clearly, lacking his eyeglasses. He imagines him with "contours from the memory of all other boys." Just knowing the boy is there fills Reeve with "excitement and shame." The wounded ephebe sports a baseball-size bandage on his thumb. He "spends much of the day just looking at it, cradling it mournfully in his intact hand." Reeve is unsure at first, but feels the boy may possibly not yet have perceived his queerness; the tubes and bandages are his disguise, his "flame is shaded if not extinguished."

The writing is sharp and insightful, as here when Reeve is caught staring: "He looks back at me, his eyes unreadable, nothing behind them. He isn't really looking into me; the shades of cruelty that pass over his face are just the flickering blue light of the television. It is only in my imagination that straight men look right into me. "

The friendship between the young student Reeve and his mentor Slater was rife with friction and irreconcilable difference. Reeve is freely promiscuous; Slater is uptight and frigid. Reeve envies Slater his prestige and wealth (and the apartment that comes with his professorship); Slater Reeve's youthful adventures and fun. Neither is prepared to enter fully into the other's life. Reeve is too self-centered, Slater too proud and proper. Reeve dreams of and pursues sexual ecstasy while Slater is obsessed with an intellectual ideal that is sadly incompatible with mere sex. One day Reeve asks what Slater's new book is about (he was just finishing *The Invincible City*).

> To my regret, this remark happened to catch him on a day when he was ready to talk about it. He started to try to explain the book, the message he thought was in it and that no one else ever quite drew from it, the revolution as the triumph of comradeship. I may have been visibly

> squirming, thinking of the comradeship I was missing just
> down the hall.

When Slater makes a remark about Melville's long-frustrated desire, Reeve confesses that "I was so young and self-centered, I took that as directed at me. I was starting to answer that I had been ready enough." There's a wide distance between the two: young Reeve is on the near side of sensuality, Slater on the far. Back in the novel's present, with the now older Reeve hospitalized and besotted with his indifferent companion, the roles are reversed, and the young man's self-centeredness reminds Reeve of his own. He understands, though he doesn't quite admit, that he was a wholly inadequate friend and that Slater's suicide was the final indication that the abyss between the two men was indeed unbridgeable.

Reeve is ambivalently grateful for his young companion in the hospital room, just as Slater was for Reeve's company. Reeve is in the habit of seeking out companionship at almost any price, though his assignations are always unsatisfying and bereft of affection, let alone love. The tension between sordid — but potentially "sacred" — contact and lonely (but elegant) solitude is the overriding preoccupation of Merlis's rigorous, irrepressible *American Studies*.

# Charles Nelson
# The Boy Who Picked the Bullets Up

William Morrow, 1981

## Jim Marks

Charles Nelson's 1981 novel about a gay military medic in the Vietnam War is something of a conundrum. It's not that it poses a riddle without a good answer, but rather that it is a puzzle whose pieces can be fit together in different ways.

It might seem strange to suggest that *The Boy who Picked the Bullets Up* abounds in complexity since at first glance it appears straightforward. It follows a year (August 1966-July 1967) in the life of ex-Detroit Tiger farm team baseball infielder Kurt Strom, from his initial training to be a medic in Boston through the stages of his military career with occasional detours into family life. Big (six foot three, two hundred and five pounds), good-looking Kurt has an infinite relish for sex with other men, and usually encounters few difficulties in gratifying his urges.

His experience in Vietnam has two markedly different stages. In his initial deployments he works both at a large military hospital and as the medic stationed with a battalion of marines in the front line jungle. These initial deployments paint a *Catch-22* picture of military life combined with sometimes gruesomely graphic images of maimed bodies in the hospital and in the field. In his last major deployment he is stationed in a remote village as part of an early version of the pacification strategy designed to win "the hearts and minds" of the local population. The soldiers' efforts initially appear successful; however the operation ends in disaster when their compound is overrun by the Viet Cong. Kurt has a harrowing escape which he barely survives. There is a brief coda in which Kurt is once again wounded and then spirals down in a combination of drug addiction and sexual abuse, ending ambiguously on the road.

Its narrative technique gives the book charm and complexity. *The Boy who Picked the Bullets Up* is an epistolary novel, a series of letters home. Dorothy Allison has noted that the gay novel is a novel of character and this technique allows Nelson to paint Kurt's character through his own voice. At times jaunty, often ribald, with an off beat sense of humor, Kurt can wax serious and philosophical. In addition to sex, his great passion is reading and he presents himself as the company's egghead oddball when he's not demonstrating his athletic prowess. While he is a generally engaging, sympathetic character, he shows his Southern upbringing with an ugly racist streak and can at times come across as crudely misogynistic.

Kurt communicates with multiple correspondents, primarily his grandmother (somewhat confusingly addressed as "Mom"); Arch, a former teammate from his baseball days; Chloe, a female cousin roughly his age; and Paul, a gay college professor friend. For each, Kurt adopts a slightly different persona, tone and subject matter, although all but "Mom" get his sign-off "Relentlessly, Kurt." Writing "Mom" and Chloe, Kurt tends to focus on his complicated family back in Louisiana; with Arch he'll reminisce about their team days while Paul gets raunchy accounts laced with literary allusions (the novel takes its title from a poem by Arthur Rimbaud; other poems by Rimbaud preface the individual sections of the novel and the grim, disillusioned jauntiness of the decadent poet presides over the entire text). Occasionally Kurt will describe the same event to two different recipients. For instance, a light hearted thank you note to Chloe for a Christmas gift of rum, in which he sardonically mentions Mom's gift of binoculars — "Binoculars! The better, I suppose, to see this fucking country" — is followed by a more respectful thank you to Mom: "That's a dandy pair of binoculars. I look through them everywhichaways and am the envy of the compound." The overall effect is akin to the multiple perspectives Cubist painters flattened out onto their canvasses, presenting Kurt's personalities as they emerge in his interactions with the world.

Yet there is something curious about telling this story using an epistolary technique. The founding narrative of the first epistolary novels published in 18th century England (Samuel Richardson's *Pamela* and *Clarissa*) was the story of a young woman imprisoned and struggling to gain her freedom while retaining her honor. It is not hard to see how this antique story telling device can find a new lease on life in, say, Alice Walker's *The Color Purple*. But that is not the sort of story Charles Nelson is telling. His hero's episodic adventures are more in the line of Henry Fielding's picaresque *Tom Jones*. Far from being a tale born of confinement, the picaresque novel's central story is that of a young man who ventures out into the world where through his encounters and romances, he eventually discovers his true identity. In a sense, then, the technique and the narrative could be thought to work at cross purposes, where one stealthily undermines the other.

Or are they truly at cross purposes? One question haunts this novel: why did Kurt abandon a promising career for this trip to hell? And make no mistake about it; the war this novel depicts is hell. Living conditions range from the institutional gloom of a hastily constructed hospital to the squalor of forward encampments, where sanitation, as Kurt frequently and colorfully reminds us, is primitive to nonexistent. Daily life swings from boredom to terrifying encounters with a mostly hidden enemy and the ever present possibility of being blown to bits by a booby-trap.

The war was never broadly popular and lacked the kind of patriotic fervor that swept the country after 9/11. Even ostensible supporters found ways to avoid service (evidence A & B: President George W. Bush and Vice-President Dick "Other Priorities" Cheney). The huge manpower demands were sustained by the draft, and those who voluntarily enlisted tended to be earnest and politically ambitious (think of Al Gore and Senator John Kerry). Kurt's no hippie, and has a hearty contempt for his anti-war peace and love brother-in-law, but he's also too much of a loner and wise-ass to be a blind believer in the war as a cause.

So why did he enlist? His explanations, such as they are, are distressingly casual — a quart of vodka martinis, a sense of obligation as a dutiful son of the South. A potential major league athletic career is brief and uncertain in the best of circumstances; why put it off if not entirely in jeopardy? Something not told to us must have happened to precipitate Kurt's decision or there must be something in his character beyond what he reveals to us that would explain or justify this decision.

This mysteriousness of Kurt's basic motivation in turn suggests that the breezy, brave front he presents to his correspondents hides as much as it reveals. His final, swift emotional disintegration also suggests a barely contained personality undone by the stresses of war. Kurt has reversed the hero's course: at one point he is actually a prisoner and, at novel's end, dependent on the good will of a Green Beret.

As it happens Kurt appears again in a second book, Charles Nelson's *Panthers in the Skins of Men*. Although it, too takes its title from Rimbaud, it is not quite a sequel. Rather than pick up the story from where it left off in *The Boy who Picked the Bullets Up*, Nelson has substituted an alternative ending that finds Kurt recovering from a baseball-career-ending wound in a New Orleans military hospital. More significantly, although told in the first person, *Panthers* does not attempt the epistolary technique of *The Boy who Picked the Bullets Up*. The change in technique illustrates how form is in itself creative. Without the multiple correspondents, Kurt is a flatter, simpler character. And without the pretense of writing a letter, *Panthers* loses the opportunity for the verbal hijinks that give *The Boy who Picked the Bullets Up* much of its ebullience. Kurt's letters are often devised to amuse; particularly when writing Paul he will switch into high camp ("Tom-toms throb with a message from Kurtala, the Jungle Queen. 'BWANA! GET ME OUT OF HERE!'" begins one letter). One letter is composed entirely of poetic doggerel:

> Simpler and far less sophisticated
> Is Barry, whom the marines have rated
> A radioman; I rate him straight A's

> He shyly grins beneath my ardent gaze.
> His mild manner and his horn-rimmed glasses
> Protected him once from my subtle passes
> But on the beach, glasses off, nearly nude
> Kurt Strom saw Superman and desire stewed.

The direct narration of *Panthers* doesn't lend itself to these kinds of verbal flourishes, taking away one additional source of interest.

*Panthers*, which appears to have been modeled on Jack Kerouac's *On the Road* (with touches of John Rechy's *City of Night*) also lacks the great compelling theme of the war in Vietnam. While the war in Vietnam has spawned many novels and films, this gay Vietnam novel is pretty much sui generis. The only comparable book would be Christopher Bram's *Almost History*, which follows a US Foreign Service officer whose career includes time in Vietnam. The contrasts between *Almost History* and *The Boy Who Picked the Bullets Up* are revealing. Bram's novels demonstrate a disciplined talent working to extend his mastery of his craft. In *Almost History*, Bram explores ways of constructing a narrative over an extended period of time, of convincingly portraying a man coming out in early middle age, of setting an individual's story against the larger narrative of his time, of convincingly portraying distant places. In *Almost History*, the reader can observe an artist imposing his will upon his subject. In *The Boy Who Picked the Bullets Up*, it is more as if the story has taken possession of its author, who is compelled to tell the tale.

For those of us who came of age in the late '60s and early '70s, the Vietnam War was the central precipitating national crisis of our lives. It was begun on false pretenses and conducted with equally dishonest claims. For those of us who opposed it, the war revealed a rottenness, a corruption, a stupidity at the heart of American polity. The Kurt we see at the end of *The Boy Who Picked the Bullets Up* reminds me of the Vietnam vets who would show up in writing workshops at the school where I was doing graduate work as the war came to its sad ending. Sent on a fools mission by a careless government, they were lost souls, more than a little bit crazed by the

attempt to square their sacrifice with the lack of honor they felt upon
returning and the knowledge that their efforts had been in vain. Kurt is no
anti-war lefty. Seen through his cynical soldier eyes, the portrait of the war
as a disaster seems not political but simple empirical fact.

*The Boy Who Picked the Bullets Up* retains its relevance. We are again
mired in a war dishonestly begun and conducted. The military remains
officially anti (openly) gay while mostly turning a blind eye to the many
homosexual soldiers whose talents are sorely needed. The trauma of the
combat has left many of those returning home as physically and emotionally
damaged as those coming home from the jungles of southeast Asia.
Literature cannot ameliorate these damages, but perhaps it can convince us
of their reality, even if, sadly, we seem unable to learn from them.

# Kyle Onstott
# and Lance Horner
# **Child of the Sun**

W.H. Allen, 1966

## Michael Bronski

*Child of the Sun:* Let's start with the cover of the 1972 paperback. The art here by noted graphic artist Frank Frazetta is shocking even for early in the 1970s. A mostly naked muscular gladiator-type – he is wearing a red thong – in a chariot, drawn by a white and a black stallion, is racing past an orating Roman citizen, who seems to be entirely naked except for part of a toga tossed over his shoulder and some sandals laced half-way up his calf. Next to him in a subservient position is a crouched man – a slave? – naked except for his sandals. At the bottom of the frame is a naked woman, her back to us, on a red blanket. She is hardly noticeable; faux heterosexual window dressing. On the back cover is a close-up of the gladiator with emphasis on his enormously muscular buttocks. Beneath this overtly homoerotic image is the pitch for the book:

> This brilliant and brutally intimate novel captures
> accurately the depravity and intrigue of Ancient Rome.
> CHILD OF THE SUN tells the story of the youth Varius
> Avitus Bassianus, destined to become Emperor of the
> Roman empire. Varius spurned women. His erotic longings
> searched out a very different type of love. Whatever or

whomever he fancied was quickly offered to him. And no
man, be he soldier or citizen, dared refuse him. As his
perverted passions grew more and more bizarre, even the
voluptuaries of Rome recoiled in horror.

*Child of the Sun*, by Kyle Onstott and Lance Horner, was originally
published in 1966 by Gold Medal, one of the most prominent and influential
mass market paperback publishers in the country. It was overtly
homosexual in theme and content and while marketed to a mainstream,
heterodox readership, the jacket copy did not hide its homoerotic subject
matter. The cover of the 1972 edition, quoted above, is even more explicit.
Curiously, neither cover makes explicit that Varius Avitus Bassianus
becomes the infamous Emperor Elagabalus – aka Heliogabalus or Marcus
Aurelius Antoninus (not to be confused with Marcus Aurelius, the
philosopher-Emperor) – whom semi-serious readers of history would have
known as the man that Edward Gibbon in *Decline and Fall of the Roman
Empire*, claimed "abandoned himself to the grossest pleasures and un-
governed fury."

*Child of the Sun* is an important touchstone in a number of
intersections of queer publishing currents. Most obviously, it is a prime
example of gay culture's – and to some degree mainstream culture's –
fascination with the implicit and explicit homoeroticism of the classical
world. This was not new to British and American queer male culture. We
see the origins in John Addington Symonds's obsession with the male body
in Greek and Renaissance art. We see it in the endless issues of *Physique
Pictorial* and *Grecian Guild Quarterly* where the hustler-models posed in faux
togas and tacky pieced-together sandals. We certainly see it in the advent of
the Italian sword and sandal epics of the late 1950s such as *Hercules,* which
starred muscle men like Steve Reeves who had already appeared frequently
in *Physical Pictorial*. The classical nude had, from just before the turn of the
century, been a coded marker of male queerness. Not very good repro-
ductions of Michelangelo's David were commonly found in gay men's
apartments in the 1950s – it was safe because it was deemed acceptable
culture, but more than obvious to anyone in the know that statuettes of

naked teenaged boys with slings over their shoulder were pretty direct code for: queer.

But *Child of the Sun* is also a more blatant homo-manifestation of the literary oeuvre of Kyle Onstott and Lance Horner. These are names that were once at the center of popular literary culture in the 1950s and early 1960s and who are now all but forgotten except as minor footnotes. Hell, they don't even have Wikipedia entries. While they often collaborated on novels, Onstott and Horner – they sound like a two-bit corrupt small town law firm in a Eudora Welty novel – wrote their own works as well. All of these works were historical novels that featured sweaty, heaving sex scenes, light on explicit details and heavy on innuendo, that were very heterosexual except for the fact that the authors were far more fascinated by the male physique and genitalia than they were by the female. Onstott became famous for *Mandingo* in 1957 – a lusty, raucous, and racist look at interracial plantation life before the Civil War. And yes, all of the men, especially the African slaves, had very large penises. *Mandingo* was followed by *Drum*, and then *The Master of Falconhurst* – all set in the south and all dealing, in erotic ways, with slavery. Onstott and Horner then collaborated on sequels to *The Master of Falconhurst*, such as *Falconhurst's Fancy* and *Heir to Falconhurst*. Like Grace Metalious's *Peyton Place*, published in 1956, *Mandingo* and its sequels took advantage of the new leniency in mainstream publishing that was allowing more erotic detail and adult plots. And while the African-American Civil Rights movement was struggling for equality under the law and basic human rights Onstott and Horner were providing lurid, sexualized fantasies of interracial sex, enormous amounts of sexualized violence, and a sexualized historical revisionism of the old South that made Margaret Mitchell's *Gone with the Wind* look like a nursery rhyme.

It is something of a relief, at least for a culturally sensitive reader, that Onstott and Horner left the American south for other realms. *The Tattooed Rood*, ("More Terrible, More Wonderful than the Unforgettable *Mandingo*" reads the back cover) set during the Spanish Inquisition, was published in 1960, and Horner on his own published *Rogue Roman* ("Bloody and Barbaric as *Mandingo*, Corrupt and Sensuous as *La Dolce Vita*") in 1965.

*Child of the Sun* was published a year later and – like *Mandingo* and the other novels – both badly, even terribly, written but compulsively readable. These are men who cannot leave a cliché unearthed, who believe that lurid adjectives are more impressive when used repeatedly, and who eschew subtlety with the faith of a novice. But what is so interesting about *Child of the Sun* is that Onstott's and Horner's queer sensibility is able to come to the fore as they detail the depravity of an actual queer person. While this may be startling in the framework of Stonewall which was not to happen for another three years, they are moderately behind the times in regard to other openly gay works of fiction (though its depiction of gay marriage as desirable and just was certainly ahead of the curve).

Novels such as Gore Vidal's *City and the Pillar* (1948), James Barr's *Quatrefoil* (1950) and Fritz Peters's *Finistere* (1951) had all seriously addressed queer themes nearly two decades before. And, in terms of explicit sex, John Rechy's *City of Night* shocked readers with its life and times of queer hustlers in 1963 and his even more explicit *Numbers* would be published in 1967. More saliently, Mary Renault had been mining the classical-age of homo-lit with *The Last of the Wine* (1956), *The King Must Die* (1958) and *Fire from Heaven* (1969). Of course Renault's elegant literary peregrinations won her accolades of good taste and insightful characterization – the inverse of the heaving and pulsating antics of *Child of the Sun*.

So can anything positive actually be said about *Child of the Sun*? Well, it is fun to read as long as you don't expect much in the way of literature. Like *Mandingo* and their other American historical novels, Onstott and Horner know how to tell a story in the most basic, page-turning, sometimes even mind-numbing, manner. Here is the end of Chapter Seven after Antoninus has just killed a priest making a sacrifice and is taking control of the royal palace:

> Despite the pain, he was smiling. His spoken words were only for himself. "They obeyed me! When I spoke they cringed before me. They feared me. This is how it will be when I am Caesar. Ah, 'tis a good feeling. I like to command.' He walked a few steps across the hall, hearing Ganny's steps behind him. He smiled. 'But there are times when I like to be commanded.'

As with all of the other Onstott and Horner novels there is a strong leitmotif of sadomasochism here, and they play it to the hilt. At the end of Chapter 28 Antoninus has Agrippa, a member of the Praetorian Guard, in his room and when the man refuses his advances – calling him a "bath-boy who sells himself for money" – has him tied to a rack and gagged so that he can fellate him. Agrippa is humiliated and Antoninus, who considers this a divine act, is deeply perturbed. It is all very odd, and you can't help wondering what is going on here – emotionally – for the writers. *Child of the Sun* is relatively sexual and moderately titillating, but it has none of the deeply disturbing aggressive, deeply disconcerting, sexuality that *Mandingo* has. That is because at heart this is less of an adult novel than an old fashioned boy's adventure book filled with essentially romantic interplay between men who are less interested in sex then in being chums and soul mates: think *The Adventures of Huckleberry Finn* or *Moby Dick*. For all of its sheen of depravity of ancient Rome, homosexual orgies, and sexual intrigue, *Child of the Sun* is actually fairly sweet. Onstott and Horner are intent on humanizing the horrible Heliogabalus and making him, at heart, a sort of sweet, if totally deranged, queen. This charming historical revisionism is at odds with the fact that they had no problems exploiting racism in *Mandingo* and the *Falconhurst* series. I suspect that these two, quite dissimilar novels were very different projects for Kyle Onstott and Lance Horner. While the mainstream culture of the 1960s was still, although in lessening ways, demonizing queers, they set out to reconsider and reclaim one of history's most notorious decadent queens.

*Child of the Sun* is a fascinating historical pop-culture curiosity that doesn't really connect to the great gay novels of the 1950s; by the time Stonewall happened a few years later, it felt old fashioned. This makes it both singular and special; one more tile in the complicated mosaic of what we now call 20th century gay literature.

Roger Peyrefitte

# The Exile of Capri

Secker & Warburg, 1961

(1<sup>st</sup> edition in English translation)

## Gregory Woods

A handsome Frenchman in his early 30s meets a beautiful 17-year-old
compatriot on the crest of Vesuvius in 1897. Some kind of mutual
understanding is achieved, more or less, at first sight — 'They suspected
each other of having something more in common than a taste for climbing
mountains; something betrayed in the fact that each had obviously selected
his guide for his looks" — and is then reinforced as, looking down over the
ruins of Herculaneum and Pompeii, their conversation unearths a shared
interest in classical culture and modern poetry.

On a trip across the Gulf of Naples to the 'Siren Isle' of Capri, they
witness the snubbing of Oscar Wilde — fresh out of jail — in the restaurant
of the Quisisana Hotel. The younger of the two Frenchmen sends him
flowers, even while the elder counsels him against any such association
with scandal. By this time, the boy has made it clear that his sexual interest
is, and probably always will be, in boys younger than himself. We know
already that this strikingly attractive and intelligent young aristocrat, the
Comte Jacques d'Adelsward-Fersen, is likely to lead an unconventional life,
for, as he tells his older companion, desire has a tendency to turn into
destiny.

I first came across Roger Peyrefitte's 1959 novel *L'exilé de Capri* in a paperback reissue of Edward Hyams's translation of it, *The Exile of Capri*, published by Panther in 1969. There were several signs that this was a book I would like. In the first place, I already knew Peyrefitte's earlier novel *Special Friendships* (*Amitiés particulières*, 1945), the story of a platonic love affair between two boys at a Roman Catholic boarding-school. Although — or because — I had been to such a school myself, I found that book rather dull, since the two lovers never did anything more daring than swim together and kiss.

*The Exile of Capri* looked more promising. On the front cover, it had been given the subtitle *An Elegant Study in Decadence*. This was coded, but it was a code I already knew how to read. The back cover spoke of Capri as the 'ISLAND OF STRANGE DESIRES' and as 'a refuge for the sexually persecuted of all tastes.' The blurb promised 'a superbly scandalous picture of a colourful bygone era.'

However, just as my attention had first been drawn to *Special Friendships* by the cover illustration on my second-hand paperback edition (Panther, 1968) — the superimposed photographs of two shirtless boys, one dark and one fair — so too was the main attraction of *The Exile of Capri* its peculiar cover photograph: a man in full-body striped underwear, a boy in nothing but a towel, and a potted plant on a wooden pedestal. Although the man's underwear now seems to me interestingly full, in those days I was more interested in the boy. He is looking up at the taller man from behind and to one side. What I could see of his smooth, pale chest endorsed all of the cover's other promising clues. I bought the book.

This in the early 1970s, in what was then the best second-hand bookshop in Norwich, where I was an undergraduate. The man who ran this reassuringly Dickensian establishment, the Scientific Anglian on St. Benedict Street, was an irascible old devil who, despite the fact that I was a regular customer of his for almost a decade, would never show any sign that he recognized me. He showed his disdain for paperbacks — and, I think, for those of us who could not afford to buy anything better — by writing their prices in hard-pressed ball-point on their front covers. My copy of *The Exile of Capri* cost me 18 pence; someone else had already bought it second-hand for three shillings. (The publisher's price on the back cover is six shillings or 30 pence.) I must have been more impressed by the book than its (at least) two previous owners, for I have kept it. My modest initial outlay has been good value over the years.

The novel's central character Jacques d'Adelsward-Fersen (1880-1923) is no invention. Like most of the other characters in Peyrefitte's novel, he really existed. Nor was this the first novel based on his life on Capri: that honor belongs to Compton Mackenzie's *Vestal Fire* (1927), which resulted in its author's banishment from the island in a hypocritical response to his satirical depictions of certain prominent local citizens. Yet Peyrefitte's later novel is a lot more forthright. He imagined all, but invented very little. He was well placed to research his narrative, both by consulting the relevant written records and by gossiping with all the right people. Fersen was a boy-loving man destined for a golden career in the French diplomatic service until scandal intervened. A writer of aesthetically derivative but thematically daring poetry, he never needed to earn his living — always an advantage, if you are going to behave in ways that are likely to risk your reputation in the eyes of the bourgeoisie. Being forced out of your country is obviously much less of an inconvenience if you can afford to cushion the shock of exile with a luxurious home and beautiful companions.

It was in 1903 that Fersen was fined in Paris and briefly imprisoned for the corruption of minors, his crime being all the more scandalous for having involved not mere street urchins or rent boys but well-born schoolboys whose half-formed bodies and minds were of much greater potential value to the state. On his release from prison, Fersen made his way down to Capri; but that was not by any means the last they had heard of him in Paris. In 1909 he founded an arts periodical called *Akadémos*, pretty much dedicated to the celebration of pederasty. He was not going to allow the fear of further trouble to gag him. Indeed, now that he no longer had much of a reputation to protect — other than on behalf of his unfortunate family — he could take even more risks than before.

Roger Peyrefitte (1907-2000) turned to writing after leaving the French *corps diplomatique*, under a cloud, in 1944, when he was 37. *Amitiés Particulières*, his first novel, which came out the following year, secured his unsuitability for public service. Not only was its story of love between boys set in a Jesuit boarding school like the one in which the author had himself been educated, but its juvenile lead, Georges de Sarre, partly based on himself, was of the governing class, precisely the kind of boy who was destined to become a politician or a diplomat. Indeed, in two subsequent novels, *Les Ambassades* (1951) and *La Fin des ambassades* (1953), Georges follows the author into the diplomatic service, thereby allowing Peyrefitte to satirize his erstwhile profession and the scandalous goings-on behind the scenes of national public life. Further satires followed, mainly on the Roman Catholic church. Peyrefitte's fiction often indulges in point-scoring. His consciousness of himself as an insider who had become an outsider seems to have given him a lasting need for revenge by scandal-mongering. If the resulting tone were merely neurotic or monotonously embittered, his work would probably be unreadable. But Peyrefitte always leavens his anger with glee. His vengeance is taken with a lightness of heart.

True to its roots in the author's classical education, *The Exile of Capri* often veers into didactic digressions — if yet another paragraph on the history of gay culture can be regarded as a digression at all, within a novel whose main theme is the history of queer culture. One character, usually the older, will enlighten another (and the reader) with a mini-lecture on some scandalous detail of European history, ancient or modern — not merely for the sake of the accumulation of knowledge, but as an encouragement to the life of informed queerness. I have no objection to these passages, because I have always complained about the silences surrounding queer experience, the absence of queer lives from school and university curricula. Throughout my life, but especially when I was much younger, I have compensated for these silences by seeking out the queerness in literature. Hence my career as a professor of gay and lesbian studies; hence, also, my *History of Gay Literature* (1998). Lacking a queer pedagogue of my own as a young man, I educated my queerness by reading appropriate books. *The Exile of Capri* was, and remains, one of these. It is not a great novel in aesthetic or technical respects. Its prose is, to be frank, stodgy at times and its characterization is not always complex or subtle. But of how many more famous gay novels is this also true? In this case, the dullness of the style is more than mitigated by the sheer nerve of the narrative. No reputation is left undamaged.

I read the novel for the second time, in a copy I had picked up in Naples, in the original French. Again, this copy was second-hand. I assumed it had been left in some hotel room by a departing French tourist, a gay man perhaps, who had brought it down to the Mezzogiorno to use as a guide to the pleasures once — and some still — available in the searing south. The year was 1982 and I was now living in Italy, teaching at the ancient university of Salerno, once the haunt of the medieval alchemists. I was sharing a flat on the beach at Vietri on the Costiera Amalfitana, one of the most beautiful stretches of coast in the world. From here, I could get into Naples in an hour by bus or train. Also, in season, I could catch the early morning ferry along the Costiera from the industrial port at Salerno to Capri. This was a three-hour journey, with stops at Amalfi and Positano, before the boat threaded its way through the Isole i Galli — one of them owned by Rudolf Nureyev and, before him, by Léonide Massine — and, opposite Sorrento, crossed the narrows to the Siren Isle itself.

With the Peyrefitte in my shoulder bag on these occasional trips, I was able to visit a Capri that was in none of the official guide books. Queer Capri, you might call it. No topographical or architectural feature with the slightest relevance to the island's queer cultural history is overlooked by Peyrefitte. Every rock and cavern, every shrine and villa, seems allocated its significance on his map of the island, its every contour outlined with gossipy threads of scandal. I could labor my way up an overgrown path to Fersen's Villa Lysis (then a virtual ruin, but today re-inhabited) or even further up to the Villa Jovis, teetering on the cliff from which those who aroused the emperor Tiberius's displeasure had been thrown to their deaths. I never managed, though, to eat in the restaurant of the Quisisana — my

salary as a young academic, although numbered in millions of lire, would
not stretch to that.

It was when using the novel in this way, as an intelligent
guidebook, that I really felt the benefit of its didactic streak. It gave me some
of my life's most engrossing touristic experiences. But I measure its generosity
by the fact that it never completely absorbed me: often enough, I was distracted
from it by queerness in the flesh. I have always read books in the open air. But
one of my fondest general memories of Italy is of how often I was interrupted
by boys in need of a cigarette, a conversation, or more. I think of such
encounters in the grounds of Catullus's villa on Lake Garda, in the park beside
the Salerno opera house, on a bench beneath a naked Apollo alongside the
Naples aquarium, on the ramparts of Mantova as an eery mist was coming in
from the marshes, in searing heat among the ruins of Paestum.

In October 1984 I followed Peyrefitte's narrative down to Sicily. Fersen
and Nino go there to visit the Greek sites at Agrigento and Syracuse — where
they also pay their respects at the grave of the boy-loving poet August von
Platen (1796-1835) — and they tarry long enough in Taormina for Fersen to
write a short novel, *Une Jeunesse*, about a French painter who falls in love with a
younger man — in Taormina. Like all other affluent tourists of their day, they
visit the studio of the photographer Wilhelm von Gloeden (1856-1931), famed
for his evocative images of Taorminan boys, generally naked, in classical
locations and pseudo-classical poses. I had been to Sicily several times, but
never to Taormina, which had a reputation for touristic chic that I was not
interested in investigating. I found the town full of coupled German clones,
with tailored jeans and primly trimmed moustaches. Although they gave the
Corso a pleasantly gay atmosphere in the evenings, this was not the kind of
gayness one would travel so far south to find.

Among the postcards of Taormina's famous views — over the straits to
Calabria, across the proscenium of the Greco-Roman theatre to Mount Etna —
some shops still sell monochrome postcards of von Gloeden's photographs of
local boys. When I spent a long time in one such shop, making my selection, the
proprietor, an old woman perhaps in her 80s, came out from behind her
counter and led me by the hand down the street to the building that had been

the photographer's studio. It was with real warmth and pride that she said of him, 'He was the first tourist. We owe everything to him.' I still use one of those postcards as my bookmark in the Peyrefitte novel. Fersen himself may have chatted with these very boys, while they waited to be stripped and posed.

I no longer have my French edition of *L'exilé de Capri*. I suppose I lost it on one of my moves between Vietri and Nottingham, where I now live and work; but I prefer to think that someone stole it — or felt compelled to borrow it without asking me, too embarrassed to acknowledge a depth of interest. Perhaps it was one of my students, seeking an extra-curricular supplement to what I had already taught him; sentimentally, I hope so. Re-reading the novel now, in English, in England, I feel far removed from its center of gravity, distant in both space and time, but still close in sensibility (to use an unfashionable term).

When he settles on Capri, Fersen buys the promontory beneath the Villa Jovis and builds himself a beautiful home, the Villa Lysis. (Lysis is the boy in Plato with whom Socrates discusses the nature of friendship.) Here he brings Nino Cesarini, a 15-year-old laborer he has picked up in Rome. He has Nino educated and sculpted — nude, of course. And so begins a life-long idyll of sacred estheticism and profane love. Although Fersen makes several long trips abroad — to north Africa, for instance, and to Ceylon — all he has to do is stay put on Capri and, eventually, the whole of the queer world will turn up on his doorstep.

This is, therefore, a book full of queer cultural celebrities, some of them greatly admired by Peyrefitte, but some just shown making fools of themselves. With Fersen we encounter writers, artists, musicians — Jean Cocteau, Camille Saint-Saëns, Norman Douglas, Renée Vivien, Nathalie Barney, Jean Lorrain, André Gide, the scions of the Ballets Russes — along with an assortment of aristocrats and riff-raff from all over Europe. Some of them are hiding from scandals at home; others generate fresh scandals that will follow them back.

Peyrefitte offers us a version of early 20th century history in which all of the world seems queer. It is a vision of sybaritic privilege, doubtless distasteful to many, in which indulgence in the arts looks oddly like an eighth deadly sin. To be sure, reading *The Exile of Capri* is like the most reviled yet most mundane of the solitary vices, offering the temporary pleasure of a dream, without any real or lasting personal connection. A disappointing pleasure, perhaps, but worth indulging in, all the same.

Paul Reed
# Longing
Celestial Arts, 1988

## Bill Brent

> Published in 1984, *Facing It* was acclaimed by Rita Mae
> Brown and others as the first AIDS novel. *Longing*, the tale
> of a young man's search for love in San Francisco's gay
> community, was praised by the *New York Times* for its
> evocative style. *Vertical Intercourse*, his final novel, deals
> with aging and loss in the gay male community and was
> praised by media ranging from *Publishers Weekly* to the *Bay
> Area Reporter* and *Frontiers*, to *The Stranger*, Seattle's weekly
> alternative newspaper. — *From Paul Reed's obituary*, Bay
> Area Reporter, *Feb. 2, 2002*

Paul Reed published three novels over a span of 16 years. While he
completed and published work in other genres for multiple publishers in
the 12-year hiatus between his second and third novels – journals, short
fiction, nonfiction; even a whimsical meditation on the respective virtues of
cats versus dogs – I glean that the work he considered most important was
his book-length fiction. As with so many veterans of the epidemic, Paul's
creative work was impeded by the exigencies of the AIDS crisis, including
his own health issues. That he was able to turn this adversity to his
advantage, and maintain his prolific and varied output, is testament to his
ingenuity and perseverance.

Paul rose to prominence as the first wave of AIDS was claiming the lives and community of many gay Americans. Thus, the reporters and reviewers who brought Paul's work to the public's attention – mostly gay – would have had a strong emotional investment in promoting such work. In that era, promoting the gay movement in general was conducive to job security and the formation of a gay identity. Therefore, it is hard to claim that, with this "gay agenda" (the true agenda of any persecuted group is not predation, but survival), and lacking an historical perspective, any reviews or reports were entirely unbiased. Paul was in the right place at the right time.

More than a quarter century after Paul's first novel was published, enough time has passed to permit a more objective review of his work. I can hardly claim complete objectivity, as I had a personal and professional relationship with the author that spanned nearly a decade. I own a signed collection of his complete works, which he bestowed upon me over the years much as a parent might pass down a collection of family memorabilia to a child. It was a shrewd strategy on Paul's part, who, having witnessed at close range my penchant for subcultural documentation, must have realized the wisdom of gifting me with his 14 volumes. His three journals *(The Q Journal, The Savage Garden,* and *The Redwood Diary)* now strike me as precursors to the well-rendered blog, in their detailing of the day-to-day shifts in consciousness of someone dealing with a life-threatening illness (and, as in *The Q Journal,* a highly unorthodox treatment regimen).

> He was a very intense and intellectual person, very sexual, and very funny. There's an ambitious truth-telling quality to his fiction that has staying power. – *Jerry Rosco, author, and Paul's corre-spondent for 15 years*

In reviewing these books, and *Longing* in particular, I felt as though I were getting to know for the first time about a part of Paul's life that I had intuited while he was alive, yet which remained largely unknown to me then. While couched in the conventions of fiction, Paul took his settings and plotlines primarily from direct experience. Of his three novels, only *Facing It* relies on research to a significant degree. Paul was an intensely private individual, yet through his works, he reveals his vulnerability and his idealism with remarkable candor.

Above all, Paul was a deeply humanistic author. He expressed his humanism with subtlety and sensitivity to "the spirit of the times," as Dr. Kiljoy remarks in *Vertical Intercourse,* and that is a remarkable gift indeed.

When we wish to examine the transcendent forces operating beneath the surface of everyday life, it serves us to scrutinize our existence at its most severe and least prosaic level – in a word, survival. This is where Paul's work pays dividends to the astute reader. Let us examine how Paul's choices of character, setting, and conflict point to his underlying intensity and grit, in light of what I consider to be his literature's primary theme: psychic survival in harsh times.

In his novels, Paul describes or alludes to the state of longing to the point of pervasiveness. He even uses *Longing* as the title of his second novel. Longing denotes an absence, a desire for an unattained Other. There may still be hope for attainment, though often there is not. But longing is more painful to bear than hope, which often wears an optimistic, happy face. Likewise, dismissal implies a more final judgment than pessimism, one that often eradicates the object or banishes the concept entirely from consideration. In other words, both positions on the axis are more absolute and penetrating than their more everyday counterparts.

Thus longing is Paul's most haunting idea, one which spans his entire novelistic career. There are glimmers of it even in his debut, *Facing It,* whose very title implies a longing for life before the deadly epidemic. The argument scenes between the parents of Andy, the dying protagonist, demonstrate this battle between longing and dismissal. Edna wants to visit her gay son before he dies, while her husband Chuck, who has long disowned Andy, forbids it:

> 'You have no idea how difficult it has been for me to
> dismiss Andy all these years. Of course I detest his
> perversion; it's wrong and hurtful. But I can't ignore the fact

that he is dying just because of his perversion. It hardly
seems related.'

'But it is!' he protested, but seeing the rage in
Edna's face, he was silent again.

'No, no …' She was shaking her head. 'I gave up
myself to raise these children, and to stand by while part of
my life dies is just an impossible request. You're asking me
to give up everything in that case. Don't you see? I am
submerged in the lives of my children, and if I can't be with
Andy when he dies, then everything is waste.'

Even at the time Paul died, he had a new novel-in-progress set in Maui,
"longingly" titled *Another Island:*

A friend once told me that he spent a great deal of his time
longing for the past, for a time and place of complete
perfection. Hours of his life were spent sitting beside a
window, gazing as afternoon light shifted, his mind empty
of everyday concerns. He would simply stare – watching
the afternoon fade into dusk – and he would think about
the things he hoped would happen in his life, things he had
once hoped to do. This became an art form for him, this
longing, this constant, poignant reappraisal of everything
that would not, after all, come to pass.

Dismissal manifests variously in Paul's novels, but primarily as refusal
to accept people in their totality (e.g., homophobia); and refusal to take
others seriously (often by teasing, scolding, or belittling them).

Paul juxtaposes the visciousness of *Longing's* gym queens in chapter
five, against the underlying condescension of the straights toward gays in
chapter six, for what they judge to be an inferior way of life. Thus he shows
the reader how the gym queens got so viscious – because their enclave is the
only sure defense against a dismissive if not downright hostile straight
world, which offers them little but the anguish of longing:

> I left the disco and walked the streets, angry and befuddled,
> disgusted. I loved him, but there was nothing doing. What
> could I do? Did it make any difference? I sat in the square
> downtown and stared at the intersection before me, three
> corners – a Taco Bell, a Jack-in-the-Box, and a service
> station. I studied the plastic signs and disparaged the poor
> taste of heterosexual life. I understood what it was that
> drove people to hurl themselves from bridges or to stick
> their heads into ovens after watching something on TV.
> Why should one go on living in a world of breasts and
> plastic?

Of course, the gay ghetto is quite capable of replacing one superficial world
with another, as the protagonist realizes soon enough:

> 'How long is this sort of thing going to go on? This drug
> stuff and this dancing stuff and all this body worship and
> just plain nonsense? Are gay guys ever going to grow up?'
>
> 'That's a fine remark coming from you, Miss Musclething,
> Miss Gym Bunny.'
>
> 'Gym Rat,' I correct him. 'I'm too old to be a bunny, of any
> sort.'

Yet the solution to the *Puer Aeternis* dilemma is not simply to snap one's
fingers and get over it. The Castro and similar neighborhoods in other large
American cities became a gay ghetto not to ensnare those rich enough to
afford them, but initially to protect them from an even greater hostility
without. However, a constant defense gains no ground. In the end, the
inhabitants often turned that hostility inward, via the twin battlements of
bitterness and ennui, in their flight from it. Dismissal is nothing if not a
desire to travel more lightly.

One can certainly understand this desire to feel less burdened, even at
the cost of psychic self-neglect, or the risk of seeming callous in the eyes of
others. One side effect of the AIDS epidemic is something that Paul refers to

twice in *Vertical Intercourse* as "compassion fatigue." As the protagonist observes, "It seems that all things, all this, the epidemic, the dying, the renewal, the hope – they are all experienced in some mode of delayed response. They do catch up, but sometimes it takes weeks, or months, or years."

What *Vertical Intercourse* posits as the antidote to the twin toxicities of the ghetto and the epidemic is not to seek it outside oneself, but within: to develop one's psychic muscle.

> [Thomas] is one of those "real" men, a solid, masculine pillar of strength. He is certainly the epitome of the strong, silent type. I admire this. But I wonder, does he ever lose it, just go nuts, break down and cry or something? It's hard to imagine Thomas in tears, but it wouldn't be a shock to me. My admiration would undoubtedly grow, to see a man who knew the right time and the right moment to shed his tears of grief, of impending loss.
>
> Thinking about Thomas, in this way, I find him very attractive. For a moment, I think of sex with Thomas, as though I could somehow absorb his masculine strength by taking him into myself. And in the next moment, I think that, when Michael dies, perhaps I can have a fling with Thomas. But I banish the thought at once.

I find it refreshing and even inspiring to hear a gay protagonist sorting out his definitions of manhood in an American novel. Thinking of James Bond, he ventures: "coolheaded, even in a crisis, always strong." What *Vertical Intercourse* points out is a self-respect that elicits respect from other men, without even trying. We can locate these qualities in many places within the American psyche (the Boy Scout Law[5] comes to mind), yet how many gay men get to express themselves fully while participating within the institutions that espouse such values, even today?

---

[5] "A Scout is Trustworthy, Loyal, Helpful, Friendly, Courteous, Kind, Obedient, Cheerful, Thrifty, Brave, Clean, and Reverent."

Paul weaves this contemplation of maturity into the novel at many different levels, both subtle and obvious. Clearly his protagonist is preoccupied with it; it even creeps into his grumpy observations on panhandlers, most of whom he would encourage to "grow up:" "He makes me ill. I just want to punch him in his sniveling mouth and tell him to get a job. After all, there's a help wanted sign in the café right where he stands on the corner." Further along, the situation recurs, this time revealing the narrator's growing compassion, and implying a growing maturity:

> One man, a boy really, dressed in retro-punk gear, asks for a dollar. He's so cute that I give him one, and then feel guilty that I have responded to his cuteness, his youthful beauty. Does that make him more worthy than the other beggars? Can I be so superficial as to step over the decrepit hag who slurs the phrase spare change, sir? so that it comes out as spurhansser? Or the obvious tweaker, jittering in front of the bus stop?

Oddly enough, this wisdom on what it takes to be a man is espoused by his female therapist, just as it is often echoed by American society's preeminent women. Thus, when the therapist tells him, "I think you want to be a new, improved version of yourself, and I think that what you want is to be a man," it may bring to mind Judy Garland's advice to "be a first-rate version of yourself, not a second-rate version of somebody else," and perhaps even what Maureen Dowd meant when she proposed that "the moment you settle for less than you deserve, you get even less than you settled for." But of course – who has the perspective to see these men as they are, rather than as they wish to be seen? Their feminine counterpart.

Such strength of character, then, has little to do with physical attributes, which brings us back to *Facing It*. David's transformation occurs when he is forced to acknowledge his past limitations, which shocks him into a new way of seeing his lover Andy's relentless decline:

> 'David!' It was Andy shouting, standing before David and yelling his name. 'David? Snap out of it! Lord knows I

never expected to have to be the strong one at this point ...'
He didn't finish the sentence. David looked up at his lover,
so pale and thin, so dignified as he faced the severity of his
illness. And David realized that he had no right to behave
as he was, to draw away into his own world of selfish cares
and fears.

That he should be the strong one, David said to
himself. That he should be the strong one ... David was
filled with a sudden strength, a vitality borrowed from
Andy's dignity. What had seemed so pathetic only a
moment before – Andy's ghastly gray pallor, his thinning
hair, the hideous lesions on his skin – what had seemed so
pathetic now seemed the inverted symbol of Andy's
strength.

He has stuck it out! David told himself. He's been
strong and faced it at every turn, while I ran and hid in my
fucking press coverage of the damned crisis. It was nothing
new, really, but it was, for David, one of those rare
moments of crystal clarity, when the tragedies, as well as
the victories, of the world somehow fit, a moment when
David saw that what had already been accomplished had
been good, had been real.

He stood and held Andy close, saying nothing. It
was a moment when the whole of Andy's illness became a
true reality, when both of them saw together that they had
weathered a storm, and moreover, that there was more to
come: they accepted Andy's illness. And they gathered their
strength for what was left.

Paul's writing is consistently convincing and emotionally powerful,
despite occasional lapses into cliché (e.g., "weathered a storm," above),
flowery language (in *Longing*, "the relationship blossomed, like a traveler's
vacation planned over weary winter months, finally coming to fruition"),
and stilted dialog (from *Vertical Intercourse:* "You know that from time to
time I indulge a dusky taste," meaning a predilection for sex with black males!).

In general, however, the personality at work behind the fiction does not call
undue attention to itself. Only the resolution to *Longing* rings rather hollow,

with its love story, which arrives late in the novel and feels rushed to an obvious conclusion. Paul's truth here was bleak – not uncommon in the twentieth-century Bildungsroman,[6] even within the gay canon (witness *Massage,* by Henry Flesh) – but it lacked resonance, at least for me. I didn't hear the side of the bleak truth that leads to triumph. Learning hard lessons is more than harsh; it's useful. What is useful is what we take from that experience into the next phase of our lives. It's not all bitter fruit.

At its best, Paul's literary work soars. While rich in descriptive detail, Paul's novelistic style is concise; observe in *Longing* how seamlessly he connects two pivotal and contrasting years at the beginning of the AIDS epidemic:

> How many hours did we eventually spend on those steps? How many months did we sit, as languid as lovers after orgasm, doing nothing but staring out into Castro Street, accepting everything that crossed our vision as utterly believable, including the decrepit old man who scooped up his poodle's poop with his bare hands and deposited it in the garbage bin? We saw everything from those steps, from which we declined every suggestion and every invitation with a haughtiness deserving of Cleopatra on her barge. We saw the world of the Castro change before our eyes: One season we reclined and observed tap-dancing blonds, leathermen, and drag queens, hundreds, even thousands of bare chests sporting hair, tattoos, pierced nipples (left and right), handkerchiefs and bandanas the colors of the rainbow and then some. By the next season we saw fear and caution, green and orange hair, too many police, young men shuffling with canes, an unusual outside-world mix of women and children, and men not clad in tight jeans, and a group of nervous, confused Filipino women wearing masks of

---

[6] German, meaning "novel of formation": that is, a novel of someone's growth from childhood to maturity. In their grappling with the *Puer Aeternis* ("eternal youth") dilemma of many gay men, all of Paul Reed's novels involve elements of the Bildungsroman.

white hankies over their noses and mouths as they stood
awaiting the 24 Divisadero.

Such vignettes also reveal Paul's skill as a chronicler – specifically, of urban
America's rising gay middle class during the latter decades of the twentieth
century. The most truthful tellers of tales make the best historians. No less a
literary light than Richard Labonté has asserted that Paul's importance in the gay-
lit pantheon rests in large part upon this knack for cultural reportage.[7]

Certain elements are universal to any social crisis. Once the sudden
shock of the new subsides, the deeper toll lies in the details. In *Vertical Intercourse,*
a decade and a half after the ordeal depicted in *Facing It,* the protagonist expresses
deep grief over having no mentors or trusted support left to grow old with. He
has seen the epidemic take several waves of friends to early demise, and now
watches in resignation as his friend Michael declines in health. This trajectory
seems to mirror the decline of San Francisco's streets, once pleasurable to stroll,
and now a repository for society's dismissed.

Thus, the slow, grinding collapse of one man's social edifice is quite akin
to what has happened on a grand scale in America during the early years of the
new century: malaise, a dearth of spirit that can lead to a death of spirit. Death is
the ultimate dismissal, as it is no respecter of person, position, or time. The
protagonist's observation that "I've lost most of the witnesses to my life" is
plaintive, and speaks to a larger longing for trusted support within community.

Within the crucible of grief, however, forms a promise of increased
wisdom and maturity, and with it a perspective that, in its highest form, brings
what Paul refers to as "the renewal, the hope."

Such longing is universal to the human condition, and Paul accurately
captures the sense of it. As an incisive chronicler of social upheaval, and an author
skilled at depicting internal states with ringing honesty, his humanism transcends
the spirit of his times. Thus, many may yet find his tone enjoyable, his vision
acute, and his wisdom instructive.

---

[7] Via email with Bill Brent, 24 January 2009.

## Paul T. Rogers
# Saul's Book
Pushcart Press, 1983

## Paul Russell

Even now, 25 years after I first read it, *Saul's Book* retains a certain terrible majesty. I remember buying a copy at a bookstore in Provincetown sometime in the early '80s — though whether on my first rapturous visit to that Sirens' Cove or my second (and last) disastrous one the following summer I can't properly recall. So much of the past is a painful blur. But I still have that original copy — a foxed and dog-eared Penguin paperback (the hardcover original had been published in 1982 by Pushcart Press) on whose lurid cover a young man, cigarette dangling from his mouth, looks wistfully toward a marquee advertising LIVE GAY BURLESK BOLD RASCALS XX MALE MOVIES XX. "A Times Square Hustler's Passionate Love Story" proclaims the book's own tawdry marquee. I think I bought *Saul's Book* because the cover also claimed, in what seemed a forlorn stab at legitimacy, that the novel had won the first annual Editors' Book Award (whatever happened to *that* award, I wonder?). The brief biographical note described the first-time author as "a schoolteacher and a social worker," and assured (reassured?) the curious (skeptical?) reader that "he knows firsthand the people and places found in his book."

What I found within the book's covers was exhilarating. I was in my 20s, a newly minted Ph.D. trying to make my way as a writer and college teacher and out gay man. The world of the novel bore no resemblance at all to my own, and yet I found myself avidly dreaming its prurient dreams, escaping gratefully into its ghastly fantasies with all the swooning surrender of a Victorian virgin allowing herself the excitations of *The Mysteries of Udolpho*. Like all sweet escapes it beckoned me to dangerous places I had always secretly wanted to visit, places where my own carefully managed self might, under controlled circumstances, be allowed to come apart, lose itself completely, be utterly annihilated — if only momentarily and in perfect safety. For the space of its pages, in other words, I could become that doomed young hustler I had always, ridiculously and at the same time profoundly, thought was somehow my most authentic self. For the exemplary citizen, after all, the idea of throwing himself away can be very tempting, as if in revenge for all those years of good behavior, all those suppressed impulses that are the casualties of his outward success (I had my Ph.D. from Cornell, I was teaching at Vassar College).

The 12- and 16- and 20-year-old narrator of *Saul's Book* is a Puerto Rican street hustler and drug addict nicknamed Sinbad the Semen. The setting is ostensibly Times Square and its immediate environs but is really the whole world. Hustling is thus the subject immediately at hand and a metaphor for human relationships generally ("Everybody's running some kind of game"). The same goes with addiction, in tropes that will be immediately familiar to readers of William Burroughs. As Sinbad says,

> Everything around the Square is burnt out, beat up, shit.
> Nowhere. The Square is the pits, the asshole end of the
> world where everything is garbage and nobody gives a fuck
> about anything anymore except themselves and just making
> it through the day, burnt out like the buildings, or as Saul
> says, "It's the isle of the dogs."

Saul is the middle-aged john, seducer, tormentor, alcoholic, teacher and trickster to whom Sinbad is bound by mutual dependence, exploitation, betrayal and perhaps love:

> From the time I was twelve I existed only in relation to Saul,
> so I have nothing that is my own. I lived my life through

him — in him and in spite of him. I found no pleasure in
living for myself. I despaired, I loved, and I survived. But
who is to say whether survival is a virtue or a vice? Who is
to say that he did not force me to survive merely because it
amused him to do so?

In the vicious circles of this world, Saul is at once the dope and the
methadone, damnation and salvation.

*Saul's Book* is, among other things, a *Bildungsroman*. Picking Sinbad
out of the gutter, Saul instructs the hapless, addled kid in the ways of
survival amid the wiles of the world. "Assume the mask appropriate," he
advises. "If you're hustling, then act like a hustler should. Don't let the trick
know how much you hate him. Don't let him know that he, not you, is the
piece of shit. And don't, under any circumstances, flaunt your beautiful
body."

There are three fundamental laws, Saul goes on to say. Understand
them, and you can begin to navigate this absurd world. The first is: "Things
are always as they seem." The second: "Things are never what they seem to
be." Which is right? Sinbad demands to know.

"Both of them."

"But that's impossible!" he exclaims.

"Aha, intelligent, just as I surmised. You have arrived without
coaching at Saul's third law."

The novel is filled with Saul's cryptic apothegms. "If you're absolute
certain about something," he tells Sinbad, "then most certainly you are
wrong." "That's the adventure, to plunge into the pool without knowing
whether or not it is filled." "The only way to be satisfied is to suspend
judgment. Without laughter one soon becomes morally fastidious, unfit for
human company." And perhaps most memorably, "Every act of love
ordains an act of betrayal." And so it does, again and again in these
tumultuous pages, equal parts pornography, philosophy, pederasty and
pedagogy. Dostoevsky looms large here, as well as Nietzsche and Genet,
and by the end perhaps Beckett also, for these two battered figures that

somehow manage to remain standing on the author's bleak stage-set even to
the bitter end, "him, a pot-bellied old faker and me, a washed-out hustler,"
resemble no one so much as Vladimir and Estragon, or perhaps I should
say, were we to know everything about that play, offstage as well as on,
Godot and his boy (and you thought we were just reading about hustlers
and johns, didn't you?).

At a climactic moment (Sinbad is threatening to leap from a window),
Saul taunts him:

> What exempts you from absurdity? ... You abandon
> yourself to vanity by refusing to laugh at it all. You know
> what life owes you? A swift wrench out of the womb into a
> comfortless world, and not a fucking thing else. After that
> you're on your own, no guarantees, me bucko. But you, you
> don't have the balls of a crab louse. If you did, you'd accept
> the challenge, make up your own rules as you went along,
> change the rules of the whole fucking game whenever you
> wanted to, and laugh at all the silly fuckers who complain.
> You know what a man is? A man is a creature who shouts
> from the highest mountain, "Fuck you, God, fuck you and
> get off my back because I can damn well damn you if I want
> to."

All this might seem like so much text-book adolescent existentialism were
Sinbad and Saul not such marvelously realized characters embedded in a
vibrant plot. Young, unloved Sinbad's descent into the underworld of drugs
and prostitution is gripping. Part Two of the novel (it is in five parts) is a
black-farcical tour-de-force account, at once comical and heartbreaking, of a
day in the life of a hustler so drug-impaired that he can barely keep himself
together. Part Four is a suspenseful, noirish episode in the baths as Sinbad,
newly out of prison, comes looking for Saul while the Mafia are at the same
time looking for *him* (or in this novel teeming with sleights-of-hand, perhaps
they are looking for Saul, or perhaps no one is looking for anyone at all).

The epilogue involves not only a spooky séance with a *bruja* but also a final stunning revelation about the scope of Saul's seductions that makes grimly perfect sense.

The novel's narrative voice is compelling as well, shifting as it does among several different modes, sometimes first person, sometimes third, in an attempt to convey the various stages of Sinbad's evolution, ranging from the semiliterate voice of the 12-year-old: "I was just, you know, hanging out. I bought a coke at the hot dog stand and was just standing there, sucking up the last little bit from the bottom where all the ice gets stuck. I didn't even know the guy was standing there until I felt him staring at me;" to the world-weary adult: "In the beginning I suppose there was a God, but he must be too bored by now to care about anyone or anything and certainly too preoccupied to take any note of the chipped plaster saints, the multicolored candles, the fragrance of incense, the dishes of mangoes and bananas and pennies, the gilt prayer cards: in short, all the elaborate equipment of Santeria which my mother assembled." If to some extent we are the words available to us, then Sinbad's moral growth is charted through his gradual acquisition of articulate speech. It is only in prison, he tells us, that he finally discovered the books and words that eventually set him free.

Perhaps what I found most attractive in *Saul's Book* circa 1984 was its searing, let's-see-through-all-of-it brand of truthfulness. Sinbad at one point rages,

> Fuck that house shit. For what? So you can have a wife and kids to feed? So you can fuck the same pussy night after night and look at the same four ugly walls and snotty kids with all their bullshit who are always getting sick? For what? So that one day you can go bananas and chop them all up, or you just give it all up and lay around all day watching TV because you know you're trapped and it's not gonna be any different for your kids either because they're gonna be trapped in the same bullshit too ... Fuck all that work bullshit. You bullshit around all your life and what

> happens? You got nothing to show for it, you go bald, your
> teeth fall out, you catch cancer or some shit and still you
> don't want to croak.

I suppose such lucid nihilism is always bracing, but it seemed particularly
so amid the smarmy pieties of the Reagan/Bush years.

Saul himself is a formidable presence, loathsome and repellent, yet
capable of strange charm and an almost supernatural ability to confound
Sinbad at every turn. He is at once cruel and gentle, monstrous and
benevolent, arbitrary and accommodating, a storm of conflicting aspects —
and Sinbad's vexed relationship with Saul, at first merely that of a desperate
user with his fix, in the end comes to figure for something much grander
and more disquieting: namely, man's perplexed, enraged, disappointed but
necessarily ongoing relationship with God Himself, who is evoked
throughout these pages as an exhausted deity, bored with humanity "but
still petulant enough to play his pranks upon a world long wearied of his
improvisations."

Two years after the publication of *Saul's Book,* Paul T. Rogers was
beaten to death with a plank and his body burned in an incinerator by his
20-year-old adopted son Chris, to whom the book had been dedicated "with
my love and devotion, now and forever," and a 27-year-old drifter who had
been living with the two men in Queens.

One always takes a risk in rereading after many years a novel that has
had a powerful effect on one's younger imagination. Certainly my early
(and long out-of-print) novel *Boys of Life* could not have been written
without its predecessor's cadences haunting my brain. That novel owes a
great debt to Rogers' laser-like focus on all the currency of lies and
hypocrisies that prop up respectability, as well as to his spicy stew of the
prurient and the literary. But I realize I have moved on since then — in large
part, I suppose, simply by growing older. When I am sometimes asked by
readers (and editors) if I might ever again write so fierce a novel as *Boys of
Life,* my answer is invariably no. I couldn't even if I wanted to, and I no
longer want to. I no longer possess the righteous anger of the young and
disenfranchised (if a college professor can ever be disenfranchised, no

matter how unconventional his sexual tastes). For eventually one gets over reality's affront to one's innocence. One grows accustomed to the melancholy fact that we all sell ourselves at one time or another, that whoring is the dirty little secret of our success as human beings. Exposing that obvious truth no longer seems very interesting. One instead becomes rather more curious about the intricate and elaborate lies themselves: for how varied, ingenious, poignant, demented and inspired those charades can be!

I used to want to write only about out gay men, those noble beings who had left behind the camouflage and subterfuge of the closet in order to live their lives openly and proudly. I looked forward to celebrating a world liberated from shadows, where everything was lit by the kindly glare of honesty. Now as I head into the more wistful landscape of middle middle-age, it's the closet and its shadows — the deeper, darker, more well-defended the better — that fascinate me, for I'm increasingly convinced it's only here, amid the cobwebs and mummified mice and the boxes of rejected photographs, the old letters one can no longer bear to read ( I'm thinking of lost friendships, of violated loves, of those irrecoverable visits to Provincetown so many years ago), it is only here, as I say, that the wondrous awful secret of what we have made of ourselves is most likely to be found.

That I've voyaged beyond *Saul's Book* in the last quarter century doesn't in the least discount its vital importance as an early port of call on that very long and continuing journey. Everything about *Saul's Book* is still true. And none of it ever was.

# Patrick Roscoe
## Birthmarks

Penguin, 1990

## Andy Quan

Infatuation involves who you are at the time, who your object of affection is, and who you believe him to be. The reasons can be perfectly evident, or opaque.

In the summer of 1992, I fell into infatuation (I think the word 'love' should be used sparingly and truthfully) with a writer named Patrick Roscoe and his book, *Birthmarks*. Just as one often remembers the small details of affairs, so I recalled the concrete object: the cover, a face of a boy appearing in hot red as if from a tray of photographic chemicals, the print removed before the image was fully developed; the pages were slightly degraded, as I had found the book in a used bookstore after its 1990 publication by Penguin.

Also important to this story is who I was when I read the book: 23-years-old, awkward in knowing how to put my desire for men into practice, taking a break from my university in a small town in Ontario, Canada to work as a host at the Canadian Pavilion at Expo '92 during a hot summer in Seville, Spain. I had written many poems and only one short story and was many years from being a published writer. The main concern in my life was finding out who I was; the main question: would I ever find a place where I belonged, where I was accepted? I had already traveled a lot and wondered whether I'd ever settle down or whether I'd always be travelling.

So it was predictable that I was hooked into *Birthmarks* by the very first story — introduced to a family of nomads by the grandmother who visits them while they're still in Africa. Meeting her grandson years later, she comments on that generation while shaking her head, "All she knew was they switched jobs and countries the way people used to change socks." I predicted, correctly, that this would describe how I would be as well as the people I'd meet.

Roscoe's book veers off into unpredictable directions from there: short fiction divided into four sections, inhabited often by a young man named Richard, Rickie, Reeves; by parents who abandon and children who were abandoned; and by glittery mother figures who may or not have been forgotten movie stars.

One way to piece together various narratives: Patrick Roscoe was one of four children, born in Tanzania to parents who had given up stable work to live in Africa. At the end of their time outside of Canada, for nearly a year, they rolled through Europe in a cramped minivan with little money. His parents were distant, unable to connect with or nourish their children. He leaves home at a young age, takes up prostitution and drugs, is taken under the wing by a woman of faded glamor, and turns tricks and survives in Oregon, California and Toronto with an occasional visit to his mother's home.

Of course, this is only a simplistic sketch. What also drives the book are other stories which may or may not be part of Roscoe's own history. In an early story, a child is kidnapped, beaten and kept in the dark for years. A boy (a runaway?) is taken in by an older hooker. A boy (the same?) lives with a woman – his foster mother? – who dreams of California, where the boy ends up as a sex worker. A pedophile arsonist's plans go wrong. Rickie tells the story of his years in an orphans' home with his best friend Frances (imagined?). The clash of the real and imagined reaches a climax in 'A Child of Man.' At last the narrator makes an emotional connection with another man. His past history and hurts are on full display. He trusts himself little to stay around. He feels a child growing within him. Family members from other stories come into the narrative. The speaker's voice becomes charged with poetry as the child is born. But if any expectations are raised for the narrator to explore an intimate relationship, the very next story confounds with a claustrophobic tale of a hemophiliac harassed by silent phone calls.

The blueprint of the book becomes clearer in the final stories. In 'Rorschachs V,' the author takes on the voice of a psychologist, in charge of a grand experiment, watching himself and describing what he sees. To get at his outcome, it's necessary to "erase the outlines of my personality, blur the contours of my character." He explores who he is both by telling his life history, and by inhabiting other characters. The astonishing 'Dying to Get Home' recounts a writer and a man in an AIDS hospice watching each other through their windows; each takes turns speaking.

It's risky writing. In one story, an omniscient narrator not only describes himself as a separate character, he occasionally addresses the reader. Passages often take off like kites into bouts of poetry and life philosophy, but without details to anchor them to a lived experience. There are long, focused explorations of a single emotional state, with few external descriptions to distract: you are going to live these characters, inside their heads, like it or not.

Still, the book worked for me not only because I could hear the beating heart underneath the narrative flourish, but because the stories created a whole: the loner, poet, psychologist and the self-explorer are the same. In the last story, Roscoe faces his family history and himself without disguise. He tells his brother he needs to finish writing "this damned book." The voice is honest and emotional. He's tough on himself. In telling his story, he is also recounting how memory plays tricks on you. How complex, untrustworthy, and important our stories are. "We will never tell you the true story of our lives." At the end of the book, Roscoe does offer a few slim pages of warmth as the long-alone narrator seems to have found companionship.

With so many other gay books on my shelf at the time – the *Men on Men* collections, Edmund White, David Leavitt – it's odd that this is the one that stuck with me, because it does little exploration of gay identity, which I was obsessed with and went on to explore in my first short story collection. The various Richard incarnations show no allegiance to a gay "community," nor do they take part in any gay "culture." There are mentions of bars and clubs, but they are places the narrator returns from, not where any action takes place. AIDS appears, but at a distance from the narrator. If there is identification here, it is as a sex worker.

Birthmarks was not alone as a book featuring gay narrators who stepped outside of the prototype of middle-class gay white men in New York City or San Francisco. But while I'd read other authors who portrayed tough, hard gay men and boys who lived on the wrong side of the tracks and had thoughts that weren't pretty, Roscoe felt the most authentic. The hallways of hotels where "[o]ne of the other prostitutes or addicts had stolen the bulb," and the narrators who knew "[h]ow to make the most money. How to fix the shots. How to mistrust strangers." seemed not a literary experiment but a smudge of blood on the page.

If Birthmarks is a gay book, it is in the sense of portraying an outsider's experiences, of exploring the self, of being an outlaw. The stories portray a darker existence than I would ever experience. I would never engage in sex work. It would be years before I would recognize the drugs that are mentioned. On rereading the book, I'm still shocked by the story, "My Lover's Touch," where a young boy is imprisoned, kept slave, and beaten brutally, and as a young man searches for this same man who will make him feel this "love" again.

Yet all of these stories are about wanting to connect, and understand one's self. The deep aloneness that seeps out of the pages was what I often felt those years, feeling that everyone else was happier than me, and that I would never quite fit in with the world as it was. I longed for something that would make me feel happy, accepted, perhaps a boy, who would appear, as in "Angie, Short for Angel." "I found you, he would say, for the first time speaking my real name out loud, and that would be the final end of being lost."

It was not only a sense of missing romantic love. There is a disconnection from family, a state of being broken; more than another banal story of a broken heart. Something went wrong long before that, almost at the beginning. The always slightly altered narrator of Birthmarks is detached from his own family, and from nearly everyone. He has a profound sense of difference from the world that for many of us is our first sense of being gay.

Far away from the land of my birth, I was in Spain when I read *Birthmarks*, but reading stories of my birthplace of Vancouver, parts of British Columbia where I'd studied and done outdoors trips; Toronto, the closest city to my university; Europe, where I'd backpacked in the last year; and even the "Third World," though my Ecuador was far away from his Africa.

How strange that the book would end in Seville. Yes, I'd read the author bio at the front of the book that told me Roscoe "currently lives in Seville, Spain" but the timing still shocked me. I was on a bus from Sagres, Portugal, headed back to Seville at the same time that Roscoe's narrative moves to Spain, where he meets his younger brother and recounts his parents in "perpetual motion," dragging their children with them through Africa and Europe, leaving Roscoe's narrators as restless drifters uncertain of their next destination.

That, too, was a similarity I was drawn to, for after my summer in Spain, I was only to live in Canada two more years before returning to Europe for four years and then Australia ever since. Unlike Roscoe, I had no particular reason for feeling such wanderlust but I could feel the strand of rootlessness that runs through the book and let myself become also entangled in it. Another commonality that I hoped to share but could only imagine was that I wanted to be a writer.

Of course, it is what writers do: imagine. He'd published books. He was living the life of a writer. I later heard that he did not give "readings;" instead he performed and recited long parts of his work from memory. More so, there was something about both the author and the book that allowed me to dream that I would have my own books. The contents of *Birthmarks* were not traditional stories, they were pieces of lives, and he was using his own experience as material, crafting and shaping it, and then bringing it out into the world. They showed me how momentary portraits and events can hint at larger stories. You can deal readers a few hands, and they'll play. You don't have to give them the whole deck. Most of all, it was the intensity and fire of his voice, his vulnerability and openness: I wanted to do that. *I could do that.*

Crushes are about fantasy as much as anything and it helped that I was great at living in my head rather than trying to figure out the world as a young gay man. The book didn't have an author photo, but a newspaper interview I'd seen at the time showed a darkly handsome, athletic man in a crouching pose, I believe. I think his arms were bare and he was possibly wearing only underwear. His expression and eyes were intense and I found him beautiful. Meanwhile, the interview and the book told of his work as a prostitute. At the time, sexually naïve, he possessed a sexual wisdom which I wanted. It was a silly young crush, all the more ridiculous because I'd never seen him in the flesh, but I remember an erotic surge at the two clicks as his name ran off of my tongue.

I like to think that there was something more to the attraction that can't quite be pinned down, a connection perhaps, a book's "aura, the ineffable, almost psychic pulse emitted by its pages" as Tom Bissell said on Salon.com, discussing writers we know have great talent, but don't connect with. What is it that attracts us to our favorites? And why do we remember of them what we do — magic talismans we wear around our necks, invisible to all, but still leaving the imprints of their chains?

Rereading *Birthmarks* 14 years later, I wonder about others' opinions of the book. For me, it was like an encounter with a handsome stranger that no one you knew ever met, someone so compelling that you thought about him for years after, but didn't know what your friends would have thought. These days, I've settled down, I've found a home, that old loneliness only seldom returns, but reading the book again, I felt some of the same excitement of long ago. I remembered how it felt to be drifting from place to place and wondering if I'd find somewhere to settle down. I was doubtful at the time that I'd ever feel close to my parents and family – though have since been proved wrong.

I was reminded that it was not only the sadness in his pages that I echoed, but hope and beauty, characters that rose up from the gritty pavement to a whirling, swooping sense of joy: "We are singing, and every wondrous shape we wish for appears like the present stars above."

Douglas Sadownick

# Sacred Lips of the Bronx

St. Martin's, 1994

## Tom Cardamone

In proposing and then editing *The Lost Library: Gay Fiction Rediscovered*, I felt a certain amount of sheepish guilt approaching my own contribution. Having asked so many writers to champion a book they cherish, I never actually finished the one I stated I would write about. Yet there was a very strong reason why I never completed Douglas Sadownick's *Sacred Lips of the Bronx*, one that made me revisit the text and my first months in New York.

Moving to the city in August of 1998 with two bags, my old life in storage and a new one waiting to be discovered, I had purposefully chosen New York City as the place where I could finally be gay. I was coming from such a closeted existence in Florida that when I made my first foray into a gay bar (friends still don't believe this) I was genuinely baffled to find only men and no lesbians. Utopian solidarity aside, as I looked for myself by walking down new streets and into midnight bars, I also foraged the city's bookstores. I knew nothing about gay books or gay authors, only that I have always relied on books to take me *there*, not caring or knowing where I was going, the journey being of more importance than the destination. So I stumbled through the shelves at the Strand; the first two books I bought were filled with cold sex and predictable prostitutes giving their bodies to everyone, their hearts to none. I was turned off.

I burned through several couches and friendships before landing in Brooklyn, renting an unfurnished room from a pregnant woman with a baby who didn't necessarily want me there but needed my four hundred bucks a month. I slept in a sleeping bag on the bare floor, temped a variety of strange jobs in different neighborhoods and absolutely marveled as the leaves changed; growing up in Florida, I had never experienced the seasons and was excited by the prospect of snow. The Central Library of Brooklyn, an Art Deco masterpiece designed to resemble an open book, was across the street and allowed me to continue my journey. Within this secular temple I hit pay dirt. It's interesting how we can identify the queer essence of a text by the poetry of the title, the cover art which might not communicate obviously gay content with the now typical torso but nonetheless it draws our eyes to it. My radar was flickering to life. I read most of Edmund White's *A Boy's Own Story* while standing in the stacks. Much later I intuited that Mark Merlis has something to tell me as well. Douglas Sadownick's *Sacred Lips of the Bronx* was an early find. Something about it grabbed my attention. Enough so that, riffling through a few pages, I put it back on the library shelf and bought the remaindered hardback at the Strand. I knew there was something here to covet.

The story was mildly complicated; chapters alternated between the main character Mike Kaplan's gay journalist adult life in Los Angeles and vignettes from his teen years growing up within a shrinking Jewish neighborhood in the Bronx. I skipped the contemporary chapters with their ominous politics and difficult relationships and devoured only those of his youth. The young Mike's emerging sexuality seems to mirror the ethnic changes within the Bronx of his boyhood; the Puerto Ricans moving into the neighborhood threaten his cultural roots in the same way his gay desire subverts the identity his faith and family expect of him. He is attracted to shirtless, menacing boys. The social circus of high school teaches him to camouflage his desires. But one boy, Hector, sees through his facade. I read and re-read certain passages, hungry to capture for myself what I found on the page.

Hector approached and nervously put his lips on mine. So sudden. I had never kissed a guy I knew. I had kissed girls, male strangers who were older than me and hungered for my saliva – like it was a drug. To lock lips with a boy you had just talked to? To press up against a boy who acted as if he knew and loved your mother? To want to devour breathless moans like they were M&Ms with someone you had just taken the bus with? I felt self-conscious. Hector put his tongue on my lips. The wet spasm: it was like receiving a knock on the head or a whiff of airplane glue or a sudden and uncalled-for football pass. I broke free.

'Hey, wassup?'

I fell onto the bed, like a person collapsing into himself after a dirty joke. I needed a moment to think. Hector folded his thin, soft-skinned body onto mine, confused.

'I'm not sure,' I said.

'Not sure of what?'

'Not sure of I don't know what.'

Lips found mine and tried to drum out the doubt. But he couldn't. Layers and layers of hungers and hesitations got fused together like an elixir with each touch – and from a buzz or a drone I thought I felt in the air. I had questions: What if your mother comes home? Do you believe in God? Will you go away? Is there a membership to this club? But he wasn't interested in questions. He kissed me like he had a right to; I thought I was going to die.

Reading that over and over I knew I was going to live.

At the time this book clarified an important aspect of my budding existence as a young gay man. "Gay" didn't define the type of sex I was after, but the type of love I required and wanted to give. But I had only read half of the novel. The contemporary chapters I couldn't read represented the reality I still did not want to face. And this was absolute, so much so that when a new friend to whom I had praised the book passed me a copy of Douglas Sadownick's nonfiction follow-up, *Sex between Men: An Intimate History of the Sex Lives of Gay Men Postwar to Present*, abandoned by one of a succession of roommates, I quickly shelved it. The cover, half of a pair of naked men, one shamefully covering his face while clutching the genitals of the other, who in turn reaches to conceal his compatriot's cock as well — doubly obscured by the outsized and reddened "sex" of the title — frankly embarrassed me. I didn't want to dissect sex, know our history or in any way examine life. I was too busy chasing overdue kisses. I felt that my previous life had been a dishonest waste, that I had lived past the opportunity to experience young love; so I rushed to fill every moment, dance to every song. I was too madly busy for introspection, politics, and even, sometimes, condoms; they represented caution, the opposite of the natural youthfulness and freedom I was desperately looking to recapture. I used my next move as an excuse to dump *Sex Between Men* at Housing Works Used Bookstore and Café, a bookstore in SoHo that, at the time, I considered more a convenient downtown bathroom stop than a place to browse.

I continued to feverishly re-read favorite sections of *Sacred Lips of the Bronx*. I loved the furtive smooching, the proud outbursts of public handholding as Mike and Hector became a secret but very real couple. They went on dates and then they went on double dates with girls to keep their cover. They met one another's parents. They explored sex with an ingénue earnestness I wanted to replicate. When I went to work, I would hide the book in the bottom of my sleeping bag because I didn't want my roommate to know I was gay. I was thrilled by the temporary power we instill a "secret" with –- to better make it ours, to reverse shame from a noose to a whip. At night I would push it further down with my toes, conspiratorially considering the book contraband.

How a decade can change everything. I shed the sleeping bag and got my own place and a straight, male roommate (a Puerto Rican from the

Bronx no less) who sussed out my sexuality with a shrug. I soon had too many gay novels to hide around the apartment and started putting them on shelves. The regret toward those years in the closet faded (the crowded pace of New York City is most unsuitable for the retention of such bulky grudges). One night, with tears burning my cheeks during the last act of *The Normal Heart*, Larry Kramer's seminal drama about the onslaught of AIDS, I had a harsh, working epiphany: I had *always* been in the audience. So I started volunteering at the aforementioned Housing Works Bookstore, a nonprofit benefiting the homeless with HIV and AIDS. My writing strengthened. The necessity of this book formed.

And so I re-read *Sacred Lips of the Bronx*, now in full; ten years hadn't rubbed away any magic from the book; the urban prose popped, the few bits that flagged, like the reoccurring ghost of Mike's grandmother, did little to hinder my initial assessment that the novel is a good, solid work. But the fever of coming out had subsided; Jewish faith and folklore were more central to the book than I remembered, how the constancy of family made burgeoning sexuality all the more exacting. I'd forgotten Mike had a brother whose social rebellion provided a cover for Mike's sexual one. I'd forgotten that Hector had a terrible secret. The chapters which concerned the older Mike, grappling with the politics of a modern plague and a cheating lover, still seemed to interrupt the narrative rather than complement it, but here I sensed a reality the author was facing and I was learning: lost love weighs heavier than lost time; as the older version of Mike thinks he sees Hector in a park, he is really straining for a simpler age, when his love was more real. I closed the book aware of the character's mistake. When you want something as powerful and necessary as love, you don't reach back, you reach forward.

2009: one of my New Year's resolutions was to join facebook (I keep my resolutions easy). My boyfriend's crazy about the site and I figured it was a great way to catch up with old friends. Douglas Sadownick's name popped up early on in the *People You May Know* function. So of course I contacted him and learned that he teaches at Antioch University and is the Director of the first LGBT specialization in Clinical Psychology in the country. In researching this essay I located a New York Times article from 1994: *Coping: Growing up Gay in the Heart of the Bronx*, a short profile of the author in the year his novel was published. The article contained a surprising confession: Hector didn't exist. While Mike found first love in the Bronx, in real life the young Sadownick never repeated any of his rendezvous with the boys he met on the Grand Concourse. "Hector in the book was a way for me to redeem what I see now as a lot of missed opportunities."

How discourteous to contradict an author's interpretations concerning his book, much less his own life, but Sadownick made that observation while still pretty young; the longing and unusual jealousy that *Sacred Lips of the Bronx* inspired dissipated once I kissed the right boy. What I had considered "missed opportunities" were simply the necessary preparations for the experiences that ended up counting the most. That rush to recapture what I had mistakenly considered lost had nearly cost me everything. The book at the bottom of my sleeping bag was in no way illicit but a rather splendid and sturdy diving board.

# Glenway Wescott

# The Apple of the Eye

Dial Press, 1924

## Jerry Rosco

Even as a very young man Glenway Wescott (1901-1987) spoke as beautifully as he wrote. He was a distinguished writer and personality — the *New York Times* remembered him as "one of the last of the major expatriate American writers who lived in France in the 1920's and 30's." Three of his four novels would be reprinted over the decades. When he stopped writing fiction, he remained a fine essayist and critic, and his posthumous *Continual Lessons* (1992) is one of the great gay journals. Syndicated columnist Liz Smith remembers him as a wonderful New York social figure. All this reflects who he was. But a big part of his story is in his first novel, the one that made his career possible, the one that ought to come back in print.

When *The Apple of the Eye* (1924) appeared to universal good reviews, 23-year-old Wescott's publisher gave him a small advance toward another novel. A generous female patron who loved the book gave him more — enough for Wescott and his lover Monroe Wheeler to join the expatriate writers in France. His second novel, *The Grandmothers* (1927), was a huge success and for a short time he was more famous than Ernest Hemingway and F. Scott Fitzgerald. Later, he would remain a respected literary figure, with recurring moments of celebrity in the 1940s and 1960s, and he was blessed with a long and fortunate life. But it all began with a humble start.

A regional novel of the Midwest, *The Apple of the Eye* is written in beautiful lyrical prose, but it's no dreamy Romantic story of the American heartland. Instead, it's about the impoverished early-century midwest that Wescott knew on his father's poor Wisconsin farm. It's about the oppression of puritanism, which seems familiar to us nearly a century later. It's about the cruelty of nature no less than its beauty. And the novel's autobiographical character, Dan, is a farmboy obviously in love with a young farmhand who is dating his cousin.

All of the autobiographical material in the novel becomes obvious, but how Wescott came to put it into a novel is part of the story. He was first known as a poet. At age 16, he made it from Kewaskum, Wisconsin farm country to the University of Chicago on a scholarship. He was boarded in an attic room by distant relatives and had a weekly allowance of $3.50. Having barely gotten over a high school romance with a straight boy, he was worried about his sexuality, and intimidated by a large sprawling campus of athletes and more affluent students. But he was intimidating too. His professors couldn't believe the amount of reading he had done, especially of contemporary playwrights worldwide. His literature teachers dealt with the teenager as a grad student. More importantly, he saw a notice one day that the campus Poetry Club was taking applications for new members. He wrote his first poems and submitted them. "It was just a trick," he said. Sure, so is all writing of every kind. The impressive Poetry Club members were impressed. They included the important Imagist poet and critic Yvor Winters; his future wife, novelist Janet Lewis; Southern novelist Elizabeth Madox Roberts, 20 years their elder; and others. Janet Lewis remembered that when they heard Glenway's speaking voice, they made him president, and at meetings he would read their poems aloud. But Winters was the real leader and a great influence.

Wescott nearly died from the Spanish Influenza of 1918. He dropped out of college but stayed connected with the Chicago poetry group, which included *Poetry* magazine editor Harriet Monroe, and patron Harriet

Moody (widow of poet William Vaughan Moody), and he met major poets
of the day. His own poems and book reviews began appearing in all the
literary journals, and his new (lifelong) lover Monroe Wheeler printed a
fancy chapbook of his poetry, *The Bitterns*. Wallace Stevens wrote, "It's
difficult to make poetry as sophisticated as this fly, but you certainly make it
tremble and shake."

In his early 20s, Wescott didn't know which direction his talent
would take him, but he was already making the transition from poet to
prose writer. His long story "Bad Han" would become the opening five
chapters of his first novel. The character Hannah Madoc was based on a real
woman from his early Wisconsin years. Because the woman had worked in
a bar and been a prostitute, she was an outcast in the farm community. But
Wescott's mother Grace, with a different notion of Christianity, was friendly
and kind to her. And the woman became a kind of saint, living alone,
tending to and healing farm animals, smoking a pipe, learning the power of
herbs, and increasingly working as an extra hand, a midwife and a healer
for the very people who condemned her. In the words of Wescott's story,
"To her simple eye nothing was degrading, nothing evil; everything formed
a single difficult pure coil — moralless and pure. So she spoke more plainly
and more strongly than other men and women, the faultless, the
prosperous, or the strong."

In "Bad Han," Hannah became old and eccentric in middle age.
"Solitude in the form of anguish did not exist now; and sometimes the face
of her lost boy lover appeared in her dreams." In fact, the lost boy lover was
Jule Bier, now a middle-aged farmer who lived with his wife and daughter
nearby. In their youth, Jule had loved Hannah but her bad reputation in the
Christian community was a problem and he married another. Yet, many
years later, Jule was kind to Hannah. Sometimes he'd sit on her porch and
they'd talk quietly or just look out at the fields and marshlands. Though she
had her little farmhouse, sometimes she would stay all night in the woods
and fields, or would sleep in the barn. "Once she found a herd of cattle on
the brow of a hill, and lay down among them." Finally, she had an accident
and the country doctor knew that with her broken hip, broken leg and bad

heart, nothing could be done. She took his hand to say goodbye. Her bed was pushed near a window so she could look outdoors to the changing fall colors. And the man who had been her only friend, Jule, came to share her last two days, lifting her, feeding her, giving her morphine.

> Jule sat close to Hannah. Their eyes, when they did not run
> out over the marsh, were fixed upon each other; his gaze
> abstract, as if it gleaned then from her sunken unlighted
> face her wisdom and her peace; the dying woman's wistful
> and proud, who entrusted her existence, from that moment,
> to his thought.

By the time "Bad Han" was published in the January and February 1924 issues of *The Dial*, Wescott had continued writing fiction until he had a fully-drafted novel, as well as some short stories. He had moved east with Monroe Wheeler and was living in Greenwich Village in a front, second-floor apartment at 17 Christopher Street. The building is still there, next to the Oscar Wilde Bookshop. Their neighbor at nearby 14 Saint Luke's Place, Marianne Moore, became a lifelong friend.

When the new book division of Dial Press published Wescott's first novel that fall, novelist Sinclair Lewis offered the book jacket blurb: "I have finished with the greatest delight *The Apple of the Eye*. It seems to me to have something curiously like genius." Dozens of glowing reviews followed. So did success and a decade of glamorous life in France.

What Wescott remembered was that Marianne Moore, who was editing *The Dial* magazine then, thought the novel shouldn't be published. She thought Glenway should be paid for it — he and Monroe needed the money — but that the novel's sexual content would ruin his budding career as a poet and critic. In fact, the publisher's lawyers had suggested many deletions on the final proofs. And Wescott, seriously sick with the mumps in his little apartment, put all the deletions back into the text. He had earlier edited out some overblown romantic passages, but even in his early 20s he had a writer's sense of what should stay.

There had been sexual content in the "Bad Han" chapters, but what followed went further. "Rosalia," the five chapters of Part Two, is named for Jule Bier's teenage daughter. But Jule also had a teenage nephew, Dan Strane, who lived on a nearby farm. Dan preferred visiting and helping out at his Uncle Jule's farm, because his own father had no use for him. His father considered Dan a "moody, indolent creature — like a girl he thought — clinging to his mother, sarcastic and sensitive, a bundle of nerves." Gaydar, anyone? Dan Strane was Wescott's autobiographical character.

In fact, I should say here that I knew Wescott in his last years, wrote essays about his work and life, and eventually completed his biography (*Glenway Wescott Personally*, 2002). That included a decade of research visits to the Beinecke Library (Yale) and the Berg Collection (NY Public Library). But when Glenway was still around, I interviewed him and sometimes just asked a stray question that I thought was important. In his more famous works that followed, his autobiographical character was always Alwyn Tower. Although the answer was obvious, I once asked what no one else had: "Isn't Dan Strane actually Alwyn Tower?" Glenway just said, "Of course."

Dan's early century schoolmates were rough farmboys, many of them German, and to them "his careful polite speech seemed an affectation." One day, Dan saw the playground empty and when he looked in the woodshed, "all the boys were in there in a compact circle facing the center — an impenetrable mass of little backs, rigid with interest in something unseen." Poor Marianne Moore — she was a great poet, but she couldn't imagine any place in literature for a schoolboy circle jerk!

Rejected by his father and his schoolmates, Dan also felt oppressed by stifling Puritanism. He was sensual but knew nothing of sex. Then Mike Byron appeared. When Jule hired the 25-year-old farmhand, Dan was attracted to him and felt liberated by his worldliness. Mike had some experience in college and working for a newspaper. He taught Dan the facts of life. And when Dan was spouting some confused nonsense about Christian purity and duty, he was amazed when Mike replied, "In my opinion, everything is pure, everything is good that doesn't hurt somebody else. Life is dull enough if we have all the fun there is."

What develops from there is Mike's attraction for Dan's pretty cousin Rosalia and the problems that causes. Dan is a little young to understand his own sexual feelings, but for him nothing could be more profound than a handsome, older male friend who makes him feel positive about himself and gives him the vision of a bigger, freer world. With his use of lyrical prose and sensitive wordplay, Wescott takes the reader to the edge of forbidden territory for a mainstream writer of that time — sensual feelings, a wet dream, masturbation, and intercourse. And for Dan there isn't jealousy but a feeling of freedom, as when he sees Mike kissing his cousin: "The boy's heart stopped for a beat. A pang shot through him. Following it, there surged a tumultuous happiness. He was no longer shut out; life had opened and let him in."

However, the dreamy, triangular love of the three young people in summer could not last in a culture of sexual repression. Rosalia's mother would never approve of Mike courting her daughter. Uncle Jule, still inspired by the lost Hannah, had a talk with Mike, and told him his relationship with his daughter would cause problems — but he would support him. But that was enough to scare off Mike. Dan was shocked one day when his uncle said that his farmhand had given notice.

Days later, when they met at night to say goodbye, Mike told Dan that his leaving was the best thing for Rosalia. Dan suspected, and others had rumored, that Rosalia would meet him later in Milwaukee and they'd marry. Mike also knew Dan loved him, and threw his arm around him. "Don't cry, Dannie. I'll see you again. We'll meet somewhere." Mike did his best to cheer up the boy, but Dan's tears returned. Finally: "In their short, brusque kiss there was an implication of something like despair."

Rosalia, meanwhile, was devastated, and not just in the healthy, first-love, broken-hearted way that Dan was. The girl was totally consumed by her mother's fierce, unforgiving brand of Christianity. She not only thought that Mike had left her, she imagined that he had left her pregnant. Her behavior became strange, and she disappeared. The rumors of the young couple eloping surfaced, and the parents were upset but at least believed that their daughter was safe.

The last third of the novel, "Dan Alone," has autobiographical material drawn from Wescott's problems with his father. Dan's self-education and his determination to leave finally bring him to the emotional day when he leaves his parent's farm for the life that awaits him. But before that, the tragedy plays out. In early spring, a neighbor comes to tell Jule and Dan that he has found Rosalia's body in the marshlands, in the bad part of the swamp where it was dangerous to walk. Jule swore them to secrecy; Rosalia's mother must never know. They set out to the swamp and buried her in a rise of ground under a tree. The father's face turned grey. "He sank upon a great protuberant root, and covered his face with his hands."

The tragedy and the lessons end on a hopeful note, with Dan boarding a train for Madison, the great liberal city of the Midwest — just as it is a century later. More than the story, the genius of the book is in its poetic language, its interwoven battle of humanism versus puritanism, and in the omnipresent force of nature. In more ways than can be described in a short essay, nature itself is at the core of the farmers' lives: "The April spring being an illusion of light, the setting sun left the farms clasped in a hand of darkness and wet ominous air." *The Apple of the Eye* was a remarkable first novel — by a 23-year-old.

What followed was early fame. While writing his second novel in France, Wescott was well paid for some short stories. An agent got Harper & Brothers to buy the rights to *The Apple of the Eye* along with the next novel. In 1926, new editions of *The Apple* were released by Harper and the British publisher Butterworth. In 1927, *The Grandmothers* was nothing less than the great American novel — in a chronicle-style format that became a model for writers. The ($10,000) Harper Prize-winning novel went through 26 printings in six months, and saw many future editions. Readers today can easily recognize half a dozen gay characters. A book of short stories, *Goodbye, Wisconsin* (1928), followed.

After less successful nonfiction works, and then a fallow period in America, Wescott wrote *A Visit to Priapus* (drafted 1938), a very explicit long story about a gay writer who visits an extremely well-endowed artist in Maine. Unpublished in his lifetime, it was printed as a chapbook in 1995 and then in the 2004 anthology, *The New Penguin Book of Gay Short Stories*. The importance of *Priapus* is that it gave Wescott the "voice" for what would be nothing less than one of the great short novels in English, *The Pilgrim Hawk* (1940). Praised by everyone from Christopher Isherwood to Susan Sontag, this little masterpiece is the dry champagne peak of Wescott's career. Like *The Grandmothers*, it was reprinted many times, including foreign translations, and is part of the Dell anthology, *Six Great Modern Short Novels*. And in 1945, his World War II novel *Apartment in Athens* was a Book of the Month Club bestseller, and was also republished in foreign editions.

The literary reviews and essays and the gorgeous personal essays of Wescott's late career are worth remembering. His lover Monroe Wheeler was a world-traveling curator and innovative director of publications for the Museum of Modern Art. Together, they hosted a salon at their Manhattan apartment for a Who's Who of writers, artists and celebrities. They also had a country home called Haymeadows at the western New Jersey farm of Wescott's accomplished brother and wealthy sister-in-law.

It was a great life, complete with a succession of younger lovers. Richard Hall once mocked that life in a short story in his *Fidelities* collection. But years later Hall told a mutual friend, John Gilgun, that the story was inspired by his brief glimpse, as a young writer, of a Wheeler/Wescott social event — and he respected others' perspectives. The fact is that Wescott spent four decades at the American Academy of Arts and Letters getting grants and awards for many young writers — and neglected older ones.

While rereading *The Apple of the Eye*, I didn't want to handle my Dial Press first edition and used the 1926 Harper book and a 1935 Grosset and Dunlap edition. It's annoying when readers make notes and underscores in a book, but in my 1926 copy, someone with small, sharp-pencil script, "Leonard Amater, 1927," wrote a number of perceptive remarks. Among them, he wrote at the start of Part Two: "The following four chapters are equal to anything in American literature. I think it reaches a higher level than Crane, to whom Wescott has been compared." At the chapter "Around the Dead," he commented on the fine-line sensitivity of Wescott's lyrical skills: "This is a magnificent chapter. There is poetry in it as there is realism, and understanding of peoples' hearts."

Over the last decade, Wescott's other three novels (especially *The Pilgrim Hawk*) have appeared in new English and foreign editions — German, French, Italian, Greek, Spanish and Portuguese. *The Grandmothers* and *The Pilgrim Hawk* are masterworks, and *Apartment in Athens* holds up as one of the best World War II novels. *The Apple of the Eye* doesn't rank with them, but it should be reprinted for two reasons: It's a classic regional novel of the Midwest, and it's the first novel of a notable author. That doesn't require a big mainstream release, but it's enough reason for it to be in print.

I've been slowly putting together a last volume of Wescott journals, and recently I found a few of Glenway's late comments on his first novel. He called it "one of the crossroads of my entire life." And he wrote to editor Robert Phelps, "I spent an hour reading *The Apple of the Eye* — I don't suppose I have done so for twenty years…I felt proud of the descriptive passages, like mediaeval illuminations or Eastern enamel."

# George Whitmore
# Nebraska

Grove Press, 1987

## Victor Bumbalo

"You would never listen to me and now look what happened!" Mama fainted dead away. "The next thing I knew, I woke up with my leg gone." So begins George Whitmore's stunning novel, *Nebraska*. The time is 1956. It is summer, and Craig, age 12, is on the "sleeping porch" recovering from the accident that took his leg. He lives with this mother, who works supporting her family at "Monkey Wards," and his two teenage sisters. A while back, Craig's alcoholic dad left Lincoln and took a job in St. Louis for "good money." He wasn't missed — he sent money. Then one day he returns and announces that he wants to be free. He leaves, and no more money ever arrives. Most of the family pretends he's dead. But he isn't.

Craig's mama, referring to her son's accident, comments, "We're going to be paying off the bills for the rest of our lives. . . . Now I guess we won't have to buy that bike. . . ."

Craig spends the summer watching TV and doing puzzles books. And then everything in this household changes. Craig's Uncle Wayne, recently discharged from the Navy, comes home.

Uncle Wayne is like a movie star. "A postcard from Uncle Wayne was a holy relic." He brings the marvel of the outside world to this struggling, working-class family and especially the boy who's confined to bed.

Uncle Wayne opens Craig's life to the birth of those millions of feelings that commence with our adolescence. It is that extraordinary, restless, summer of youth. A summer filled with yearnings, fears, loneliness and sudden erections.

Uncle Wayne is a wonder to his nephew. The boy develops a crush on his uncle that is beyond sexual. It's the crush that awakens Craig to life.

Uncle Wayne tells his family that he is not going to be in Nebraska for long. He's waiting for his great Navy buddy, known as the Chief, to send for him. They are going to go into business together, opening a garage in California. The Chief seems as magical to Craig as California. The friendship between these two men seems ideal, uncorrupted and trusting; the stuff that dreams are made of. The kind of dreams that lodge themselves in a 12-year-old boy and will haunt him for the rest of his life.

Uncle Wayne talks to the Chief monthly, but the summons to California never seems to come. His "wait" extends as the dream of California fades. He takes a job on line at Chicks, the local factory, and starts drinking heavily. This is a different Uncle Wayne, and a door seems to be closing on Craig's imagined escape from his claustrophobic life.

One night, Craig's friend Wesley sleeps over. Wesley tells Craig about being in the Scouts. He asks to feel Craig's stump and Craig lets him. Craig asks Wesley if he could feel Wesley's prick. He tries to convince Wesley that everybody does it. Boy Scouts do it. He fibs and tells his friend that his Uncle Wayne told him that they even do it in the Navy. After all, they have to get rid of their "jizz."

"Uncle Wayne told me, Wesley. He even showed me how."

Wesley is not buying it.

The fib takes on a life of its own.

Sometime later Uncle Wayne is arrested with seven other men for "lewd and lascivious behavior at the municipal bus depot." Uncle Wayne pleads guilty. His service record is revealed. Wesley's father comes forward, and Uncle Wayne is gone.

1957. Craig's crazed dad appears . . . now sober, but with newfound religious fervor running rampant through his veins. He kidnaps his son and takes him on a horrific journey through a Nebraska blizzard. He believes he is saving his son from Uncle Wayne and Craig's mother. He is going to take his son to Denver for a new life together. His vision of the perfect boy's life for the perfect boy filled with erector sets, Lincoln Logs, Monopoly and Chinese Checkers.

One night they stop in a cheap, cold cabin. That night Craig tries to escape. His father finds him and the nightmare continues. Reality slips away in the snow. Both are raving when they arrive in Denver.

The last section of the novel takes place in 1969. Craig is now 25. His life is as broken as the lives of the Chief and Uncle Wayne. Craig sets out for California to find them. Will there be redemption, forgiveness? And if there is, what action can cause it to occur? The action Craig takes is brave, loving and totally unexpected.

What a pleasure to go back to this gem of a novel. Its language is direct, spare and poetic. Sentences and dialogue will haunt the reader, as will off-hand observations.

"When I was in the hospital, I heard the nurses say about a little girl who died …'They opened up that little tyke and found such a tumor there she must have been in terrible pain all her life. But you see she didn't never know it. She must of thought This is life.'"

Within the first two pages, most of the characters, the tone and setting are thoroughly in place. No time is wasted.

George was one of my dearest friends. We had known each other since our days at Bennington College. I have to refer to him as "George." To call him Whitmore may seem more respectful, but for me it's too off-putting. It distances him further from my memory. And the further that distance, the more of me that dies.

George was sophisticated, political, urbane, and preferred female novelists. He was a pacifist. In lieu of military service during the Vietnam War he worked at Planned Parenthood in New York. But this novel reveals the secret cowboy in him. This is an intimate work. Not biographical, but depicting a world that George was very familiar with. There is never a moment of condescension in his view of this working-class family. George was born in Denver, Colorado, but parts of his family came from Nebraska and were indeed cowboys. As I was reading *Nebraska*, I wondered what George would have thought of Cormac McCarthy's *All the Pretty Horses* and

what McCarthy would think of *Nebraska*. Both their young men share a
similar dark and lonely vision.

George wrote thoughtfully about men, both gay and straight.
*Nebraska* is aggressive, masculine and muscular. This novel will not age. It
stirs the senses in many ways. One can smell the summer nights as well as
Craig's youth. The dankness of the motel room where Craig's father abuses
him creeps into your bones.

George wrote *Nebraska* first as a play, but the play didn't work — too
much of the major action took place off stage. George tried to solve the
problem, but after many drafts, he still was not happy with the play. George
and I would share our work with each other. In a discussion we had about
the play, we came to the conclusion that it might be a novel. George applied
and was accepted at the MacDowell Colony. Off he went to that wonderful
artists' haven in New Hampshire. Five and a half weeks later he handed me
a copy of *Nebraska*, the novel. George wrote quickly and was astonishingly
precise. This can be attributed to his experience as a journalist and the poet
that was an integral part of his being.

The novel was published by Grove Press and garnered many well-
deserved excellent reviews. *Vogue* called it "lean, uncompromising." *Kirkus
Reviews* said, "A lyrical, evocative novel . . . A tough, economical, and finally
haunting book." *Village Voice*: "*Nebraska* is *Huckleberry Finn* gone awry. . . .
Wonderful."

George was living with AIDS. It should be remembered that he
sued the Northern Dispensary, a Greenwich Village clinic, after it refused to
treat him because he had AIDS. The clinic was fined $47,000 by the City's
Human Rights Commission. It closed.

After the book party for *Nebraska*, a group of us went to a
restaurant. George, always a great looker, was in a wonderful mood and
looking quite handsome. He was surrounded by his friends and his dear
lover, Michael Canter. I was unusually quiet. At one point George turned to
me and asked, "What's wrong with you?" I lied and told him that I was fine.
George could read me, and I could tell if I continued to sit there withdrawn,
he would get really pissed. So I started to yak it up, but didn't do a very

good job of acting. I couldn't stop myself from foreseeing what was going to happen to my friend. We'd seen too many friends in hospitals and sat together at too many of their funerals. That night I was down that road, somewhere in the future. And in doing so, I was ruining that most special moment — mainly for myself. I was missing the opportunity to bathe in the love and success of a close friend who was such a part of me. George, wiser than I was, did not ruin that night for himself.

*Nebraska* was George's second book. His first was *The Confessions of Danny Slocum*. This book is part novel, part autobiography and a totally hilarious and penetrating look at gay life in the late 1970s. After *Nebraska* George went on to write *Someone Was Here: Profiles in the AIDS Epidemic*, a compassionate, harrowing and beautiful book. Later he would write about his own experience as an AIDS patient. That article became a cover story for *The New York Times Magazine*.

In his life, he loved order, quiet, loyalty and the company of his friends. In his work he was a true daredevil.

I miss the brave books I'm sure he would have written. But I miss his humor and his penetrating smile more. I miss his phone calls. The missing never stops. George died in 1989, two years after *Nebraska* was published and a year after *Someone Was Here.* He was 43 years old.

# Donald Windham
# **Two People**

Coward-McCann, 1965

## Philip Gambone

I first came to know of Donald Windham through his association with the great gay American playwright Tennessee Williams, who was Windham's friend and literary mentor for 25 years. In 1977, Windham published the correspondence he had received from "10," as Williams often signed his letters, under the title *Tennessee Williams' Letters to Donald Windham: 1940-1965*, a book I devoured. I had come to love Williams' plays and to admire his courageous portrayal of shocking, taboo subject matter, especially homosexuality. As an aspiring writer still in his 20s, I combed those letters (Windham's replies were not included) looking for the courage to write my own stories, looking for tips on how to be half as fabulous a gay man as Williams was, looking for clues as to how to cultivate a literary friendship such as the one he and Windham had.

The letters were such fun to read. I loved Williams' campy patois, the coded language, the gossipy news: "The 'crowd' here [Provincetown, 1940] is dominated by a platinum blond Hollywood belle named Doug and a bull-dyke named Wanda who is a well-known writer under a male pen-name." I loved the outrageous honesty: "There are only two times in this world when I am happy and selfless and pure. One is when I jack off on paper and the other when I empty all the fretfulness of desire on a young male body." Loved, loved, loved Williams' descriptions of writing *The Glass Menagerie*, the rehearsals, the subsequent triumphs, and the later flops. The

205

letters were peppered with famous names, witty aperçus, and candid confessions of sexual shenanigans.

Windham and Williams had met in New York in January, 1940. Windham, then 19 and "practically penniless," had recently fled Atlanta with his 21-year-old boyfriend. They were living in a single furnished room. The romance of all that delighted me. As I read the letters, Windham seemed like the writer-in-training and literary acolyte I longed to be. Nevertheless, I didn't feel any strong desire to delve into his novels. Perhaps that's because Windham's books were hard to find, mostly out of print; or perhaps because, in the last years of the 70s, newer gay voices — Andrew Holleran, Ed White, Joseph Hansen, Larry Kramer, Armistead Maupin — had begun to appear. Whatever the reason, it was 30 years later that I finally got around to reading one of Donald Windham's novels. It happened, really, quite by chance.

One day, browsing in one of my favorite used bookstores in downtown Boston, I came across a copy of Windham's novel (his third, it turns out), *Two People*. I might have easily passed it by but for the author's name, which triggered happy memories of reading the Williams-Windham correspondence so many years before. I pulled it off the shelf. The dust jacket — a sketch of the Spanish Steps in Rome, a few people lolling about — seemed innocuous, even old fashioned. And the title, such a generic one, seemed innocuous as well, promising little more than a safe plot, a pleasant read. But the book — its heft, its sheer physicality —piqued my curiosity. It was an immaculate copy, not a mark or tear, and the pages, creamy white, had the soft, thick, luxurious texture that hardback paper used to have. I checked the publication date: 1965. A quick glance at the dust jacket blurb — "The story of an American man and an Italian boy in Rome . . . a situation that another author might have made melodramatic or sensational" — clinched it. Code for a gay story! That night, curled up in bed, I began to read.

In the opening sentences, Forrest, the American, who is hanging on in Rome after his wife has left him, picks up a stray newspaper and reads that several people have jumped from bridges into the Tiber. Their intention, he soon realizes, was "diversion, not suicide," just the Roman way of celebrating the New Year. This moment, which might pass as nothing more than a bit of scene setting, is, in fact, Windham's deft way of announcing one of the novel's main themes: that a diversion, even one that is "unique and unfathomable," is preferable to emotional suicide.

A shy, amiable New York broker, Forrest is conventional in every way. He's from the Middle West; he has two children. Twice a week he plays handball after work. His days in Manhattan have been "as much alike as the business suits" he wears to work. We soon learn that an aimless year in Greenwich Village and "some early promiscuous encounters" are long behind him. At 33, he counts on his life being settled. But then, on the Spanish Steps, he meets Marcello, a 17-year-old, whose attitude toward the American is "carefully balanced between the indifference of a departure and the deliberateness of an approach." A casual *buon giorno* on Forrest's part leads to a conversation, tentative at first, and then, when Marcello turns to him with a smile that's "a part of the sunshine," to an invitation back to the American's apartment, where they make love.

At first, Forrest feels that he has made a mistake, that he has "started something that he would regret or that would end without anything having come of it." A jaded gay acquaintance warns him that he'll be robbed or blackmailed. When Forrest tells Marcello, "My friend says that boys in Rome began doing this after the war," Marcello answers, "Your friend is wrong. Roman boys have been doing the same thing since ancient times." It's the matter-of-factness with which Forrest (and Windham) treat homosexuality that makes *Two People* so interesting, both from an historical and fictional perspective. Forrest becomes neither a possessive lover nor the boy's surrogate parent. As a result of a much earlier homosexual experience, the American has learned that "categories do not account for everything," and he seems content to let this affair play itself out in the "innocent male conviviality" that is Rome.

Marcello is "serenely beautiful." At one point, he is described as "a youth on a Greek vase," but in general Windham does not indulge in the kind of prurient encomiums to comely ephebedom that characterize, say,

Mann's descriptions of Tadzio in *Death in Venice*. This restraint is one of the novel's many appealing qualities. And unlike Tadzio, Marcello is old enough — and Italian enough? — to have learned how to pick up guys in cinemas. (Windham notes that "promiscuous encounters are to Italian boys what ice cream sodas at the corner drugstore are to their American counterparts.") There's a dual practicality to these hook ups: "Instead of having pleasure alone, he had it with someone and was given money."

A second encounter, a week later, leaves Forrest bewildered, unable to explain his new desire. "The boy's figure, lean and rounded, evoked neither masculinity nor femininity, rather the undivided country of adolescence; and his silent receptivity, open equally to tenderness and passion, spoke of no special desires, but of a need for love so great that it prevented him from asking for it." Those looking for hot scenes of passionate man-boy sex will not find them here. If you read the novel too quickly, you could almost miss the references to the times Marcello and Forrest go to bed. Still, there are beautiful passages that nicely capture the limpid dynamics of their lovemaking:

> As soon as they were in bed, Marcello's distance, awkwardness, and waiting vanished. His childish eyes, which had sought the floor or had looked into a nowhere just above their lowered lids — with a reflective quality that made it impossible for Forrest not to feel that the mind behind them was full of unspoken thoughts — sought him as directly as the hands and lips.

Although Forrest gives Marcello money and gifts, it's clear that the relationship is about something more than prostitution. With Forrest, Marcello is alternately friendly and shy. In one particularly telling passage, Forrest offers to buy a present, and after some coaxing, Marcello hesitantly tells him he'd like a new shirt. With that, the boy opens an Italian grammar book he has brought along and inscribes it "*A Forrest con simpatia.*" Later, Forrest consults a waiter, asking him about the exact meaning of *simpatia*. Closer to love than friendship, the waiter tells him.

The chapters alternate between Forrest's point of view and Marcello's. Windham, who was 45 when *Two People* was published, does an extraordinary job of getting into the head of a teenager, and a non-American one at that. The intense and confused needs, the egocentrism alternating with shyness, the self-consciousness, the moments of brutal honesty, the feelings of loneliness and loss and confusion. Marcello's father, a Sicilian tile contractor, treats his son "as though he were an employee that he wanted to make a profit on." He expects the boy to follow in his footsteps. He treats Marcello's interests in other careers with grudging tolerance. Sundays are the worst, for then the whole family spends the day together — church, visits to relatives, dinner — where the two usually end up fighting.

Rome, too, is a character in this novel, a place of romance, beauty, eroticism, chaos, squalor, mystery. A city "charged with an elixir," Henry James once said. All over Rome, Forrest encounters "sights that drew him out of himself, not through an attraction that he recognized in them, but through an obscure affinity that returned and persisted beyond under-standing." It's the seductive elusiveness of Rome — the impossibility of pinning it down — that Windham offers up as the city's most appealing quality. Like Marcello (or Forrest, for that matter), the city resists easy pigeonholing.

A further complication is that Marcello also has a girlfriend, Ninì, a girl with full breasts and skin whose "plumpness and whiteness . . . was more suggestive of a woman than of a girl." In the context of his playful, but chaste, times with Ninì, Marcello thinks of his continuing relationship with Forrest as a "friendship." The sex he and Forrest have, Marcello tells himself, is a stopgap measure before he can "properly make love" to Ninì. Forrest is, Marcello assures himself, "no competition to his feelings for Ninì, anyway."

Windham doesn't treat this arrangement ironically. His intention is not to write a novel about a "bi-curious" kid who is deluding himself. It's about two people — note that the age discrepancy is absent in the title — each in search of something. For Marcello it's autonomy, identity, maturity, experience. And indeed, through his relationship with both the girl and the

American, he gradually enters into an understanding of "the process by which love, when the world expands, limits responses and makes intensity possible." It's the intensity of the adult, not the child.

And for Forrest? What is he searching for? What Forrest most wants from Marcello is to "enter the boy's life," to enter the life of Roman Italians, indeed, to enter "any life at all." Like so many generations of travelers before him, he discovers that in Italy "the heaven and the earth are mixed up." Goethe called Rome the place in which to be reborn. Forrest is not exactly "reborn" here — Windham is too sober for that kind of earth-shattering epiphany — but he does achieve a kind of quiet, peaceful reconciliation to what has been, to what is possible, to what may be. For Forrest, Marcello has made things — Rome, and everything — real again. Glad is the word Forrest applies to himself toward the end of the novel — "glad that he had been in Rome and glad that he was returning home."

E. M. Forster, who also became a literary friend and correspondent (his letters to Windham, a much slighter volume, were privately published in 1975), appreciated Windham's art and volunteered to write an introduction to Windham's collection of stories. In that little essay — a model of economy, lucidity, and insight — Forster notes that "warmth" is the hallmark of Windham's style. "He knows that human beings are not statues but contain flesh and blood and a heart, and he believes that creatures so constituted must contact one another or they will decay. Isolation means death."

If there is anything "political" about *Two People*, it's to be found in an understated subplot involving some research that Forrest is doing at the Vatican Archives on Giordano Bruno, the 16th-century Italian monk and philosopher, who was burned alive for not retracting his heretical works. Forrest is interested in Bruno because the monk did not "falsify his declarations to achieve a nominal accord." Perhaps Windham threw in these references to suggest a parallel with Forrest's unapologetic acceptance of his relationship with Marcello. This is not a novel that pleads for understanding or tolerance, or indeed makes any apologies for Forrest's behavior, an amazing stance for a pre-Stonewall novelist to take.

I will not give away the ending. That would spoil the sweet, poignant pleasure of reading the novel's closing chapter, pages in which Windham nicely, but not facilely, wraps up the several themes he's been weaving. Instead, my original intention was to encourage you to go out and find a used copy of this long-out-of-print little gem and read it for yourself. But how wonderful to discover, just before I finished the final draft of this essay, that Mondial, a small, independent publisher of "rare and unusual books in English and Esperanto," has reissued *Two People* in a new, paperback edition graced with a handsome cover drawing by Fritz Bultman.

And while you're at it, pick up as well a copy of Windham's *Emblems of Conduct*, published two years before *Two People*. A memoir about his youth in Atlanta during the Depression, it's another model of clarity, wisdom, and restraint. Toward the end of that book, Windham wrote:

> The wonder of beauty is that it does not lie in any identifiable quality. It cannot be isolated; it exists outside the sum of its parts; and until you are aware of it, nothing is wonderful. But once you are aware of beauty, the wonder goes out of it into all that is beyond your understanding. You may make no effort to understand it, or you may track it down as far as 'wholeness,' 'harmony,' 'radiance.' But it remains outside what you can pin down. And from it wonder enters life.

A quiet wonder will enter the life of any reader lucky enough to read *Two People*, or any of Donald Windham's other gracious, generous, intelligent, and beautiful books.

# Come Again

## A History of the Reprinting of Gay Novels

## Philip Clark

An anthology like *The Lost Library* initially looks rather grim: See all the wonderful gay books that are out of print? Except for some small coterie of dedicated fans, these books are dead. No one's going to reprint a gay novel — a midlist title, at best — in this era of media conglomerates, corporate profits, and blockbuster bestsellers.

At first glance, a downbeat assessment seems accurate. In this digital moment, where books themselves sometimes appear to be on their way to extinction, will even new gay-themed fiction survive, let alone titles from what may now seem the musty past?

If a look at the history of the reprinting of gay novels is any indication, these books may enjoy a longer and more varied life than we can imagine.

While there are echoes of a gay presence in such mid-19th century works as Herman Melville's *Typee* (1846) and *Moby Dick* (1851), travel writer Bayard Taylor's *Joseph and His Friend* (1870) is generally considered the earliest example of a consciously gay novel. This makes the publishing of gay fiction a relatively recent endeavor. Oscar Wilde's *The Picture of Dorian Gray* (1890-91) was reprinted as early as 1895, directly before Wilde's trials, and then again in Paris in 1905. A few other isolated titles received quiet republication in the first half of the 20th century, but the effort to reprint earlier gay novels in a gay-specific context is even more recent.

H. Lynn Womack, the founder of Washington D.C.-based Guild Press, was already publishing male physique magazines like *Fizeek* and *Grecian Guild Pictorial* in the late 1950s. With the assistance and encouragement of bookseller Howard Frisch, owner of New York City's Village Books and Press, Womack briefly dabbled in hardcover books. These included American editions of British titles like *The Leather Boys* (1965; Anthony Blond, 1961) by "Eliot George;" memoirs such as journalist Michael Davidson's "life story of a lover of boys," *The World, the Flesh, and Myself* (1962; Arthur Barker, 1961); and reprints of more obscure gay works. Famed French writer Georges Eekhoud, little-known in America, had his novel *Strange Love* (1909) reprinted in a small quantity by Panurge Press in 1930 before Womack stepped in with a new edition in 1965. Similar re-releases awaited John Selby's melodramatic *Madame* (1963; Dodd, Mead, 1961) and the interracial World War II "problem" novel *The Invisible Glass* (1965; Greenberg, 1950) by the pseudonymous "Loren Wahl" (Lawrence Madalena). This initial run soon faded as Womack realized there was more profit to be made in a steady diet of pornographic novelettes and magazines than in hardbacks, either original or reprint. Still, Womack deserves to be recognized as a pioneer for his pre-1967 output.

The gay liberation movement, increasing in size and intensity after the Stonewall Riots in 1969, provided impetus for more gay publishing activities. Two major projects in the 1970s were the Arno Press series on homosexuality spearheaded by historian Jonathan Ned Katz and Winston Leyland's founding of Gay Sunshine Press. While working on the research for his monumental *Gay American History* (1976), Katz came into contact with Arnold Zone, Arno Press's president. Zone was willing to hire Katz to edit a series of gay reprints, especially since Arno had printed a similar, successful series of books on black history topics edited by Katz's brother, William. The Arno reprints were mostly nonfiction, but also lesbian fiction (Jane Rule, Gale Wilhelm, and Ann Bannon, among others) and a few decades-old gay-themed novels. These notable works included Reginald Underwood's once-scandalous *Bachelor's Hall* (Fortune Press, 1937), A.T. Fitzroy's immediately censored anti-war novel, *Despised and Rejected*

(Daniel, 1917), Blair Niles's New York City-set *Strange Brother* (Liveright, 1931), and *Imre: A Memorandum* (privately printed, 1908) by the pseudonymous "Xavier Mayne." Mayne was actually the American travel writer Edward Iranaeus Prime-Stevenson, author of *The Intersexes* (1908), an apparent attempt to gather between two covers every known fact – and quite a bit of gossip – about homosexuals and homosexuality. *The Intersexes* would make the lineup in Katz's Arno series, and, improbably, *Imre* would again receive new life in the 1990s in the form of an abridged paperback reprint from erotic publisher Badboy.

At the same time that Jonathan Ned Katz was beginning work with Arno Press, Winston Leyland was pursuing expansion of his publishing activities on the West Coast. The founder of the San Francisco radical gay liberationist newspaper *Gay Sunshine Journal* in 1970, Leyland began Gay Sunshine Press in 1975. Originally publishing mostly poetry (the second modern gay poetry anthology, *Angels of the Lyre*, and Erskine Lane's translations of Arabic boy-love poetry in 1975; Aaron Shurin's *The Night Sun* in 1976), Leyland soon diversified the Gay Sunshine Press list. Beginning with short stories and novel excerpts in *Now the Volcano: An Anthology of Latin American Gay Literature* (1979), Leyland would release both fiction originals and reprints for the next two decades, many of them in translation. These include books of such high quality or noted historical value as Gore Vidal's short stories in *A Thirsty Evil* (1981; Zero Press, 1956); *Bom-Crioulo: The Black Man and the Cabin Boy* (1982), an interracial, intergenerational love story written by the Brazilian author Adolfo Caminha and first published in 1895; Charles Warren Stoddard's early gay American novel *For the Pleasure of His Company* (1987; A.W. Robertson, 1903); K.B. Raul's *Naked to the Night* (1986; Paperback Library, 1964); gay mystery writer Joseph Hansen's *Pretty Boy Dead* (1984) – the second title change since its original publication as *Known Homosexual* by Brandon House in 1968; and *Teleny*, the 19th century erotic novel attributed to Oscar Wilde and a possible host of other hands. Leyland would continue his contributions to reprinting gay fiction well into the 1990s, with such anthologies as the Japanese-themed *Partings at Dawn* and *Out of the Blue: Russia's Hidden Gay Literature* (both 1996).

As Leyland continued expansion of Gay Sunshine, the 1980s would mark the largest outpouring of gay reprints, with presses in both England and America publishing more titles than ever before. A conscious effort was being made to preserve gay novels in danger of disappearing from the scene. Adding to its larger line of original gay novels, London-based Gay Men's Press (GMP) inaugurated the Gay Modern Classics series, bringing such rare works as Charles Henri Ford and Parker Tyler's *The Young and Evil* (Obelisk Press, 1933) back to public attention. Francis King (*The Firewalkers*; *A Domestic Animal*), John Lehmann (*In a Purely Pagan Sense*), Kenneth Martin (*Aubade*, first published when Martin was just 16), Michael Nelson (*A Room in Chelsea Square*), and James Purdy (*Eustace Chisholm and the Works*; *I Am Elijah Thrush*; *Narrow Rooms*) were some of the other authors to receive the Gay Modern Classics treatment. Further, GMP followed Arno with second reprints of A.T. Fitzroy's *Despised and Rejected* and Blair Niles's *Strange Brother* and Gay Sunshine with Wilde's *Teleny*. They even found time to print a new edition of the "Eliot George"-penned *The Leather Boys* (Guild Press, 1965; Anthony Blond, 1961) under its author's real name, Gillian Freeman.

In order to get its titles marketed widely in America, Gay Men's Press entered into a distribution agreement with an American publisher newly minted for the 1980s: Alyson. Still in business today as part of the Regent Media conglomerate, Alyson Publications was originally founded by Sasha Alyson in Boston in 1979. Some of Alyson's earliest publications were reprints of gay novels. The "Phil Andros"/Samuel Steward erotic classic *$tud* (1982; Guild Press, 1966); Richard Friedel's still popular *The Movie Lover* (1983; Coward, McCann & Geoghegan, 1981); Richard Hall's *The Butterscotch Prince* (1983; Pyramid Books, 1975), a mystery that was ill-promoted in its first edition; "Richard Meeker"/Forman Brown's much-beloved *Better Angel* (1987; Greenberg, 1933); and *Quatrefoil* (1981; Greenberg, 1950), a long out-of-print response by its author, "James Barr"/James Fugaté, to a suicidal and doomed fraternity brother's plea: all reappeared in Alyson's distinctive paperback format. These were obviously popular with readers, as Alyson continued to reprint a book like *Quatrefoil* into the 1990s. Alyson was even willing to reprint works of historical value by truly obscure authors; the radical German-bred anarchist John Henry Mackay's *The Hustler* (privately printed, 1926) resurfaced in an English-language edition in 1985, nearly sixty years after its original publication. It remains one of Mackay's only novels to be printed in English. Alyson would provide a home for republishing gay work into the late 1990s, with editions of such novels as John Weir's *The Irreversible Decline of Eddie Socket* (1999; HarperCollins, 1989) and Paul Monette's *The Gold Diggers* (1999; Avon, 1979) as part of its Alyson Classics Library. This imprint also worked to keep gay genre fiction alive, with mysteries by Nathan Aldyne, Michael Nava, and George Baxt. Alyson was one of several publishers to revive Baxt's *A Queer Kind of Death* (Simon & Schuster, 1966).

Even some major publishers made an attempt to attract gay book buyers by launching reprint projects in the late 1980s and into the 1990s. New York's independent giant, St. Martin's, had shown commitment to gay work for many years. In fiction, they had had success with books ranging from Edmund White's *Nocturnes for the King of Naples* (1978) to Renaud Camus' controversial *Tricks* (1981) to Steve Kluger's gay baseball novel, *Changing Pitches* (1984). In 1987, editor Michael Denneny proposed an all-gay and lesbian imprint, the first of its kind at a major publisher. Dubbed Stonewall Inn, the imprint went on to publish over 120 titles in its first ten years. While most titles were simply paperback versions of novels St. Martin's had originally published, Denneny and his successor as series editor, Keith Kahla, brought a diverse group of reprints under the Stonewall Inn banner. These included novels with devoted followings, like John Preston's *Franny, the Queen of Provincetown* (1996; Alyson, 1983); offerings from writers in the Violet Quill gay writing collective, such as Felice Picano's *Late in the Season* (1997; Delacorte, 1981); and novels from writers who gained more fame for their work in other genres, as with *Taking Care of Mrs. Carroll* (1988; Little, Brown, 1978) by Paul Monette.

In a similar vein to Stonewall Inn was the Quality Paperback Book Club's line of Triangle Classics. With an inverted pink triangle emblazoned on their spines and featuring back cover photographs of the authors,

Triangle Classics spanned the twentieth century. Early century books like Henry Blake Fuller's *Bertram Cope's Year* (1998; Alderbrink, 1919) were for the first time formally acknowledged as gay novels. Mid-century favorites – Christopher Isherwood's *A Single Man* (1996; Simon & Schuster, 1964), James Baldwin's *Giovanni's Room* (1993; Dial, 1956), John Rechy's *City of Night* (1994; Grove, 1963) – were newly hailed as gay masterpieces. Finally, QPB reprinted important gay liberation-era novels, ensuring their continued access for a new generation of readers. Robert Ferro's *The Family of Max Desir* (1995; Dutton, 1983), Andrew Holleran's *Dancer from the Dance* (1993; Morrow, 1978), and Patricia Nell Warren's *The Front Runner* (2001; Morrow, 1974) were a few modern novels to receive Triangle's canonization as classics. It was no coincidence that David Rosen and Retha Powers, who founded Triangle Classics for QPB, would go on to spearhead the creation of the first all-gay and lesbian book club, Bookspan's Insightout Books, in summer 2000.

Post-1980s gay reprints, though, were in no way the exclusive province of large publishers. Throughout the 1990s and into the present, a variety of independent publishers have taken on the task of continuing their predecessors' work. The *New York Review of Books* began a handsome set of paperback reprints in 1999 that has thus far included multiple gay titles. Novelist and critic J.R. Ackerley's revelatory memoir *My Father and Myself* (1999; Bodley Head, 1968) and A.J.A. Symons' "experiment in biography," *The Quest for Corvo* (2001; Macmillan, 1934) show the range of *NYRB*'s gay entries, while Sylvia Townsend Warner's Edwardian *Mr. Fortune's Maggot* (2001; Viking, 1927), Glenway Wescott's *Apartment in Athens* (2004; Harper, 1945) and *The Pilgrim Hawk* (2001; Harper, 1940), and James McCourt's opera comedy *Mawrdew Czgowchwz* (2002; FSG, 1975) are representative of the fiction series.

On a smaller, sumptuous scale, Elysium Press busily continued its publishing activities in the tiny town of North Pomfret, Vermont, where it began in 1980. Founder David Deiss dedicated his publishing ventures to reviving attention in long out-of-print or overlooked gay writers and artists. Writers like Denton Welch (*A Lunch Appointment*), James Lord (*Stories of*

*Youth*), Lord Berners (*The Girls of Radcliff Hall*), Stephen Tennant (*Two Stories*), Philippe Julian (*Marraine*), and Count Jacques d'Adelsward Fersen (*Lord Lyllian*) have all had their fiction given the lavish Elysium Press treatment, bestowed such trappings as marbled endpapers, custom-made slipcases, letterpress printing, and linen or silk bindings. Just as much collector's items as the highly-desired original editions, Elysium's books are reminiscent of the small, careful, often private press runs that much early gay writing received.

To bring this history up-to-date and to counter the naysayers predicting gay fiction's demise, there is Canada's Arsenal Pulp Press. In conjunction with longtime Canadian gay bookstore Little Sister, Arsenal Pulp has for several years been rescuing older gay and lesbian novels through its Little Sister's Classics reprint project. Each introduced by a leading gay or lesbian writer and containing fascinating and valuable historical materials, the Little Sister's authors include pulp novelists (Richard Amory, Valerie Taylor), modern writers (Larry Duplechan, Sarah Schulman), cult favorites (John Preston), and classic authors (Jane Rule, Fritz Peters). As this very essay was written, Little Sister's Classics brought back Agustin Gomez-Arcos's *The Carnivorous Lamb*, discussed by Richard Reitsma in the book you now hold. This serves to show that, with the dedicated effort of independent publishers – and with the financial support and interest of all readers who value gay literature – classic gay novels, those that should never be lost, can continue to find their way into the next generation's hands.

# Contributors

**Christopher Bram** is the author of nine novels, including *The Notorious Dr. August* and *Exiles in America*. His fifth novel, *Gods and Monsters*, was made into the movie starring Ian McKellen and Lynn Redgrave. He lives in New York City and is currently teaching at New York University. A collection of his essays will be published this fall by Alyson Books.

**Bill Brent**'s sex-and-drugs memoir, "This Insane Allure," comprises one-seventh of *Entangles Lives: Memoirs of Seven Top Erotic Authors*. His nonfiction article, "Martin Luther Goes Bowling," appears in *Everything You Know About God is Wrong*. His best-known work is probably *The Ultimate Guide to Anal Sex for Men* (published in French as Le Plaisir Anal {pout lui}). Bill has completed one novel, about a drug-dealing whoreboy who runs away to join the circus. Follow Bill's antics at LitBoy.com. A detailed biography of Paul Reed and his career is at http://www.glbtq.com/literature/reed_p.html. For information on current availability of *Vertical Intercourse,* please email: info@blackbooks.com.

**Michael Bronski** is the author of *Culture Clash: The Making of Gay Sensibility* (South End Press;1984) and *The Pleasure Principle: Sex, Backlash and the Struggle for Gay Freedom* (St. Martin's; 1998). He has edited *Flashpoint: Gay Male Sexual Writing* (Richard Kasak Books 1996) and Taking Liberties: Gay Men's Essays on Politics, Culture and Sex. (Richard Kasak Books; 1996) and *Pulp Friction: Uncovering the Golden Age of Gay Male Pulps* (St. Martin's Press, 2003.) His essays have appeared in nearly forty anthologies. As a journalist, cultural critic and political commentator he has been published in a wide array of venues including The Village Voice, The Boston Globe, GLQ, The Los Angeles Times, The Boston Phoenix, and Z Magazine. He is also the editor of the "Queer Ideas" and "Queer Action" series at Beacon Press. On the non-literary side, he has been involved in gay liberation as a political organizer, writer, editor, publisher and theorist since 1969, and has

been a Senior Lecturer in Women's and Gender Studies and Jewish
Studies at Dartmouth College since 2000.

**Victor Bumbalo** is an award-winning playwright whose plays have been
produced worldwide. He is the recipient of an Ingram Merrill Award
for playwriting. Bumbalo was a finalist two years in a row for a
Lambda Literary Award for his plays, *Questa* and *Niagara Falls.*
Broadway Play Publishing Inc. has published *Adam and the Experts*,
*Niagara Falls*, *What Are Tuesdays Like*? and *Questa* . SHOW appears in an
anthology published by Applause Theatre Books Publishers, and *Tell* is
included in *Gay Lesbian Plays Today* published by Heinemann.
Bumbalo has written for several popular television series: *NYPD Blue*,
*American Gothic*, *Relativity*, and HBO's *Spawn*. He has also written
several movies of the week. He is the founder and president of the
Robert Chesley Foundation.

**Tom Cardamone** is the author of the erotic fantasy novel, *The Werewolves of
Central Park* and the short story collection *Pumpkin Teeth*. His work has
appeared in on-line magazines and journals as well as several
anthologies. He has reviewed books for *The LAMBDA Book Report* and
*Books To Watch Out For*. You can read some of his fiction at his website
www.pumpkinteenth.net. While there you can drop him a note about
any out-of-print gay fiction you would like to bring to his attention.

**Philip Clark** is a Washington D.C.-area editor and writer; he has been
named to the board of directors for D.C.'s Rainbow History Project and
is at work on research for a potential book about H. Lynn Womack and
the D.C.-based Guild Press. Essays have recently appeared in *The
Golden Age of Gay Fiction* and *50 LGBT Books Everyone Should Read*. An
anthology he co-edited, *Persistent Voices: Poetry by Writers Lost to AIDS*,
was released by Alyson Books in late 2009. He welcomes correspondence
at philipclark@hotmail.com.

**Wayne Courtois** is author of the memoir *A Report from Winter*, published by
Lethe Press. His novel *My Name Is Rand* was published by Suspect
Thoughts Press, and a second novel, *A Pardoner's Tale*, is forthcoming
from Lethe. His fiction and nonfiction have appeared in many
anthologies, including *Best Gay Erotica* and *Country Boys*, and in
journals such as *The Greensboro Review* and *Harrington Gay Men's
Literary Quarterly*. As a grantwriter in the nonprofit sector, he has
helped to raise millions for HIV/AIDS services, hospice care, and the

arts. He lives in Kansas City, Missouri with his longtime partner. Please visit www.waynecourtois.com.

**Jameson Currier** is the author of a novel, *Where the Rainbow Ends*, and three collections of short stories, *Dancing on the Moon*; *Desire, Lust, Passion, Sex*; and *Still Dancing*. He blogs regularly on GLBTQ publishing at QueerType.

**Larry Duplechan** is the author of five acclaimed gay-themed novels, including *Blackbird* and *Got 'til it's Gone*.

**Philip Gambone** is an award-winning writer of fiction and nonfiction. His collection of short stories, *The Language We Use Up Here*, and his novel, *Beijing*, were each nominated for a Lambda Literary Award. Phil's longer essays and memoirs have appeared in a number of important anthologies, including *Hometowns*, *A Member of the Family*, *Sister & Brother*, *Wrestling with the Angel*, *Boys Like Us*, *Gay Travels*, *Obsessed*, *The Man I Might Become*, *Wonderlands*, and *Big Trips*. Phil's collection of interviews, *Something Inside: Conversations with Gay Fiction Writers*, received praise for "both the depth of Gambone's probing conversations and for the sheer range of important authors included." Phil has taught writing at the University of Massachusetts, Boston College, and Harvard University. Currently, he teaches English at Boston University Academy and fiction writing at the Harvard Extension School. His latest project is a book of profiles of important LGBTQ Americans.

**Michael Graves** is thirty years old. His fiction has appeared in several literary journals, including Velvet Mafia, Lodestar Quarterly and Cherry Bleeds. His work is also featured in the print anthologies, *Eclectica Magazine's Best Fiction Volume One, Best Gay Love Stories 2006* and *Cool Thing Best New Gay Fiction from Young American Writers*. One of Michael's short stories was recently nominated for a Pushcart Prize and The Million Writers Award. Michael's non-fiction book reviews and articles have been published in numerous publications such as Lambda Book Report, Philth Magazine, Edge Boston and Grub Street's Free Press. Michael earned an MFA in Creative Writing from Lesley University in Cambridge, Massachusetts. He lives with his partner, Scott, and their bunny rabbit, Bumbles. Contact Michael at MBoyBlunder@aol.com.

**Stephen Greco** is Executive Editor of Classical TV, a broadband portal for full-length performances of opera, ballet, modern dance, jazz, and theater. Formerly Executive Director of Dance Theater Workshop, Editor-at-Large of *Trace*, the international magazine focusing on "transcultural styles and ideas," Editorial Director and a co-founder of Platform.net, the first online community for worldwide youth culture, and Senior Editor of *Interview* magazine, Greco also serves as Executive Director of the Ferro-Grumley Literary Awards, Inc., America's premier honors for LGBT fiction. Greco's first book, a collection of erotic fiction and non-fiction entitled *The Sperm Engine* (Green Candy) published in 2002, was nominated for a 2003 Lambda Literary Award and praised by *Out* magazine for its "breathless bravura."

**Aaron Hamburger** was awarded the Rome Prize by the American Academy of Arts and Letters for his short story collection *The View from Stalin's Head* (Random House, 2004), also nominated for a Violet Quill Award. His next book, a novel titled *Faith for Faith for Beginners* (Random House, 2005), was nominated for a Lambda Literary Award. His writing has appeared in Poets and Writers, Tin House, Details, The Forward, and Out. He has received fellowships from the Edward F. Albee Foundation and the Civitella Ranieri Foundation in Umbria, Italy. Currently he teaches creative writing at Columbia University.

**Jonathan Harper** is slowly but surely working on his thesis for his MFA in Creative Writing at American University. His fiction has most recently appeared in the anthology *Wilde Stories: 2008* edited by Steve Berman and was nominated for a Pushcart Prize in 2005. He lives in Northern Virginia.

**Jim Marks** founded the Lambda Literary Foundation in 1996 and served as its executive director until 2005. He lives in Washington DC with his partner of 29 years. He is Treasurer of the DC GLBT Center, is a member of the board of the Rainbow History Project, and does bookkeeping for Metro DC PFLAG.

**Sean Meriwether** has been trying to live up to his moniker as "The Naughty Harry Potter". He has been working his own brand of magic on the page, drafting immersive fiction and erotica and transporting boys and girls into the tumultuous landscape inside his head. He has published over thirty short stories in venues including Best of Best Gay Erotica 2, Best Gay Love Stories 2006, and Lodestar Quarterly. His collection of short fiction and erotica, The Silent Hustler, will be published by Lethe Press (2009).

**Sam J. Miller** is a writer and a community organizer. His work has appeared in literary journals such as *Fiction International*, *Fourteen Hills*, *Permafrost*, *Pindeldyboz*, and *The Minnesota Review* — who nominated him for a Pushcart Prize. He is the recipient of a 2008 Literary Fellowship and Residency from the Bronx Writers Center. Visit him at www.samjmiller.com, and/or drop him a line at samjmiller79@yahoo.com.

**Jesse Monteagudo** has been reading, writing, collecting and reviewing gay men's literature for over thirty years. His syndicated book review column, "The Book Nook," appeared in Miami's Weekly News and other gay publications from 1977 to 2006. Monteagudo currently writes a monthly book column for AfterElton.com. In addition to his book reviews, Jesse Monteagudo writes "Jesse's Journal," a monthly opinion column, and contributes to The Guide, GayToday.com, GayWisdom.org, Bilerico and other print and online gay publications. Monteagudo's short fiction has been published in over two dozen anthologies.

Canadian-born, Sydney-based **Andy Quan** is the author of four books, *Six Positions* (gay erotica), *Calendar Boy* (short fiction), *Slant,* and *Bowling Pin Fire* (both poetry). His work has appeared in many anthologies of gay fiction and erotica in North America, Australia and Europe. He's obsessed with succulents, is reviving the art of the mix-tape in CD form, practices reiki, sings songs, and occasionally updates his websites such as www.andyquan.com.

**Richard Reitsma** was born in California, and raised along the West Coast of Michigan. He himself was lost in libraries until he picked up the right book that told him who he was. This spark of literary identification launched an academic career. He received his B.A. from Grand Valley State University, his M.A. from Purdue University, and has studied abroad in Mexico, Cuba, and France. His Ph.D. studies in Comparative Literature from Washington University-St. Louis focused on issues of sexuality and race in plantation fiction from the American South and the Caribbean. He previously taught world literature at the College of William and Mary, and has served on the Spanish and Latin American Studies faculty at several universities, most recently Gettysburg College. He has also developed courses on Sexuality as Political discourse in Europe and Latin America. In addition, he has regularly served as a judge for the Lambda Literary Awards. He currently resides in Baltimore, MD. His research has branched out recently to examine gay themes in children's cartoons. He also continues writing both fiction and academic work.

**Jerry Rosco** is the author of *Glenway Wescott Personally: A Biography* and co-editor (with Robert Phelps) of the journals of 1920s expatriate writer Wescott, *Continual Lessons*. He is selecting and editing Wescott's last journals, and working— too slowly as always— on other projects and stories. Jerry is also a veteran, star pitcher in New York's Big Apple Softball League.

**Paul Russell** is the author of five novels: *The Salt Point, Boys of Life, Sea of Tranquillity, The Coming Storm* and *War Against the Animals*. He has also published a work of non-fiction, *The Gay 100: A Ranking of the Most Influential Gay Men and Lesbians, Past and Present*. His poetry, essays and short fiction have appeared in such journals and anthologies as *Carolina Quarterly, Epoch, The Black Warrior Review, The James White Review, Lumina, Queer 13, The Mammoth Book of New Gay Erotica, Gastronomica, Men on Men 4* and *Best Food Writing 2001*. He recently completed his sixth novel, *My Unreal Life: Memoirs of Sergey Vladimirovich Nabokoff*.

**Rob Stephenson**'s writing has been most recently published in *Invert(e), Golden Handcuffs Review, Madder Love : Queer Men and the Precincts of Surrealism, Entangled Lives,* and *American Book Review*. His novel *Passes Through* is soon available from Fiction Collective 2. The CD *dog* composed with Mikael Karlsson is now available from Please Musicworks or downloadable from iTunes or Amazon. www.rawbe.com.

**Ian Rafael Titus** has written fiction and poetry for *Velvet Mafia, Into the Abyss, Frozen Tears II* and *III,* and *Visionary Tongue,* a writers' workshop fanzine established by fantasy author Storm Constantine and Eloise Coquio. A queer vampire novel set in nineteenth-century West Indies is in the works.

**Rick Whitaker** is author of *Assuming the Position: A Memoir of Hustling* and *The First Time I Met Frank O'Hara: Reading Gay American Writers*. He is Music and Theater Director of the Italian Academy at Columbia University.

**Martin Wilson** was born in Tuscaloosa, Alabama, and was educated at Vanderbilt University. He received his MFA from the University of Florida, where his short stories won a Henfield/*Transatlantic Review* Award. His debut novel, *What They Always Tell Us,* was published in 2008. He lives in New York City and is at work on his second novel. For more information, visit his website,www.martinwilsonwrites.com.

**Gregory Woods** is the author of *A History of Gay Literature: The Male Tradition* (1998) and *Articulate Flesh: Male Homo-eroticism and Modern*

*Poetry* (1987), both from Yale University Press. He is professor of gay and lesbian studies at Nottingham Trent University. His was the first such appointment in the UK. His poetry books are *We Have the Melon* (1992), *May I Say Nothing* (1998), *The District Commissioner's Dreams* (1996) and *Quidnunc* (2007), all from Carcanet Press. His website is www.gregorywoods.co.uk.

**Timothy Young** is a curator and archivist who has written on the nature of ephemera, why singers cover famous songs, how to introduce children to research libraries, the history of Peter Pan, and the relationship between Gertrude Stein and George Platt Lynes. His most recent projects include translations of works by Blaise Cendrars and editing a book of the world economic crisis of 1720.

# Bibliography

Bronski, Michael. *Pulp Friction: Uncovering the Golden Age of Gay Male Pulps*. New York, St. Martin's, 2003

Chauncey, George. *Gay New York: The Making of the Gay Male World, 1890-1940*. New York, Harper Collins, 1994.

Crompton, Louis. *Homosexuality and Civilization*. Cambridge, Massachusetts, Harvard University Press, 2003.

de St. Jorre, John. *Venus Bound: The Erotic Voyage of the Olympia Press and Its Writers*. New York, Random House, 1994.

Gambone, Philip. *Something Inside: Conversations with Gay Fiction Writers*, Madison, University of Wisconsin Press, 1999.

Picano, Felice. *Art and Sex in Greenwich Village; Gay Literary Life After Stonewall*. New York, Carroll & Graf Publishers, 2007.

Slide, Anthony. *Lost Gay Novels, A Reference Guide to Fifty Works from the First Half of the Twentieth Century*. New York, Harrington Press, Inc., 2003.

Stryker, Susan. *Queer Pulp*. San Francisco, Chronicle Books, 2001.

Whitaker, Rick. *The First Time I Met Frank O'Hara: Reading Gay American Writers*. New York, Four Walls Eight Windows, 2003.

White, Edmund, Bergman, David, editor. *The Burning Library*. New York, Vintage Books, Random House, 1995.

White, Edmund. "The Loves of the Falcon: Books by and about Glenway Wescott," *The New York Review of Books*, Vol. 56, No. 2, February 12, 2009.

Woods, Gregory. *A History of Gay Literature: The Male Tradition*. New Haven, Conn. Yale University Press, 1998.

Young, Ian. *Out in Paperback, A Visual History of Gay Pulp*. Toronto, Lester, Mason & Begg Limited, 2007

# Novels and Short Story Collections of Further Interest

*The following writers and books, mentioned or discovered during the formation of this collection, might be of further interest to literary seekers and gay historians. This casually compiled list represents the spirit more than the breadth, quantity and quality of gay fiction that is currently out of print.*

Terry Andrews (George Selden): *The Story of Harold* (1974)

Phil Andros (Samuel Steward): The Joy Spot (1969); $tud (1966)

James Barr (James Barr Fugaté): *Quatrefoil* (1950)

Neil Bartlett: *The House on Brooke Street* (1997; reprint of 1996 British edition, *Mr. Clive and Mr. Page*)

Bruce Benderson: *Pretending to Say No: A Novella and Eleven Stories* (1990)

Burt Blechman: *Stations* (1964)

Brian Bouldrey: *Genius of Desire* (1993)

Christopher Bram: *Almost History* (1992); *Gossip* (1998); *Hold Tight* (1988); *In Memory of Angel Clare* (1989); *Surprising Myself* (1987)

Joseph Caldwell: *In Such Dark Places* (1978)

Peter Cameron: *The Half You Don't Know* (1997); *Leap Year* (1990)

Renaud Camus: *Tricks* (1981)

Christopher Coe: *I Look Divine* (1987)

Dennis Cooper: *Safe* (1985)

Steven Corbin: *Fragments That Remain* (1993); *A Hundred Days from Now* (1994)

James Courage: *A Way of Love* (1959)

Jameson Currier: *Where the Rainbow Ends* (1998)

Craig Curtis: *Fabulous Hell* (2000)

Christopher Davis: *Joseph and the Old Man* (1986); *Valley of the Shadow* (1988)

Samuel Delany: *The Mad Man* (1994)

Coleman Dowell: *White on Black on White* (1983)

Larry Duplechan: *Captain Swing* (1993); *Eight Days a Week* (1985); *Tangled Up in Blue* (1989)

Kevin Esser: *Mad to Be Saved* (1985); *Streetboy Dreams* (1983)

David Feinberg: *Spontaneous Combustion* (1991)

Robert Ferro: *The Family of Max Desir* (1983); *Second Son* (1988)

Edward Field and Neil Derrick: *The Villagers* (2000)

Pete Fisher: *Dreamlovers* (1980)

Henry Flesh: *Massage* (1999); *Michael* (2000)

Richard Friedel: *The Movie Lover* (1981)

Sanford Friedman: *Totempole* (1965)

Rodney Garland (Adam de Hegedus): *The Heart in Exile* (1953)

Paul Gervais: *Extraordinary People* (1991)

Harlan Greene: *What the Dead Remember* (1991)

Richard Hall: *Family Fictions* (1991); *Fidelities* (1992); *Letters from a Great-Uncle* (1985)

Wallace Hamilton: *Coming Out* (1977); *David at Olivet* (1979); *Kevin* (1980)

Joseph Hansen: *A Smile in His Lifetime* (1981); *Job's Year* (1983)

Ron Harvie: *The Voltaire Smile and Other Stories* (1982); *Men Working* (1984)

Scott Heim: In Awe (1997)

William Haywood Henderson: *Native* (1993)

Frank Hilaire: *Thanatos* (1971)

Gordon Hoban: *The Green Hotel* (1988)

Guy Hocquenghem: *Love in Relief* (1986)

Andrew Holleran: *The Beauty of Men* (1994); *In September, the Light Changes* (1999)

Bo Huston: *Dream Life* (1992); *Horse and Other Stories* (1989); *The Listener: Four Stories and a Novella* (1993); *Remember Me* (1991)

Gary Indiana: *Horse Crazy* (1989); *Scar-Tissue and Other Stories* (1987)

Charles Jackson: *The Fall of Valor* (1946)

Fenton Johnson: *Scissors, Paper, Rock* (1993)

Kevin Killian: *Arctic Summer* (1997); *Bedrooms Have Windows* (1989); *I Cry Like a Baby* (2001); *Shy* (1989)

Harry Kondoleon: *Diary of a Lost Boy* (1994)

Jay B. Laws: *Steam* (1991); *The Unfinished* (1993)

Stan Leventhal: *Barbie in Bondage* (1996); *Faultlines* (1989); *A Herd of Tiny Elephants* (1988); *Mountain Climbing in Sheridan Square* (1988); *Skydiving on Christopher Street* (1995)

Edward Lucie-Smith: *The Dark Pageant* (1977)

Joey Manley: *The Death of Donna-May Dean* (1991)

Robin Maugham: *Enemy* (1983); *The Wrong People* (1971)

Richard Meeker (Forman Brown): *Better Angel* (1933)

Gordon Merrick: *Forth into Light* (1972); *An Idol for Others* (1977); *The Lord Won't Mind* (1970); *One for the Gods* (1971)

Merle Miller: *What Happened* (1972)

Larry Mitchell: *The Terminal Bar* (1982)

Paul Monette: *Afterlife* (1990); *The Gold Diggers* (1979); *The Long Shot* (1981); *Taking Care of Mrs. Carroll* (1978)

Oscar Moore: *A Matter of Life and Sex* (1992)

George Nadar: *Chrome* (1987)

Michael Nelson: *A Room in Chelsea Square* (1958)

Felice Picano: *Dryland's End* (1999); *Like People in History* (1995); *Onyx* (2001)

David Plante: *The Catholic* (1985); *The Country* (1981); *The Family* (1978); *The Woods* (1982)

Joel Redon: *Bloodstream* (1988)

Paul Reidinger: *Good Boys* (1993)

Lev Raphael: *Dancing on Tisha B'Av* (1990)

Robert Reinhart: *Beldon's Crimes* (1986); *A History of Shadows* (1982); *Walk the Night* (1994)

Michael Rumaker: *My First Satyrnalia* (1981)

Paul Russell: *Boys of Life* (1991)

Darieck Scott: *Traitor to the Race* (1996)

Robert Scott: *The Finding of David* (1984)

Michael Schmidt: *The Green Island* (1982; reprint of 1980 British edition, *The Colonist*)

Leo Skir: *Boychick* (1971)

George Soulie de Morant: *Pei Yu: Boy Actress* (1991; reprint of 1925 French edition, *Bijou-de-Ceinture*)

Matthew Stadler: *Landscape: Memory* (1993)

Thomas Barnett Swann: *How Are the Mighty Fallen* (1974)

Edward Swift: *Splendora* (1978)

Joseph Torchia: *As If After Sex* (1983); *The Kryptonite Kid* (1979)

John Weir: *The Irreversible Decline of Eddie Socket* (1989)

Peter Weltner: *The Risk of His Music* (1997)

George Whitmore: *The Confessions of Danny Slocum* (1980)

Calder Willingham: *End as a Man* (1947)

# Postscript

The old Rome that he had known was disappearing and a new Rome was taking its place. All over the city there were sights that drew him out of himself, not through an attraction that he recognized in them, but through an obscure affinity that returned and persisted beyond his understanding. Certain street corners, certain glimpses of park, seemed to have a hidden importance and to hint to him that a time would come when their meaning would be revealed. They were not famous places; they were not places that he had been with Marcello; often, they were not even places that had impressed him when he first saw them. But they kept reasserting themselves in the way that, in his youth, certain books which had meant nothing to him at the time had kept reappearing until he read them. They were real in the way that the trees, the banisters, the backyard dump heap of his childhood had been real; they held no significance that he recognized, but he felt that he would live with them for the rest of his life.

— *Donald Windham, Two People*